The Politics of News
The News of Politics

Second Edition

EDITED BY

Doris A. Graber
University of Illinois at Chicago

Denis McQuail
University of Amsterdam

Pippa Norris
Harvard University

CQ PRESS

A Division of Congressional Quarterly Inc.
Washington, D.C.

CQ Press
1255 22nd Street, NW, Suite 400
Washington, DC 20037

Phone: 202-729-1900; toll-free, 1-866-4CQ-PRESS (1-866-427-7737)

Web: www.cqpress.com

Cover design: Blue Bungalow Design

♾ The paper used in this publication exceeds the requirements of the American National Standard for Information Sciences—Permanence of Paper for Printed Library Materials, ANSI Z39.48-1992.

Printed and bound in the United States of America

11 10 09 08 07   1 2 3 4 5

Library of Congress Cataloging-in-Publication Data

The politics of news : the news of politics / edited by Doris A. Graber, Denis McQuail,
   Pippa Norris.—2nd ed.
      p. cm.
   Includes bibliographical references and index.
   ISBN-13: 978-0-87289-406-8 (alk. paper)
      1. Mass media—Political aspects.   2. Press and politics.   I. Graber, Doris A.
(Doris Appel)   II. McQuail, Denis.   III. Norris, Pippa.
   P95.8.P655 2008
   302.23—dc22   2007017359

Contents

Contributors

SCOTT L. ALTHAUS is associate professor of political science and speech communication at the University of Illinois. His research interests center on the communication processes that empower ordinary citizens to exercise popular sovereignty in democratic societies. His book on the political uses of opinion surveys in democratic societies, *Collective Preferences in Democratic Politics: Opinion Surveys and the Will of the People,* received a 2004 Goldsmith Book Prize from Harvard University's Shorenstein Center on the Press, Politics, and Public Policy and a David Easton Book Prize from the American Political Science Association's Foundations of Political Theory section.

W. LANCE BENNETT is professor of political science, Lawrence Professor of Communication, and director of the Center for Communication and Civic Engagement at the University of Washington. His work focuses on the impact of communication processes on citizens' political identifications and engagement. Publications include *Mediated Politics: Communication in the Future of Democracy* (2001); *News: The Politics of Illusion,* 7th ed. (2007); and *When the Press Fails: Political Power and the News Media from Iraq to Katrina* (2007). The American Political Science Association has honored him with the Ithiel de Sola Pool Distinguished Career Award and the Murray Edelman Career Achievement Award in Political Communication.

DORIS A. GRABER is professor of political science and communication at the University of Illinois at Chicago. She is the author of numerous articles and political communication books, including *Processing the News: How People Tame the Information Tide* (1993); the award-winning *Processing Politics: Learning from Television in the Internet Age* (2001); *The Power of Communication: Managing Information in Public Organizations* (2003); and *Mass Media and American Politics,* 7th ed. (2006). She serves on many editorial boards and is founding editor of *Political Communication* and book review editor of *Political Psychology.*

BRUCE W. HARDY is a doctoral student at the Annenberg School for Communication and a senior research analyst at the Annenberg Public Policy Center at the University of Pennsylvania. His research has focused on media effects, social networks, and public opinion. His work has appeared in peer-reviewed journals such as *Public Opinion Quarterly, Journal of Communication,* and *Journal of Broadcasting and Electronic Media.*

KATHLEEN HALL JAMIESON is Packard Professor of Communication at the Annenberg School for Communication at the University of Pennsylvania and director of the university's Annenberg Public Policy Center. She has written extensively on the press, politics, and presidential campaigns. Her most recent book, coauthored with award-winning journalist Brooks Jackson, is *Unspun: Finding Fact in a World of Disinformation* (2007). Jackson and Jamieson founded FactCheck.org, which is a project of the Annenberg Public Policy Center. Jamieson founded and is codirector of the National Annenberg Election Study, on which her essay in this volume is based.

ANDREW KOHUT is president and director of the Pew Research Center for the People and the Press and director of the Pew Global Attitudes Project. He is also the founder of Princeton Survey Research Associates and a former president of the Gallup Organization. His books include *Estranged Friends? The Transatlantic Consequences of Societal Change* (1996) with Max Kaase, *The Diminishing Divide: Religion's Changing Role in American Politics* (2000), and *America Against the World: How We Are Different and Why We Are Disliked* (2006) with *National Journal* columnist Bruce Stokes.

REGINA G. LAWRENCE is associate professor and chair of political science in the Hatfield School of Government at Portland State University. She specializes in research analyzing media coverage of public policy issues like welfare reform, shootings in public schools, the obesity epidemic, the anthrax attacks of 2001, and television coverage of the September 11 terrorist attacks. She is the author of *The Politics of Force: Media and the Construction of Police Brutality* (2000) and a coauthor, with W. Lance Bennett and Steven Livingston, of *When the Press Fails: Political Power and the News Media from Iraq to Katrina* (2007).

JIM LEHRER hosts PBS's *NewsHour with Jim Lehrer*. Lehrer has been covering political news in Washington since 1972 and began hosting the award-winning *MacNeil/Lehrer Report* in 1975. He has hosted ten presidential debates over the last five elections and was the solo anchor for PBS coverage of the House Judiciary Committee's impeachment inquiry of Richard Nixon. Lehrer has published seventeen novels, two memoirs, and three plays. For his excellence in journalism, Lehrer was inducted in 1999 into the Television Hall of Fame and has received a National Humanities Medal from President Bill Clinton.

JAROL B. MANHEIM is professor of media and public affairs and of political science and was the founding director of the School of Media and Public Affairs at George Washington University. His two most recent books, *The Death of a Thousand Cuts: Corporate Campaigns and the Attack on the Corporation* (2001) and *Biz-War and the Out-of-Power Elite: The Progressive-Left Attack on the Corporation* (2004), examine the role of communication strategies—in particular, the demonization of corporations—in efforts to rebuild the labor movement and the center-left in the United States.

DENIS MCQUAIL is emeritus professor of communication at the University of Amsterdam and visiting professor in the Department of Politics, University of Southampton. His books include *Audience Analysis* (1997) and *McQuail's Mass Communication Theory*, 5th ed. (2005), a comprehensive introduction to the field that takes full account of new technologies and globalization issues. His most recent edited collection is *Communication Theory and Research* (2006), which presents outstanding studies in communications research published during the past decade. The selections are drawn from the *European Journal of Communication,* a leading international journal founded by McQuail, Peter Golding, and Els De Bens.

ELLEN MICKIEWICZ directs the DeWitt Wallace Center for Media and Democracy at Duke University, where she is James R. Shepley Professor of Public Policy Studies and professor of political science. She specializes in comparative political communication, focusing on the former Soviet Union and Eastern and Central Europe. Her books include the award-winning *Split Signals: Television and Politics in the Soviet Union* (1988) and *Changing Channels: Television and the Struggle for Power in Russia* (1997). Her distinguished scholarship and service have won awards from the American Political Science Association's Political Communication section, the Journalists Union of Russia, and Atlanta's Carter Center.

W. RUSSELL NEUMAN is John Derby Evans Professor of Media Technology at the University of Michigan. His current research concerns the political and economic aspects of new media and the impact of cognitions and emotions on political perceptions. His books include *The Future of the Mass Audience* (1991) and three coauthored works: *Common Knowledge: News and the Construction of Political Meaning* (1992), the award-winning *The Gordian Knot: Political Gridlock on the Information Highway* (1997), and *Affective Intelligence and Political Judgment* (2000). In 2002–2003 he served as a senior policy analyst in the White House Office of Science and Technology Policy.

PIPPA NORRIS is director of the democratic governance group in the United Nations Development Programme in New York and Maguire Lecturer in Comparative Politics at Harvard University's John F. Kennedy School of Government. Recent books include *Electoral Engineering: Voting Rules and Political Behavior* (2004), *Sacred and Secular: Politics and Religion Worldwide* (2004) with Ronald Inglehart, and *Driving Democratization: What Works* (2006). Norris, who is a political scientist, has served as an expert consultant for many international bodies, including the UN, UNESCO, the Council of Europe, International IDEA, the National Endowment for Democracy, and the UK Electoral Commission.

THOMAS E. PATTERSON is Bradlee Professor of Government and the Press at Harvard University's John F. Kennedy School of Government. His most recent book, *The Vanishing Voter* (2003), looks at the causes and consequences of declining electoral participation. His book on the media's political role, *Out of Order* (1993), received the American Political Science Association's inaugural Doris Graber Award as the best book of the decade on political communication. An earlier book, *The Unseeing Eye* (1976), was named by the American Association for Public Opinion Research as one of the fifty most influential books on public opinion in the past half century.

BARBARA PFETSCH is professor of communication and media policy at the University of Hohenheim, Germany. She previously was a senior researcher at the Social Science Research Center Berlin and taught at the Freie Universität Berlin and the University of Mannheim. She has been a fellow at Harvard's Shorenstein Center on the Press, Politics, and Public Policy and Georgetown University's Center for German and European Studies. Her research focuses on comparative analyses of political communication and on media and the public sphere. Pfetsch has published several books, including *Comparing Political Communication* (2004), and numerous articles and book chapters.

ROBERT G. PICARD is Hamrin Professor of Media Economics and director of the Media Management and Transformation Center at Jöncöping International Business School, Jöncöping University, Sweden, and editor of the *Journal of Media Business Studies*. His books include *The Press and the Decline of Democracy: The Democratic Socialist Response in Public Policy* (1985); *Media Economics: Concepts and Issues* (1989); and, with John Bustema, *Joint Operating Agreements: The Newspaper Preservation Act and Its Application* (1993) and *The Economics and Financing of Media Companies* (2002). Picard was a fellow at Harvard University's Shorenstein Center on the Press, Politics, and Public Policy.

DARRELL M. WEST is John Hazen White Distinguished Professor of Public Policy and Political Science and director of the Taubman Center for Public Policy at Brown University. He is the author of fifteen books in the area of mass media, technology, and elections. His current research focuses on e-government and policymaking. His books include *Celebrity Politics* (2002); *The Rise and Fall of the Media Establishment* (2002); *Air Wars: Television Advertising in Election Campaigns* (2005), now in its fourth edition; and *Digital Government: Technology and Public Sector Performance* (2005), winner of the Don K. Price award for the best book on technology.

Preface

The relationship among journalists, politicians, and the public is obviously troubled. The issue in contention revolves around who does, and who should, influence press coverage of the public policy agenda in democratic political systems and thereby shape current politics. With venues for news coverage multiplying steadily and reaching ever-larger audiences around the globe at lightning speed, the control over news creation and dissemination is more crucial than ever before.

The precise roles that journalists, politicians, and the public should play in democracies remain ill-defined and controversial. Should journalists be impartial observers or advocates who participate in the political game? Do current news management practices by political actors and private interest groups impede the free flow of news? Do the fragmentation and segmentation of the media make it harder to supply the general public with the information it needs about the political world? Have megamergers in the media marketplace produced a convergence between news and entertainment, tipping the balance toward the latter?

These and similar concerns have been widely debated in the United States and abroad, but they were rarely subjected to close scrutiny by scholars and practitioners within the covers of one volume. That changed in 1998 with the publication of the first edition of *The Politics of News: The News of Politics*. The book had an interesting history. As part of its efforts to foster discussions about the role of the press among scholars, journalists, and policy makers, the Joan Shorenstein Center on the Press, Politics, and Public Policy at Harvard University's John F. Kennedy School of Government invited Doris Graber from the University of Illinois at Chicago and Denis McQuail from the University of Amsterdam in the spring of 1996 to spend a semester at the center. Graber, founding editor of *Political Communication*, was the center's visiting Lombard Professor, and McQuail, founding coeditor of the *European Journal of Communication*, was a visiting fellow. They combined forces with Pippa Norris, associate director of research at the center and founding coeditor of *The Harvard*

International Journal of Press/Politics. It was a perfect opportunity to collaborate on a volume that addressed key issues in "the politics of news." The book's development benefited immensely from the resources available at the Shorenstein Center.

Nearly a decade has passed since then, bringing momentous changes in the news business. The time was ripe for another major effort to shed light on the forces whose interactions produce the news that shapes politics. The editors therefore asked six of the original contributors to tell their stories ten years later, focusing on the same broad subject area with new insights and new examples. To broaden the scope of inquiry, the editors also invited seven renowned experts in political communication, who had not contributed to the first edition, to join the team. The result, as before, is a book that features analyses by distinguished scholars and practitioners about how the news media operate as an intermediary for communication between governments and citizens, among various political actors, and even among citizens. The book is an indispensable resource for students of politics and government as well as for every reader interested in learning more about how news is made, where the problems and tensions lie, and how they can be resolved.

As editors, we owe a deep debt of gratitude to the contributors to this volume, who carefully tailored their essays to fit into our designated goals. Profound thanks are due as well to the editors at CQ Press, who saw the project through to completion; to the staff members who ably guided production; and to our home universities who lent us their assistance. We hope that this volume is a fit tribute to their efforts and support.

The Editors
March 2007

Introduction:
The Politics of News in a Democracy

Doris A. Graber, Denis McQuail, and Pippa Norris

Reporting political news is a political process, regardless of the intentions of journalists and other news disseminators. What they choose to cover, what they ignore, and how they frame political stories influence the perceptions of elite and mass audiences. In turn, these perceptions affect political priorities and actions.

Totalitarian societies keep a tight reign on the publication of news. They control which topics are covered and which remain hidden, and they set the guidelines for framing the news so that it reflects the meanings the government prefers. The degree of control over media varies. It ranges from minimal in democracies to high in countries such as North Korea, Belarus, and Chad. Freedom House classifies these countries as having serious restrictions of print and broadcast media and strict government censorship of messages contrary to the regime.[1]

In democracies, gatekeeping—the decision of what news will be published and what news will be ignored—and framing of news—expressing it in ways that convey particular meanings—are matters of political struggle. The struggle occurs because democracies encourage the expression of diverse views by people whose policy interests and orientations vary widely while leaving it up to them to find venues for expressing their views. Democracies have no czars who decide what should be covered and how it should be framed. Providers of political news even disagree about the kinds of political news that audiences want and need.

In democratic societies, most people believe that no single government leader, interest group, or news organization should serve as the sole gatekeeper for access to the news channels, but they may disagree over what sort of diversity is required. A high level of concentration of control in the hands of governments, parties and interest groups, or media enterprises is deemed dangerous to democracy. What level of concentration is too high, however, remains controversial. Moreover, multiple ownership and a rich proliferation of media channels do not guarantee diversity of media content and news reporting, which is the rationale for seeking diversity of control. Separate news entities frequently operate like clones.

The Changing News Venue Scene

In 1998, when the first edition of this book was published, most of the parties struggling over the selection, framing, and publicizing of political news were striving for coverage by daily newspapers, over-the-air television, and radio. Competition for space and time was keen because the supply of news venues was insufficient to meet the demand, condemning most of the news available for publication to oblivion. The problem of news channel scarcity has vanished thanks to the proliferation of new venues for news. They include cable television, Internet and satellite news sites, and a plethora of personal Web sites that allow citizens to air their views about political issues.

Even so, the battle over access to news venues continues because players in the game of politics want their voices heard in the channels that are most likely to reach policymakers and potential supporters of their causes among the public. The prime targets in this competition for megaphones to the politicians' and the public's ears are still the "old media"—newspapers, over-the-air television, and radio, plus one newcomer, the Internet, which disseminates news in a variety of ways.

Poll results confirm the continuing predominance of old media. When people were asked in a nationwide poll in June 2005 about the venues they used for national and international news, 74 percent mentioned television, and 44 percent mentioned newspapers, with the Internet and radio trailing at 24 percent and 22 percent, respectively.[2] Disaggregation of the responses about television confirms that over-the-air television remains the chief supplier of news. Audiences for cable newscasts were only one tenth as large. The interviews also revealed that most news consumers relied on multiple sources, with the news packages leaning heavily to offerings by traditional venues. All in all, the audience sizes for newspapers and network television have shrunk, and the control of these media over the flow of political news into the political system has diminished. Nevertheless, they still dominate the political scene, and stakeholders continue to struggle for inclusion of their stories in the most esteemed newspapers and network television channels.

The Nature of "Political News"

The battle over controlling what is published and what remains unpublicized takes place in a wide-open arena. No one sets hard and fast rules about what constitutes political news, what criteria should determine priorities for publicizing stories, and who has—or ought to have—a right to attract wide public attention. The choice of what becomes published political news can be left to message senders eager to foster their own political agendas, such as government officials, party spokespersons, and interest group leaders. Alternatively, print and broadcast journalists, editors, and media owners can be the chief gatekeepers who determine which political messages will be publicized through news media channels and how they will be framed. What kind of political expertise entitles them to perform this function? Should they be regarded as public trustees or as purveyors of special interests, including their own? The answers have always remained unclear. Besides, message senders drawn from the same segments of society often operate in vastly different ways. For example, some journalists are significant initiators of news content, while others take their cues largely from major political actors. Journalists also vary in their ideological fervor. Some remain detached from partisan or ideological competition, while others take sides and become advocates for various causes.

Regardless of the nature of the actors who dominate news selection, theorists agree that pluralist competition among diverse outlets is essential for civil liberties and freedoms in democracies. Communication should be open so that many political interests can advance their causes, no matter how popular or unpopular their views. Journalists must therefore be free from political coercion in choosing stories to cover and in selecting story frames. Journalists should have credible evidence to support the accuracy of the factual information they present. Privacy and libel laws should protect individuals from undue media intrusion and defamation of character, although the appropriate dividing line between the public's right to know and individuals' right to privacy may be difficult to locate.

Which opportunity to publicize a political issue becomes an actuality? Which claimants among the noisy throng at the media gate will get a hearing? There are no fixed rules for selection, aside from the fact that claimants who represent power by virtue of their office or their human or material resources move to the head of the line of eager contenders for media coverage. The political significance of the story is rarely a commanding concern. In fact, it remains an open question whether the news media in a democratic society are obliged to facilitate political discourse when they are business ventures that need profits to survive. The mergers of news and entertainment organizations in the United States have heightened the commercial pressure to make political news a blend of information and entertainment aptly dubbed "infotainment." Public service broadcasting traditions in other countries have resisted this tendency.

The unwritten rules of democratic political culture do assign a public service role to news media. That role requires devoting time and space to the public policy agenda in order to reveal to political leaders and citizens the strengths and weaknesses of various policy proposals. Information should also be available about the performance of politicians and the qualifications of new aspirants to public office. Corruption, abuses of power, and other misconduct in the handling of public affairs should be reported, irrespective of the prominence of the parties involved, although appropriate standards of conduct in public life remain a matter of contention. In addition, the unwritten rules of democratic political culture require news media to apprise the political community about the political opinions, concerns, and interests of various publics. How much time and space and analysis these matters receive is discretionary.

The Stakeholders

Who are the stakeholders in this struggle for control of political news? There are three major types.

- First are the news producers—print and broadcast journalists, editors, and owners—who develop and write political news that links government officials, interest groups, and citizens. Journalists' news-writing objectives may be clashing. Their desire to maintain professional standards irrespective of mass audience appeal may conflict with their desire to entertain audiences, thereby enhancing the profitability of the news enterprise.
- Second are politicians and other power seekers who want to shape public policy and enhance their prestige. They try to influence the choice of stories that the media publish or keep beyond public scrutiny. They also try to control how the media frame particular stories.
- Last, but by no means least, are members of the public who watch or read and use the particular blend of information and entertainment that news stories provide. The Internet has blurred the line between citizens and professional journalists somewhat. Growing numbers of citizens are publicizing news as if they were reporters, using Weblogs and videos, and taking photos of breaking news events.

All these stakeholders seek to protect their unique interests and concerns as well as possible within the norms of the democratic political culture. Unfortunately, their arrays of goals do not mesh comfortably. In addition to the internal conflicts within each group of stakeholders, many boundary-spanning conflicts erupt among groups.

News Producers' Dilemmas

Intragroup conflicts and tensions appear most pervasive among journalists, guided by their editors and owners, because there are no objective guidelines to determine what political news should be selected for publication. To deserve publication, political news should involve an issue that is politically significant for some organization, group, or person because of its consequences and/or the actors involved. Deciding which situations meet these vague criteria (and deserve priority over other possible story subjects) involves multiple subjective judgments. What should be the news producers' role in making such judgments? Should journalists act as "impartial" observers and informers of the public, functioning like common carriers who accept all legitimate messages and transmit them in roughly the order in which they were received, or should they take the position of advocacy that makes journalists direct players in the political game? Should they play watchdog or investigative roles that cast them into a position of law and ethics enforcement as well as performance evaluation? What are the implications of these choices for democratic politics?

More specifically, how should the news media cover the political process? Should they concentrate on the substance of issues or focus more on the players? Each is a defensible approach but with different consequences. What role, if any, should journalists play in policy initiation? Should their role be deliberate, choosing to investigate a political situation to support particular policy entrepreneurs? Or should media serve as go-betweens, responding to the initiatives of pressure groups and government? Or should they ignore the consequences of their publication policies and thereby play an inadvertent role in policy initiation, agenda-setting, and in the implementation of policies? The answers are moot.

Critics have voiced concerns about the ability of newsrooms to report the complexities of modern societies when their staffers do not reflect society in terms of class, gender, race, and ethnicity. Which group's interests do the major news media serve? Does fair coverage of all groups require that newsrooms are facsimiles of society? Or are newsroom demographics immaterial in the choice and framing of stories? How should journalists react to commercial pressures?

Attempts to woo the largest possible audiences and to please the most power-ful advertisers or news sources may lead to lighter, fluffier news.

Should journalists cater to the large numbers of citizens who know and care little about politics, or should they address the minority who are truly inter-ested in politics, relatively well-informed, and most likely to participate? Pack-aging techniques designed to attract mass audiences—an emphasis on conflict, drama, and novelty—may become barriers to serious political reporting. Tabloid journalism may highlight the strategies of political battles and neglect the tedious facts about the merits of various resolutions of the conflict. But, if audience-pleasing tactics are not used, will this decision mean a sharp drop in audience size because mass audiences are supposedly bored by hard news pre-sented without sensationalism? How are journalists reacting to changes in the reporting of politics brought about by new technologies and new commercial pressures? Are these changes leading to a "new" journalism? Will they make the reporter's job easier, harder, or merely different?

Finally, how does journalism differ in autocratic states and in various tran-sitional and consolidating democracies? Do journalists in these nations have special responsibilities? Do they have the option of playing a "neutral" role when much political news reflects antidemocratic tendencies and preexisting political power? How can they safeguard freedom of the press from groups and actors that threaten the rights of free expression?

Political Actors

The roles open to journalists may raise the most questions, but political actors must also cope with vexing dilemmas. Public officials face their greatest challenges when open political communication jeopardizes government plans and tactics. The concerns vary widely, ranging from the serious to the not so serious: issues of secrecy to protect national security, political bargaining when major public policies are under consideration, and problems that threaten a public agency's good image and its ability to retain its status and funding. When such questions are at stake, is it legitimate in a democracy to cross the illusive boundary line between dispensing information and dispensing propaganda? At what point does public education give way to impermissible persuasion?

Government officials are also plagued by uncertainty about the best ways to manage their political news. Should the job be assigned to in-house public rela-tions experts or possibly contracted out to elite public relations firms? Can gov-ernments conduct effective information campaigns through press briefings, officials speaking on the record, the release or withholding of government documents, or the control of journalists' access to government officials? What ethical concerns limit government efforts to persuade people to behave in ways designed to enhance the common good along with their personal welfare?

Political parties and nongovernmental interest groups face many, but not all, of the same concerns as government officials. They must determine what strategies and tactics best serve their needs, considering their goals and their ability to command media attention. For example, how does targeting the policymakers directly compare in effectiveness with targeting the public via the news media? How successful are direct advertising appeals to the general public or other stakeholders compared to indirect public relations efforts through news media stories? Do information campaigns matter? What kinds of relationships should interest groups maintain with various types of journalists? How can interest groups maximize their access to media, especially if they are newcomers to the political arena and their causes lack glamour or involve highly complex issues?

Election campaigns occupy a unique position in the realm of political communication. Their outcomes have an extraordinarily large impact on the policy agenda, and they elicit more citizen participation than any other event. For this reason election campaigns in democratic societies follow a unique set of rules and regulations. These rules, which vary considerably in different societies, are both more and less stringent than those applied to other types of campaigns. Matters such as the amount of money that campaigns can spend, the standards of accuracy that candidates must meet in publicized messages, and the rules of fair play often are subject to stricter regulation.

The Public

Intragroup conflicts within the public realm are more acute among analysts of the role of citizens than among citizens. Commentators debate the amount of political information that citizens need and how much they actually absorb. They argue about the adequacy of the information supply and its suitability for maintaining the necessary levels of civic competence. They question whether the public is becoming harder to reach, and harder to influence, because of the proliferation and segmentation of the media.

Controversies rage about the best ways to communicate essential political messages to the public. In the United States advocates of "public" or "civic" journalism blame the decline of political interest on the media. They suggest that news selection and framing should be more directly guided by the interests of their audiences. Critics of civic journalism believe that such a policy impoverishes the news and that it is likely to detach citizens from larger concerns about their society and the world. Whether civic journalism strengthens or weakens democracy is a matter of continued debate in the United States, but seems to have little resonance in other countries.

Finally, the definition and interpretation of the public voice in the democratic process also spark controversy. Disputes continue about how well opinion polls and focus groups reflect the public's thinking, and how accurately the media report these opinion measures. Do polls articulate the concerns of citizens, or are they simply pseudo–news events that distort public opinion and displace real news? Does the choice of poll questions bias the responses? Do poll reports create bandwagon or underdog effects? Answers to such questions vary widely.

Boundary-Spanning Conflicts

Boundary-spanning conflicts among stakeholders can be approached from several perspectives. One can view them as conflicts between journalistic ideals and economic goals designed to maximize profits. In the commercial sector, accountants for media enterprises, especially within conglomerates, want to keep news operation costs low and revenues from viewers and advertisers high. Journalists, editors, and producers may share these concerns, or they may be more concerned about their clashing professional goals. Within news organizations, divisions compete for space and time. Likewise, traditional news beats within the government may compete for attention with newcomers such as the science or education beat.

Conflicts abound among stakeholders who represent separate institutions within the same groups. Among media, for example, newspapers compete for audience with other newspapers, with television, with radio, and with the Internet. Each medium vies for the largest market share in a particular area or among a particular audience. Its product is shaped at least in part by the pressures to win the competition for audiences, advertisers, and prime sources. If the market is naturally segmented, certain television channels may serve particular social groups or interests, such as linguistic or ethnic minorities, while others are designed to appeal to mass audiences.

Political actors compete with each other for access to news channels and for favorable treatment of their stories. They structure their tactics for gaining attention in light of the tactics of other contenders. Among audiences, some segments are favored while others are slighted. The demands of sports fans, for example, have always taken precedence over the demands of people interested in local politics. Weather forecast fans get more attention than fanciers of news about the public schools or devotees of consumer purchasing tips.

How do the conflicting interests of journalists, political actors, and the public mesh in their classic power struggle over a limited resource that is vital for each group? The answer is "compromise"! All of these actors, each with some degree of relative autonomy, are part of an evolving ecology of games, part of a "dance" in which actors have by virtue of their different skills and status positions, varying access to participate. Because they continuously anticipate each other's moves, their activities are, as a matter of course, mutually constituted.[3] As is typical of gaming situations, the payoffs for each group vary from game to game, but zero-sum games are rare. Compromises in the struggle to control the news are made easier by the fact that these stakeholders whose interests conflict also have many shared interests. In fact, although they can survive without each other, they are essentially interdependent.

Journalists rely heavily on political actors as sources. They make extensive use of information controlled by the executive and legislative branches, by administrative personnel, and by experts from semi-official and unofficial organizations. Investigative journalists can dig out some of this information without cooperation from political actors, but that task is difficult without the aid of insiders.

Just as journalists need political actors, political actors need journalists as venues to disseminate their messages to large audiences and to other elites. Political actors also require some control over the flavor of the messages about them that find their way into the news. They, too, have alternative ways for reaching the public, such as advertisements, public rallies, call-in talk shows, and messages on the Internet. Besides, many public policies can and do emerge without any media or public scrutiny. In fact, policy advocates often devote more energy to keeping news about their projects away from media scrutiny than on gaining access to news channels.

Finally, journalists and political actors both must cater to public tastes because they need particular audiences. If their audience finds political news unappealing, it can turn to alternative ways to get information or it can abandon hard news for infotainment or straight entertainment. The popularity in America of radio and television call-in talk shows and chat groups on the Internet is testimony to the public's flexibility in choosing appealing information sources. So is the widespread use of video- and audiotapes and the popularity of cable or satellite television and customized news offerings on the

Internet. The advent of digital terrestrial television promises to fragment the mass audience even more.

The upshot of mutual interdependence is the necessity to bargain even when the parties are unequal in strength. Each party receives and grants concessions in return for a measure of influence over the news product. Groups that seek publicity supply the type of story material that they believe journalists want, in a format tailored as much as possible to a particular news medium's needs. In return, journalists grant coverage seekers publicity in a format that may be a cross between what journalists might ideally prefer and what the coverage seekers want. The audience's power lies in limiting its attention to news offerings that meet its needs and in accepting the substance and perspective of news stories only if the stories seem persuasive and in tune with its sensibilities.

The Environment

The compromises that emerge from the struggle over political news are greatly influenced by the environment in which the players are forced to interact, even though they control the environment to a degree through public policies and by manipulating each other. The environment includes the physical universe that creates problems and opportunities and the political culture that encompasses the notion of democracy. As mentioned, that notion requires the press to be receptive to news from all quarters so that an open marketplace of ideas can foster democratic governance.

The environment that affects the struggle over news also includes the legal context regulating freedom of the press, technological developments that are transforming news, and a vast global communications network. Equally important are general economic conditions and the structures of media ownership. Concentration of control over media enterprises in the hands of large corporations, major entrepreneurs, or government officials may endanger the free flow of information that is essential in a democracy. Well-funded public television, if independent from state political controls, can mitigate the corrosive tendencies of commercial culture.

Many of the environmental factors are in flux. In some democratic societies, for example, ownership of media is becoming more concentrated; in others, it is becoming more fragmented. In the United States both trends are in evidence simultaneously, which raises serious questions about the impact of media ownership on democratic governance. It is clear that new technologies are transforming political communication. But it is unclear how journalists, political actors, and the public will adapt to the new technologies. Will novel presentation opportunities, such as interactive forms of communications, benefit or harm the flow of political messages? Will the new technologies attract new audiences? Will they create a global village, or a Tower of Babel? Will they change the substance of political communication?

If democracy seems endangered, is regulation of the news media warranted as a protective measure? Should limits be placed on socially harmful messages, such as obscenity or violence, and politically harmful messages, such as terrorist threats or ethnic hate messages? Should laws be enacted to mandate socially desirable messages, such as debates among political candidates or educational programs for children?

Even without government intervention, should the participants in the political communication game engage in more self-restraint? The "guilty until proven innocent" journalism, which crested in the United States after the Watergate scandal forced President Richard Nixon to resign in 1974, still contributes to public cynicism that discourages people from participating in public affairs. Should social controls be used to curb such stories? Should the privacy of public figures be respected in matters that lie outside the political realm? Should "responsible" journalists downplay reports of battlefield reverses that are likely to demoralize the troops and the public and bring pressures to end a military engagement prematurely? Should they permit good programs to be scuttled through bad publicity? These issues and many others are debated and examined by the contributors to this volume.

Organization of the Book

The book is organized in four sections starting with journalists, followed by political actors, the public's voice, and finally the changing context of political news.

Journalists

In the first section of the book, Thomas E. Patterson highlights the sharp distinctions among how journalists see their jobs by comparing their perceptions in five advanced industrialized democracies: the United States, Britain, Germany, Sweden, and Italy. Based on surveys of reporters, editors, and news managers in each country, the study identifies two principal behavioral dimensions. The first refers to whether reporters are active in shaping, interpreting, or investigating political subjects or whether they are passive, taking their cues from government officials or other actors outside the news system. The second dimension distinguishes between journalists who perceive themselves as neutral in partisan or policy disputes and journalists who see themselves as advocates.

Using these classifications, Patterson develops a fourfold typology of reporters: passive-neutrals, passive-advocates, active-neutrals, and active-advocates. Reflecting traditional perceptions of public service journalism, British broadcasters were closest to the passive-neutral type, and Italian journalists fit best into the passive-activist category. American journalists were closest to the active-neutral group, and German journalists resembled active-advocates. Patterson reflects on the consequences of these approaches for cross-national differences in media systems. He envisions future expansion of journalists' impact on politics.

In chapter 2 Ellen Mickiewicz considers the role of prominent broadcast journalists in contemporary Russia. Compared to the social context of the Soviet Union, the new democratic system allows television anchors to be active advocates. To illustrate how the journalists' positions changed during transitions from dictatorship to a more open regime, Mickiewicz traces the careers of three anchors who moved from humble roles as revolutionary journalists to leadership positions as "icon-anchors." The comparisons also demonstrate that personality and context differences produce unique professional and personal reputations for each of the three journalists.

The chapter makes a major contribution to media studies by using multiple focus groups to assess the Russian public's reactions to the new types of anchors. Reactions varied according to demographic group and region of the country, but the predominant sentiment was a longing for the past anchors who simply read government-approved scripts. Many citizens had a difficult time connecting with new anchors who seemed too young, attractive, and wealthy. Among well-educated Russians, the wealth issue was especially problematic because Russians associate it with a loss of integrity. Wealth is perceived as a sign of corruption, of selling out journalistic autonomy for money. The respect and admiration accorded to revolutionary journalism in earlier years has given way to cynicism.

To conclude this section, one of the most widely respected figures in American broadcasting, PBS's Jim Lehrer, discusses guidelines for journalism professionals. Among his nine-point list of rules are admonitions for accuracy, fair treatment of opposing view points, respect for the audience's intelligence, and clear separation of opinions from facts. Lehrer acknowledges that these rules are tough to heed in the current media environment. The roster of competitors for audience attention is growing at a steady pace, and the blandishments that many of them offer to people eager for excitement and entertainment are luring away a goodly portion of the traditional media's readers, listeners, and viewers. Lehrer fears that professional journalists will capitulate, compromise their principles, and become audience-pandering entertainers.

His passionate message to his colleagues is that capitulation is fatal to serious news production and that it is unnecessary. He points out the continuing need for professional journalists who identify important stories, investigate them, report them carefully, and put the civic needs of their audiences above the lure of making more money by sugar-coating their product. Coming from a journalist who has practiced what he preaches, that is a powerful and hopeful message indeed.

Political Actors

In this section Barbara Pfetsch explores news management by government executives in the United States, Germany, and Britain. She contends that strategic communication by governments is increasingly vital and professionalized. It is either politically centered or media centered with the latter approach becoming more prevalent. Politically centered news management focuses on creating support for government among political elites, creating horizontal linkages, and addressing conflicts within the government system. It is the dominant type of strategic communication in parliamentary democracies such as Britain and Germany, which are characterized by strong party governments, a partisan press, and strong public sector television.

By contrast, media-centered news management focuses on creating positive news coverage and popular support for political actors among the electorate, using the formats, news values, and logistics of the media. This form of news management is more common in the United States because of its presidentially centered government, highly commercialized mass media, and the predominance of adversarial journalism. Pfetsch compares the different government institutions and structures, the government media apparatus. She discusses how actors interact with the media and the government to pursue their interests through framing the news, spinning it, or distracting attention from it. The chapter concludes with an assessment of the consequences of these cross-national differences for media cultures and for the role of journalists in each society.

Jarol B. Manheim looks at some of the themes discussed in Pfetsch's analysis through different lenses. He regards news as a manufactured product, concocted by political strategists, rather than a natural product that journalists identify and present in news stories. Most political news stories flow from the efforts of domestic and foreign politicians, political parties, interest groups, corporations, and labor unions, all of whom strategize to report their concerns to the public from perspectives that benefit the source. Public relations experts working for these actors manage to produce audience-pleasing stories that are so well attuned to the media's needs that journalists find it difficult to reject them.

Manheim describes the tactics through which news shapers manipulate journalists to make sure that news stories reflect what self-interested parties want. The awesome power to create the political reality that the public experiences thus lies in the hands of largely unseen political elites who perpetuate the myth that the news mirrors journalists' perceptions of important aspects of the political world.

While Manheim paints the picture of a largely impotent press, manipulated by political movers and shakers, Kathleen Hall Jamieson and Bruce W. Hardy take a more positive stance. They analyze the role that the press can and does take in exposing deceptive political advertisements. Contrary to Manheim's image of a powerless press that spreads the deceptive messages of self-serving elites, Jamieson and Hardy contend that the press can detect and unmask deception and report its findings persuasively. Well-informed citizens will then be spared from basing their all-important election choices on wrong information. The deceivers will have failed.

Jamieson and Hardy test their hypotheses with data from the 2004 presidential election. The disappointing findings reveal that many citizens are unfamiliar with the factual situations discussed in the deceptive advertisements. Neither citizens nor journalists have done their job well enough. Although the authors acknowledge the serious problems that journalists face in dealing with deceptive advertisement, they nevertheless censure them for insufficient attention to the misinformation that harms citizens and benefits the perpetrators.

The essay does not discuss whether most Americans pay attention to political advertisements, or to advertising rebuttals, when they are crystallizing their opinions in preparation for voting. It does not say how they react to the content of the messages, if they have paid sufficient attention to them. Are citizens selectively deaf, hearing only messages coming from favored sources? Does their attention wax and wane depending on the nature of particular issues and the contemporary political climate? Or are they, perhaps, ignoring politics most of the time and neglecting their duty to monitor the performance of government officials and holding them accountable? These issues are discussed in the next section.

The Public's Voice

Darrell M. West's chapter provides a carefully nuanced analysis of the interplay between messages conveyed by political advertisements, voters' attention to these messages, and voters' ultimate choices of candidates. West finds support for all of the major theories about the influence of advertisements. These theories range from claiming that advertisements have no impact at all, because people's opinions are usually stable, to claims that advertisements can have multiple effects, from minor to profound. West explains the various kinds of circumstances that determine the no-effect outcome to the profound effect, drawing on examples from recent presidential and congressional elections.

Among the factors that, alone or in combination, determine whether advertising messages impact voting decisions are preexisting images of candidates; the credibility of the known sponsors of the ad; the format and content of the ad, including its negative or positive tone; the times and frequency of broadcasts airing the ad; and the ideological orientation of the voters exposed to it. Besides affecting the candidates' images, commercials can also shape citizens' views about the importance and urgency of various political issues. In turn, these views may increase the appeal of some candidates and reduce the appeal of others. Although commercials can prime voters to think about particular political concerns, they can also distract them from thinking about issues that candidates want them to forget.

Moving from electoral settings and advertisements to broader concerns and news media messages in general, Scott L. Althaus presents three case studies to illustrate the public's attentiveness to political news under different conditions. His research confirms the common observation that most citizens are inattentive to political news most of the time, depriving themselves of the opportunity to hold their government accountable in a meaningful way. Althaus emphasizes, however, that inattention is an intermittent phenomenon. When citizens are alerted to major political threats that are likely to affect them directly, they turn their attention to news about the situation and to concerns about the ability of political leaders to deal with the problem. That means that the public's attention to political events and its ability to evaluate the quality of political leadership is highest during periods of political turmoil and lowest in times of peace and prosperity.

Althaus's findings are based on analysis of the public's behavior during the Persian Gulf Crisis of 1990–1991, the terrorist attacks on U.S. soil in September 2001, and the invasion of Iraq in March 2003. Rather than simply relying upon participants' self-reports, Althaus uses broadcast ratings and newspaper circulation reports to assess actual behavior. Based on these data, Althaus concludes that the public's scrutiny of news and concern about the government's performance is inadequate. That harsh conclusion is softened by acknowledging that many Americans do indeed pay attention when faced with information about immediate life-endangering threats such as war and terrorism. In other words, people are civic slackers most of the time, but they do perform their civic duties when emergencies arise.

A totally different picture of the public emerges from polling expert Andrew Kohut's essay in which he revives optimism about the public's good political sense and its substantial influence on politics. As Kohut demonstrates with a number of brief case studies, public opinion poll results, published in the news media, can provide political leaders with powerful support for their policies, or they can serve as strong curbs on presidential actions. For example, public opinion constrained President Ronald Reagan in acting against Nicaragua in the 1980s; it enabled President George H. W. Bush to send troops and use force in the 1990–1991 Gulf War. Public opinion limited Congress's ability to remove President Bill Clinton from office because of the Monica Lewinsky scandal, and it helped to prevent President George W. Bush from privatizing Social Security after the 2004 election.

Kohut also contends that although public opinion draws on information provided by the news media, it also develops independent views. The influence of public opinion has been growing steadily since the late 1960s, although it is limited to reacting to policies created by others and is vulnerable to manipulation. Kohut credits technological advancements since the late 1960s with enhancing the power of public opinion. New technologies that make polling faster, easier, and more accurate have encouraged the growth of polling organizations and persuaded news organizations to make polling reports a regular news feature. Widespread publicity about the polls then forces politicians to adjust their policies to maintain favorable opinions and counteract unfavorable ones. That process can lead to major policy changes.

The Changing Context of Political News

The relationships among journalists, politicians, and citizens operate within a general context set by the structure of the economy, the impact of technological developments, and the public policy process. The last section of the book considers these issues. Robert G. Picard focuses on the tension between the ideals of democratic citizenship and the ideals of business to produce high profits by catering to the wishes of consumers. He points out that the two goals—creating media that foster civic enlightenment and serve as a fourth branch of government and keeping media as commercial enterprises operating in a free market system—are incompatible. It is a zero-sum game of civic enlightenment versus profits. Losses on one side of the ledger are gains on the other.

The mushrooming of media outlets has sharpened the competition for advertisers and the audiences that attract them. The economic environment is turbulent, and media companies see their survival at stake. Picard tracks these developments starting at the turn of the previous century, including the impact of major laws such as the Telecommunications Act of 1996. These changes have made the leaders of news organizations less inclined to pursue their civic mission and more inclined to do whatever is necessary to enhance profits and survive. The result is reduced investment in news and public affairs content and more investment in sensational stories, infotainment, or outright entertainment geared to attract mass audiences.

In contrast to Manheim's claim that the news is driven by the machinations of elites who promote their interests, Picard suggests that it is driven by the interests of media audiences. News must serve a "demand" market, rather than a "supply" market. Media cannot focus on civic concerns to promote effective citizenship because news consumers are driving them toward entertainment. Entertainment sells; serious political information is a drag on the market. Without some counterpressure brought by civic organizations or government regulators, serious political information geared to mass interests and reaching mass audiences will remain in short supply.

W. Russell Neuman's assessment of the global impacts of technological developments is somewhat more positive than Picard's appraisals. Neuman mentions the wealth of readily available news from all parts of the world, the speed with which developments can be covered, the ease and convenience of access to low-cost news, and the ability of average people to make themselves heard in the grassroots public sphere. Citizens now have much wider choices of news than in the "golden age" when three large networks (ABC, CBS, NBC) monopolized the nightly news offerings. And, thanks to the Internet, they can pursue topics of interest in far greater depth, drawing on sources scattered throughout the globe. But Neuman also points out that these new technologies have created immense economic uncertainties and concerns for contemporary media that force them to reconsider their niche among the horde of newcomers to the media scene and the plethora of diverse offerings. He warns that all too many citizens are limiting their news consumption to a narrow range of offerings despite the substantial expansion of the menu of available political news. Another cause for concern is the digital divide between the relatively small segment of citizens who are already well informed and continue to consume high levels of news and the much larger segment of poorly informed citizens who fail to keep abreast of the political scene.

Neuman warns that speculating about future developments may be pointless even though speculation is essential for designing the new technology to best serve society. There is a big gap between plausible scenarios and actual scenarios, especially when prognosticators ignore the fact that multiple, interacting changes are occurring simultaneously. Many of the anticipated, and often feared, consequences of recent changes have not materialized. The wave of mergers has not decreased news diversity, and citizens are not isolating themselves in communication ghettos. In fact, the evolving new media age may bring more benefits than many suspect. The past was not the news utopia for which many pine. Citizens should also consider that news has always undergone change because it is socially constructed, and Americans have always managed to adapt well to these changes. The global village is not quite a reality as yet. But if and when it comes at some future time, Americans will embrace it.

The last chapter returns to a more somber note. W. Lance Bennett and Regina G. Lawrence recount the major challenges to American press freedom, driven by the pressures associated with a war environment, the relentless squeeze on profitability, and the rise of the Internet. They bemoan the impact of these pressures on the chances of having a free American press that accepts its responsibility of nourishing citizens' civic information base. The wartime environment, they argue, makes citizens disinclined to listen to criticism of the government they view as their protector from the nation's enemies. The same environment allows government to control news tightly in the name of national security and at the expense of press freedom without strong objections from the press or public. At the same time, media enterprises grow more reluctant to produce serious political news because of the financial strains produced by the competition for audiences and advertisers and by business mergers that leave the media scene dominated by economic giants.

A number of features enhance these adverse trends. They include the public's low regard for the accuracy of American news media, the symbiotic relationship between the press and government officials, and the perfection of multiple ways of spinning the news text and visuals so that they reflect the views of America's power brokers. The ability of the Internet to spawn news that becomes an agenda-setter for the mainstream press is another complicating factor. It weakens the power of these media to serve as gatekeepers of what is and is not publicized.

Bennett and Lawrence end their essay with a series of suggestions for developing a press system that serves citizenship needs adequately. In an otherwise worrisome account, these rays of hope are a welcome reminder that the roles played by political actors, the press, and the public are not set in stone. They are constantly evolving in dynamic political settings and changing perceptions of what news ought to be and how it should serve the American public and global society.

In combination, the chapters in this book cover the main political communication issues in industrialized democracies in various parts of the world. These issues are worthy of serious discussion because the ebbs and tides of political news mold the political landscape. Much remains unsettled and unsettling about the interplay of journalists, political actors, and the public in contemporary democracies. Many facts about the interaction dynamics remain unknown or disputed. Norms about what ought to be are contested, as are appraisals of what is possible and predictions about future developments. We hope that the chapters in this book will enhance the quality of the debate about the paths that journalists, political actors, and publics should follow in their struggle to control the news in the twenty-first century.

Notes

1. Freedom House, founded in 1941, is an independent nongovernmental organization dedicated to supporting the expansion of freedom in the world. Freedom of the press is a major interest. See *www.freedomhouse.org*.

2. Project for Excellence in Journalism, at *www.stateofthenewsmedia.com/2006*.

3. Paraphrased from Harvey L. Molotch, David L. Protess, and Margaret T. Gordon, "The Media-Policy Connection: Ecologies of News," in *Political Communication Research: Approaches, Studies, Assessments,* ed. David L. Paletz (Norwood, N.J.: Ablex, 1987), 45.

Section I   Journalists

1 Political Roles of the Journalist

Thomas E. Patterson

Journalists are increasingly influential political actors. Their heightened power is partly attributable to changes in communication, chiefly the emergence of television as a major medium. Journalists have also gained influence from changes in politics, particularly a weakening in the grassroots strength of the political parties.[1] Yet journalists are hardly the modern equivalents of the old-time party bosses and legislative czars because politics is not their main concern. The first fact of journalistic life is that reporters must have a story to tell. They are in the business of gathering and disseminating the daily news, and they define themselves more by their professionalism than by their partisanship. "The height of [Western journalists'] professional skill," says Denis McQuail, "is the exercise of a practical craft, which delivers the required institutional product, characterized by a high degree of objectivity, key marks of which are obsessive facticity and neutrality of attitude."[2]

Journalists, however, are not full-fledged professionals.[3] Unlike physicians or lawyers, journalists do not have a body of knowledge that tightly disciplines their practice. Moreover, although many journalists have university training in their craft, such training is not a requirement for journalists, as it is for physicians and lawyers. To be sure, journalists operate within a set of professional norms and conventions, but these constraints are weak compared with the strictures on physicians and lawyers. As a result, journalism in Western democracies is not one practice but many practices, depending on the historical, market, political, and other forces that have shaped the various news systems.

This chapter analyzes the political roles of journalists and explains how they differ across news systems. I address three topics. How *partisan* are journalists, and how does partisanship vary across news systems? How *objective* are journalists, and how does objectivity vary across news systems? How *critical* are journalists, and how does criticism vary across news systems? I conclude by presenting a framework for describing the varying roles of journalists in established democracies.

The chapter compares news systems in the United States, Britain, Germany, Sweden, and Italy. In conjunction with European scholars Wolfgang Donsbach, Paolo Mancini, Jay Blumler, and Kent Asp, I conducted a survey of 1,300 journalists (roughly 275 in each of the five countries) from 1990 to 1992. The survey questionnaires were identical except in references to particular news and political organizations and in the language employed (English, German, Swedish, or Italian). The surveys were conducted by mail, and the response rate was nearly 50 percent. The demographic profile of the respondents was consistent with other information about journalists in these countries, suggesting that the samples are not substantially unrepresentative of the populations from which they were taken.

All respondents were journalists—reporters, editors, or news managers—involved in the day-to-day news coverage of politics, government, and public affairs. Our purpose was to study those journalists who are engaged in the main work of the press: the daily production of news. We did not sample journalists who produce television news documentaries or write weekly opinion columns. We also excluded daily journalists covering topics such as sports, travel, and entertainment.

We selected the respondents at random using a stratified sampling technique based on the type of news medium and news organization in which they worked. Half of those sampled were newspaper journalists, and the remainder were broadcast journalists; additionally, we selected half of each type from what we subjectively categorized as major or leading news organizations (such as the *Los Angeles Times*, *Washington Post*, CBS News, and CNN in the United States, or the *Daily Telegraph*, *Guardian*, BBC, and ITN in Britain). The others were sampled from the remaining daily news organizations in each country.

Partisan or Neutral?

The press and political parties were once closely linked. The nineteenth-century press was rooted in partisan advocacy and supported by party patrons, in and out of government. Today, partisan news organizations are rare in the United States, and they have been in a long-term decline in Europe. As McQuail notes, the "party newspaper has lost ground to commercial press forms, both as an idea and as a viable business enterprise."[4]

For journalists, partisan inclinations have given way to a professional orientation that, for example, ranks accuracy above advocacy and places approval by peers ahead of approval by political actors. Today's journalists do not take orders from outsiders; they operate within the confines of a professional calling.

Vestiges of the old-time partisan press remain, however. Many of the national dailies in Europe are associated with a particular party or ideology. Naturally, they differ in important ways from their nineteenth-century counterparts. Financed by circulation and advertising revenues rather than government or party subsidies, their news is professionally produced and aims primarily to inform rather than to persuade. Nevertheless, the vitality of these newspapers flows in part from their advocacy role and the loyalty of their partisan readers.[5] Other newspapers also take a partisan stance but seemingly confine it to their editorial pages. Studies have found, for example, that most U.S. newspapers are relatively consistent in their editorial positions and candidate endorsements.[6]

The five-country survey indicates that there is considerable variation in the partisan tendencies of Western news systems. We asked the respondents to locate their country's leading news organizations on a seven-point, left-right scale. British journalists perceived a rightward tilt in their print news system. The *Guardian* and others on the left were outnumbered by the *Daily Telegraph*, *Times*, and others on the right. German and Swedish journalists also perceived a rightward tilt in their print news system, but to a lesser degree than Britain's. On the other hand, Italian journalists saw a left-center bias, with *Il Giornale* as the one clear right-leaning major print news outlet.

The United States offers yet another variation. Its news organizations are clustered in the middle of the political spectrum, no doubt a reflection of its century-old tradition of impartial news reporting.[7] As U.S. journalists perceive it, the ideological difference between the most liberal print outlet (the *Washington Post*) and the most conservative print outlet (*Time* magazine) is small—only 1.1 points on the seven-point scale. In contrast, the range between the extremes of major European print news organizations was substantial: 3.5 in Sweden (between *Aftonbladet* and *Svenska Dagbladet*), 3.6 in Britain (between the *Daily Mirror* and the *Daily Telegraph*), 4.0 in Germany (between *Frankfurter Rundschau* and *Die Welt*), and 4.4 in Italy (between *Il Manifesto* and *Il Giornale*).

Nor are broadcast organizations completely outside the fray of partisan politics. In Germany, Italy, France, and some other European countries, broadcasting has sometimes been structured in ways that allow the parties to control some newsroom appointments.[8] At times in Italy, the three channels of the state broadcasting system, RAI, have been apportioned among the various political parties.[9]

As perceived by journalists, broadcast organizations in the five countries are less partisan than print organizations. Indeed, although partisanship was a perceived component of broadcasting in the German, Swedish, and Italian cases,[10] the British and U.S. broadcast media were seen as having no discernible partisan tendency. (The U.S. survey was conducted before Fox News was established.[11])

Partisanship in the media, however, is not only a question of news organizations. There is also the issue of whether journalists' political beliefs affect their news decisions. Allegations of a "hidden" liberal or conservative bias among supposedly nonpartisan journalists have surfaced at one time or another in nearly every Western democracy, none more so perhaps than the United States.[12]

Systematic content-analytic studies do not lend strong support to claims that avowedly neutral news outlets systematically slant their coverage to favor a particular party or ideology.[13] It is difficult, however, to determine from content analysis whether a preponderance of negative coverage is a result of partisan bias, adverse circumstances, or other factors.

In an effort to isolate the effects of partisanship, we included quasi-experimental questions in the five-country survey. Respondents were presented with textual descriptions of four situations and asked to make news decisions about each of them. The situations came from actual news stories and were identical in each of the five questionnaires except for references to country-specific institutions.[14]

Seventeen of the news decisions had a partisan slant embedded in them, and we correlated journalists' choices in these seventeen cases with two measures of journalists' partisanship, giving us thirty-four "tests" of the relationship. The results provide strong evidence that journalists' partisan beliefs affect their news decisions. Left-of-center journalists and right-of-center journalists exhibited different tendencies in their news decisions. For example, in a situation involving a tightening of air quality standards, left-of-center journalists were more likely to emphasize the resulting improvements in air quality, and right-of-center journalists were more likely to focus on the costs to business of higher standards.

German journalists were the most partisan. In nearly every instance, the news decisions of left-of-center and right-of-center journalists tended to diverge in the direction predicted by their partisan leanings. Of the thirty-four decisions, thirty correlations were in the predicted direction among German journalists, twenty-nine among Italian journalists, and twenty-six among those in Britain, Sweden, and the United States. The probability that even as few as twenty-six of thirty-four correlations would occur in the predicted direction is less than .01. The individual correlations were relatively weak, however. The average positive correlation (Pearson's r) was .15 for Germany, .11 for Italy and Britain, .09 for the United States, and .08 for Sweden. The data suggest that the hues of journalists' partisanship tend to shade the news rather than coloring it deeply. Journalists' partisanship is a more robust influence in those systems, such as in Germany, Italy, and Britain, where news organizations are themselves regularly engaged in partisan advocacy.

The "hue" testifies to the strength of journalistic professionalism. Although partisan journalism and professional journalism are sometimes portrayed as opposite types, they can coexist.[15] Partisanship does not preclude standards of practice, such as the accuracy of factual claims.[16] A key to professionalism is autonomy—freedom from intervention by outside actors. If such intervention was once commonplace, it is now rare. Press-party parallelism—Colin Seymour-Ure's term for the alignment of news organizations with partisan forces[17]—is for today's news organization a choice rather than an imperative. To describe Britain's *Daily Telegraph* as a mouthpiece of the country's Conservative Party would require overlooking the *Telegraph*'s top priority— the gathering and reporting of news. It also would overlook the *Telegraph*'s willingness to criticize wayward Conservative Party policies and leaders. The *Telegraph* is a center-right paper as opposed to a Conservative Party paper.

Partisanship in a news system may serve to bolster partisanship in the news audience. News messages that are partisan in tone and emphasize party differences may activate and reinforce citizens' partisan tendencies. Although Russell Dalton and Steven Weldon's 2005 study revealed growing antipathy toward political parties across the Western democracies, the decline in Germany, Italy, and Britain has been less steep than in the United States and Sweden.[18] The German, Italian, and British news systems are also measurably more partisan than the American and Swedish systems.

Another question about news partisanship is whether it affects citizens' policy and candidate preferences. Researchers have had difficulty isolating such effects, and our research provides a possible reason: news partisanship is two-sided. Historically, news organizations—reflecting the partisan leanings of wealthy owners and publishers—have sided editorially with conservative parties. As journalists see it, news organizations retain this bias. When asked to place their news organization's editorial position on a seven-point left-right scale, journalists tended to place it somewhat to the right-of-center. Italy was the lone exception to this pattern. On the other hand, journalists themselves tend to have a left-of-center preference. In all five countries, more journalists positioned themselves to the left on the seven-point left-right scales than placed themselves to the right. The leftward tilt is not extreme. Journalists, to use Herbert Gans's description, are mainstream "progressives" rather than "radical liberals." [19] Nevertheless, journalists are a partisan counterbalance to the news organizations in which they work.

Objective or Subjective?

If journalists' partisanship shades the news, their commitment to objectivity more fully shapes it. Objectivity is the defining norm of modern journalism. The degree to which it governs journalists' thinking is suggested by data from the five-country survey. Even in Sweden, where the norm was weakest, 76 percent of the respondents said that it is "very important" that "a journalist try to be as objective as possible." American journalists expressed the highest level of support for the norm; 91 percent said that objectivity is "very important." Fewer than 1 percent of the respondents in each of the five countries said that a commitment to objectivity is "not at all important."

But, objectivity is a less-robust influence than it might first appear. For one thing, objectivity means different things in different news systems and to different journalists (see Table 1.1). In only one country, Sweden, did half or more of the respondents embrace the same notion of objectivity. A majority of Swedish journalists (58 percent) said that objectivity means "getting to the hard facts of a political dispute." This view was also held by a plurality of the German journalists (42 percent) and Italian journalists (30 percent), although nearly as many Italian journalists (27 percent) said that objectivity is a question of expressing "fairly the position of each side in a political debate." This latter conception—objectivity as "fairness" or "balance"—was the plurality opinion (31 percent) among American journalists, print journalists (37 percent) and broadcast journalists (41 percent) alike. The "fairness" conception also typifies a plurality (31 percent) of British journalists, but in this case the broadcast and print journalists diverged. Among British broadcast journalists (35 percent), the "fairness" conception was the plurality view. Among British print journalists, however, a plurality (31 percent) favored the "hard facts" definition of objectivity.

Such differences are partly a result of cultural variations. Although Western news systems share many characteristics, they also are a product of distinctive cultural influences in every society.[20] A news system does not develop in isolation. If journalistic norms and conventions are to some degree a result of the imperatives of daily news production, they are also shaped by a society's cultural values.

Table 1.1 Journalists' conceptions of objectivity

Which statement comes closest to your understanding of the term "objectivity"?	*Britain*	*Germany*	*Italy*	*Sweden*	*United States*
An equally thorough questioning of the position of each side in a political dispute	21%	19%	11%	7%	10%
Going beyond the statements of the contending sides to the hard facts of a political dispute	28	42	30	58	28
Expressing fairly the position of each side in a political dispute	31	21	27	22	39
Making clear which side in a political dispute has the better position	1	1	3	0	1
Not allowing your own political beliefs to affect the presentation of the subject	19	17	29	13	22

Source: Five-country survey of journalists, Thomas Patterson and Wolfgang Donsbach, research directors.

This type of influence is evident, for example, in the differing historical traditions of American and German journalism. Although the U.S. news system originated in the country's party system, it was, by the late 1800s, a commercialized industry.[21] The news had become big business. Profits outweighed politics in the minds of most publishers, and they invented a form of news that enabled them to deliver large audiences to their advertising clients. Coverage of events replaced commentary as the main content of the news, and newspapers toned down their partisanship in order to appeal to as broad a segment of the population as possible. These tendencies culminated in the development of a distinctive objective style of reporting that centered on "facts" and was "balanced" in the sense that it fairly presented both sides of partisan debate.[22]

In Germany a different cultural bias prevailed. From its beginning the press was dominated by a strong belief in the superiority of opinion over news.[23] The opinionated editor and commentator was seen as the epitome of the journalistic profession.[24] German journalism was influenced by the belief that objective or even neutral accounts of reality are not possible.[25] Unlike the liberal consensus in America, European philosophy claimed that an individual's weltanschauung would always determine his or her interpretation of reality, which hindered the emergence of the type of objectivity that typified American journalism.[26]

Studies indicate that German journalists see themselves chiefly as social analysts and critics who seek to present a well-reasoned interpretation of political reality.[27] To the German journalist, objectivity is less an issue of impartiality than a question of getting to the "hard facts" underlying partisan debate. The German journalist seeks a fuller accounting than can be found in the competing claims of the opposing sides. Although American journalists would describe this type of reporting as "subjective," German journalists would defend it as more "realistic" and in this sense more "objective" than the American style.

German journalists are therefore more actively involved in the construction of news frames than are their American counterparts. For example, American journalists rely more heavily on interviews with official and expert sources and are more likely to rely on eyewitness reports when describing events. German journalists are more likely to rely on research materials and their own conclusions when creating their news stories.

The German tendency also derives in part from what Daniel Hallin and Paolo Mancini describe as the "coexistence" within German news systems of "a high level of political parallelism . . . with a high level of journalistic professionalization."[28] Like their American counterparts, German print journalists adhere to standards of factual accuracy and sourcing, but, unlike the American journalists, they bring a point of view to their reporting, which leads them to select and frame material in supportive ways.

Journalists in the British, Swedish, and Italian news systems employ styles that fall between the American and German styles. The Swedish style, for example, combines the interpretive qualities of the German model with the less-partisan tone of the American model.

In all five news systems, journalists are actively involved in the interpretation of political reality and therefore in the framing of political alternatives. Journalists in some of these systems, however, have more freedom to engage in this type of reporting than their counterparts elsewhere. Western journalists may all subscribe to the norm of objectivity, but it is far from a universal doctrine or strict imperative.

Conceptions of objectivity likely affect journalists' contributions to the "marketplace of ideas." All democracies profess a commitment to a free trade of opinions and depend on news organizations to facilitate it. In a news system where "fairness" is the norm of objectivity, this goal is promoted through "internal diversity": each news organization gives voice to various sides in a political debate. In a news system where probing inquiry is the norm, a robust marketplace of ideas requires "external diversity": news organizations that take different positions on political issues.

Neither form of objectivity, however, guarantees the existence of a free marketplace of ideas. Internal diversity would seem the preferred model because the citizen could gain exposure to a variety of opinions through a single news source. Research on the American press, however, indicates that its conception of fairness operates within a quite narrow band, roughly that defined by the differences between the major parties and their leaders.[29] Moreover, American journalists tend not to probe very deeply into issues, partly as a result of their desire to avoid even the appearance of bias. In a study of campaign coverage of the 1996 U.S. presidential race, Robert Lichter and Richard Noyes found that 75 percent of issue references on television news and in newspaper stories were single stand-alone sentences.[30] "Pack reporting" is also prevalent among American journalists. Because their norms discourage the expression of personal opinion, they often agree on their interpretation of events. Indeed, in our five-country study, U.S. journalists were substantially more likely than their European counterparts to make the same choices when asked to make decisions about a news situation.

The form of objectivity illustrated by the German style results in a deeper probing of issues and greater individual variation in news decisions. These tendencies suggest that this form of objectivity creates in practice a more robust form of political debate. External diversity is, however, problematic if significant opinions are underrepresented in the news system as a whole or if citizens do not make use of news sources that offer alternative views.

The ideal system in terms of diversity, then, would seem to be one where external diversity is supplied by a variety of news organizations, which are spread across the political spectrum, and where internal diversity is provided by other news organizations committed to a relatively impartial but full airing of political issues. Of the five news systems in our study, the British and German appear closest to the ideal. In these countries, internal diversity is supplied through an issues-oriented broadcasting system, and external diversity through a partisan-tinged newspaper system. The Italian and Swedish systems each lack one aspect, and the American system has neither of these features. If other U.S. television outlets adopted the Fox News model, the external diversity of the U.S. system would increase,[31] though in a unique way—through its television news system rather than through its print news system.

Critical or Deferential?

Journalists are always on the lookout for fresh stories, and political leaders are a prime source. Not surprisingly, journalists cultivate relationships with politicians to gain access to what they are thinking and doing. For their part, politicians need the press to get their message across to the public. For this reason, they go out of their way to build relationships with reporters, briefing them on important plans, granting them access to official places and proceedings, and even providing them with working space.

Journalists and politicians have natural reasons for cooperation, but there are also natural sources of conflict between them. As professionals, journalists want to make their own news decisions, and they fear that self-serving officials will try to manipulate them. For their part, politicians worry that journalists will distort their message or turn against them.

These fears intensified in the late twentieth century. At an earlier time, the press in most of the Western democracies was deferential to political authority. The rules of reporting required the journalist to rely on newsmakers to define events and issues. In the 1960s, however, a lengthening list of government policy failures (such as Vietnam in the case of the United States) and a heightened sense of professionalism among journalists contributed to a less-deferential stance. Many in the news business began to feel that they should no longer merely cover top leaders but should also critically scrutinize their actions and motives.[32] "This new kind of active and critical journalism," said Jurgen Westerstähl and Folke Johansson in describing the Swedish case, "strive[s] to ensure that the troublesome aspects of society and the behaviour of the holders of power [are] under constant supervision."[33]

The transparency of the message and the credibility of the source get as much scrutiny as the message itself. Journalists regularly question officials' motives, methods, and effectiveness.[34] They are also less deferential to the agenda established through the workings of political leaders, institutions, and organizations.[35]

Westerstähl and Johansson describe critical journalism as a "news ideology" in the sense that it assumes that politicians are blatantly self-serving.[36] This assumption relieves the journalist of the need for careful investigative reporting. A common technique is to use a politician's opponents to discredit his or her claims or performance. When a politician makes a statement or takes action, they turn to his adversaries to attack it. The critical element is supplied, not by a careful assessment of the claim or action, but by the insertion of a counterclaim. "This has become a routine procedure among modern journalists," note Westerstähl and Johansson of the Swedish case. "Instead of straight news, they prefer, on supposedly professional grounds, to support a controversy. This development or degeneration of critical journalism explains, in our view, the high rate of criticism in the news."[37]

As this observation suggests, critical reporting is not by definition a more responsible form of journalism than its opposite type. Like all forms, critical journalism can be irresponsible. When it becomes a "new ideology," critical journalism can be superficial or occur within a narrow context—for example, confined to the behaviors of political leaders while ignoring the effects of public policy on society. The latter is more likely to be a hallmark of partisan journalism than of critical journalism.

Critical journalism is not equally prevalent in all Western news systems. In our survey Swedish journalists were most inclined to say that a critical posture defines their work and, along with the American journalists, were most likely to say that the news "is a means by which government officials can be held accountable for their actions" and to believe that the private lives of public officials are a relevant subject of news coverage. The Italian journalists were least likely to endorse critical journalism and least likely to say it described their work. After German journalists, they were also least likely to say that officials' private lives were an appropriate news subject.

The tendency toward critical journalism is affected by cultural factors. In the United States an abiding mistrust of authority and a tradition of muckraking journalism accelerated the process. Skepticism is also part of the Swedish heritage, and critical journalism may have gained its earliest and deepest foothold in Sweden.[38] Partisan norms also affect critical journalism. The countries where critical journalism is not as pervasive—Italy and, to a lesser extent, Germany and Britain—have news systems that are more partisan than those of Sweden and the United States. Although critical journalism is a form of advocacy, it is not the same as partisan reporting, which stems from a policy bias. Critical reporting is moralistic in tone, rooted in professionalism, and aimed at politicians of all stripes, not just those of an opposing political party.

Critical journalism may be a contributing factor to the decline in political trust that is evident in many Western democracies. The decline has been sharpest in the United States and Sweden, which, as noted, are countries where the press is highly critical of political leaders and institutions. In turn, the press in these countries has been widely criticized for weakening the bond between the public and its leadership, which, arguably, is essential to a properly functioning democratic system. But an overly compliant press is also a threat to effective governance. The Italian press, for example, does not have a tradition of aggressive watchdog journalism. The exposés of political corruption that swept Italy in the mid-1990s, for example, were the work of courageous prosecutors rather than enterprising reporters. On the other hand, Italian reporters seized on the investigations, placing them at the top of the news and in this way lending force to the charges being leveled by activist judges.[39]

These contrasting cases reveal an important fact about modern journalists. They are widely expected to be all things at once: watchdog, messenger, reporter, analyst, advocate, broker. But these roles are not fully compatible, and by focusing on one, journalists inevitably diminish their ability to perform another equally well.

A Framework of Roles

The discussion so far has broadly described journalists' political roles and how they differ across news systems. In this section, I propose a more systematic framework.

Bernard Cohen was one of the first scholars to devise a typology of journalists' roles; he separated the "neutral" role from the "participant" role.[40] John Johnstone, Edward Slawski, and William Bowman applied this typology in one of the first-ever surveys of American journalists.[41] A decade later, based on their survey of U.S. journalists, David Weaver and G. Cleveland Wilhoit proposed a three-role typology: the interpreter, the disseminator, and the adversary.[42] In a comparative study, Renata Köcher described British journalists as "bloodhounds" and used the term "missionaries" to identify German journalists.[43] Other analysts have proposed other roles, including that of gatekeeper, watchdog, and advocate.[44]

Although these typologies are useful in some contexts, they are not particularly helpful when comparing news systems. All the roles found in one Western system are found in varying degrees in all other Western systems. Typologies based on fixed descriptive categories, such as Weaver and Wilhoit's, cannot describe these variations. Those typologies that are based on a continuum (for example, Cohen's neutral-participant dimension) could be used, but each employs a single dimension only. Our five-country survey suggests that two dimensions are needed to describe the cross-national variation in journalists' roles.

One is a passive-active dimension, and the other is a neutral-advocate dimension. The passive-active dimension is based on the journalist's *autonomy* as a political actor. The passive journalist is one who acts as the instrument of actors outside the news system, such as government officials, party leaders, and interest group advocates. The journalist takes his or her cues from these actors, rather than operating independently. In contrast, the active journalist is one who is more fully a participant in his or her own right, actively shaping, interpreting, or investigating political subjects.

The neutral-advocate dimension is based on the journalist's *positioning* as a political actor. The neutral journalist is one who does not take sides in political debate, except for a preference for "good (clean, honest) government" as opposed to "bad (corrupt, incompetent) government." The neutral journalist does not routinely and consistently take sides in partisan or policy disputes. In contrast, the advocate journalist takes sides and does so in a consistent and substantial way. These sides do not have to be those of the opposing political parties. The journalist could act, for example, as an advocate of a particular ideology or group.

The two dimensions are largely independent. There was virtually no correlation ($r = .01$) between our passive-active and neutral-advocate indices. (Each was created from five survey questions.) Although it might be assumed that an advocate role conception would be associated with an active role conception, the absence of a relationship is, by itself, a justification for the use of a two-dimensional rather than one-dimensional framework.

Each of the dimensions is, in practice, a continuum, but it is instructive to temporarily regard each dimension as having two discrete categories—passive or active and neutral or advocate. When viewed this way, there are four combinations, and they encompass nearly all of the role conceptions and metaphors found commonly in the scholarly and popular literature on the news media: *passive-neutral* (neutral reporter, mirror, common carrier, disseminator, broker, messenger); *passive-advocate* (hack reporter, partisan press); *active-neutral* (critic, adversary, watchdog, Fourth Estate, progressive reporter); and *active-advocate* (ideologue, missionary).

Although this typing capacity is another indicator of the utility of our two-dimensional framework, a more critical test is whether it has the capacity to describe a variety of news systems. Figure 1.1 shows where the journalists from the five countries are positioned in the two-dimensional space. They are positioned by their mean scores on the passive-active and neutral-advocate indices. British print and broadcast journalists are located at different points, an indication that their journalistic cultures differ substantially. And, in fact, the partisan-tinged world of British newspapers is different from the air of neutrality that pervades British broadcasting. In Sweden the news cultures of print and broadcast journalists are also measurably different. In the United States, Germany, and Italy the differences in the mean scores of the print and

Figure 1.1 Role positions of journalists in five countries

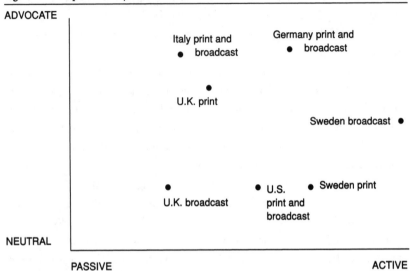

ADVOCATE

Italy print and
● broadcast

Germany print and
● broadcast

●
U.K. print

Sweden broadcast ●

●
U.K. broadcast

● U.S.
print and
broadcast

● Sweden print

NEUTRAL

PASSIVE   ACTIVE

Source: Five-country survey of journalists, Thomas Patterson and Wolfgang Donsbach, research directors.
Note: The active-passive scale is based on five survey items indicating to what degree the journalist holds a critical, adversarial position or a supportive, mediating position toward political leaders; the advocate-neutral scale consists of five items indicating to what degree the journalist prefers an advocacy or a detached type of reporting. Positions are based on deviances for each country's journalists from the grand mean for all five countries.

broadcast journalists are so small as to be insignificant. Journalists in these countries work through different mediums, but they have a shared conception of news. In other words, they have a common journalistic culture.

The spatial relationships in Figure 1.1 bear a similarity to Hallin and Mancini's models of the Western news system.[45] They posit three types: the Polarized Pluralist or Mediterranean model, which includes Italy; the Democratic Corporatist or North/Central European model, which includes Germany and Sweden; and the Liberal or North Atlantic model, which includes Great Britain and the United States. The clustering in Figure 1.1 is not as tight as Hallin and Mancini's framework might predict, but roughly accords with it. The congruence increases when the UK print system is conceived, as Hallin and Mancini suggest, as a blend of the Liberal model and the Democratic Corporatist model. As Figure 1.1 indicates, the UK print system is located between the other Liberal model systems (UK broadcasting and U.S. print and broadcasting) and the European print systems.

The mapping reflects many of the observations made earlier in this chapter. British broadcast journalists are nearest the passive-neutral point. Of all the groups, they most closely fit the image of the straightforward reporter: they try neither to "make news" nor slant it in any substantial way. U.S. journalists, print and broadcast alike, share the neutral positioning of British broadcast journalists but are more active participants, largely as a result of their commitment to critical journalism. Italian journalists are the most passive group, but they rank high on advocacy. They closely conform to the stereotype of the old-style partisan journalist; they take their cues from party leaders and organizations. British print journalists are also somewhat partisan but less so than the Italians, and they are also less passive than the Italians in their relationship with officials. German journalists rank higher than British print journalists on the advocacy scale and are also more active, a function of their role as social and political analysts. Swedish journalists rank highest on the active scale but relatively low on the advocacy scale. They function as critics of government and society but tend to remain apart from partisan disputes. These cross-national differences describe journalists who also have much in common, including their primary task: the gathering and dissemination of the latest information about current events. It is fair to say that Western journalists are more alike than different.

Nevertheless, the differences in roles appear to be consequential. The following possible implications merit further research: First, the more a news system tends toward the passive-neutral position, the less likely that journalists will have a significant influence on political agendas and public opinion. Second, the more a news system tends toward the passive-advocate position, the more likely that journalists will reinforce party politics in its various forms: party leadership, identification, ideology, and so on. Third, the more a news system tends toward the active-advocate position, the more likely that journalists will have an independent influence on political agendas and preferences. Finally, the more a news system tends toward the active-neutral position, the more likely that journalists will contribute to public mistrust of politics and to higher standards of official conduct.

A dynamic hypothesis could be explored further: in all Western societies, the trend in news systems, stronger in some than others, appears to be toward a more active form of journalism. If this is accurate, and the trend continues, the journalist of the future will be an even more powerful political actor than the journalist of today. We have established that the roles of journalists differ in significant ways in certain Western democracies. We need to go further to understand the causes and consequences of this phenomenon.

Notes

1. Russell J. Dalton, *Citizen Politics: Public Opinion and Political Parties in Advanced Industrial Democracies* (Chatham, N.J.: Chatham House Publishers, 1996).

2. Denis McQuail, *Mass Communication Theory* (London: Sage, 1994), 145.

3. Howard Gardner, Mihaly Czikszentmihalyi, and William Damon, *Good Work: When Excellence and Ethics Meet* (New York: Basic Books, 2002).

4. McQuail, *Mass Communication Theory*, 15.

5. Ibid. See also Wolfgang Donsbach, "Journalists' Conception of Their Roles," *Gazette* 32 (1983): 19–36; and Renata Köcher, "Bloodhounds or Missionaries: Role Definitions of German and British Journalists," *European Journal of Communication* 1 (1986): 43–64.

6. Cecelie Gaziano, "Chain Newspaper Homogeneity and Presidential Endorsements," *Journalism Quarterly* 66 (1989): 836–845.

7. Michael Schudson, *Discovering the News* (New York: Basic Books, 1978).

8. McQuail, *Mass Communication Theory*, 172.

9. Matthew Hibberd, "The Reform of Public Service Broadcasting in Italy," *Media, Culture & Society* 23 (2001): 233–252.

10. Thomas E. Patterson and Wolfgang Donsbach, "News Decisions: Journalists as Partisan Actors," *Political Communication* 13 (1996): 455–468.

11. Content analysis by Media Tenor and others indicate that Fox News's coverage is measurably more conservative than that of other television news outlets.

12. See, for example, Bernard Goldberg, *Bias: A CBS Insider Exposes How the Media Distort the News* (New York: Harper Paperbacks, 2003); Eric Alterman, *What Liberal Media? The Truth about Bias and the News* (New York: Basic Books, 2004).

13. But see Winfried Schultz, "A Study of the Success of the Chancellor Candidates during the 1990 German Bundestag Elections," *European Journal of Communication* 11 (1996): 33–57.

14. For a full description of the methodology, see Patterson and Donsbach, "News Decisions."

15. Daniel C. Hallin and Robert Giles, "Presses and Democracies," in *The Press*, ed. Geneva Overholser and Kathleen Hall Jamieson (New York: Oxford University Press, 2005), 13.

16. Daniel C. Hallin and Paolo Mancini, *Comparing Media Systems: Three Models of Media and Practice* (New York: Cambridge University Press, 2004), 191.

17. Colin Seymour-Ure, *The Political Impact of the Media* (London: Sage, 1974).

18. Russell J. Dalton and Steven Weldon, "Is the Party Over? Spreading Antipathy Toward Political Parties," *Public Opinion Pros*, Comparative Study of Electoral Systems (CSES) Project, May 2005.

19. Herbert Gans, *Deciding What's News* (New York: Vintage, 1979).

20. Jay Blumler and Michael Gurevitch, "Towards a Comparative Framework for Political Communication Research," in *Political Communication*, ed. Steve Chaffee (Beverly Hills, Calif.: Sage, 1975).

21. Michael Schudson, "The Objectivity Norm in American Journalism," *Journalism* 2 (2001):149–170.

22. Theodore Peterson, "The Social Responsibility Theory of the Press," in *Four Theories of the Press*, ed. Fred Siebert, Theodore Peterson, and Wilbur Schramm (Urbana: University of Illinois Press, 1956).

23. Dieter Paul Baumert, *Die Entstehung des Deutschen Journalismus* (München: Verlag von Duncker, 1928).

24. Rolf Engelsing, *Massenpublikum und Journalistentum im 19. Jahrhundert in Nordwestdeutschland* (Berlin: Duncker u. Humblot, 1966).

25. Morris Janowitz, "Professional Models in Journalism: The Gatekeeper and the Advocate," *Journalism Quarterly* 52 (1975): 618–626, 662.

26. Stanley Rothman, "The Mass Media in Post-Industrial Society," in *The Third Century America as a Post-Industrial Society*, ed. Seymour M. Lipset (Stanford, Calif.: Stanford University Press, 1979), 346–449.

27. Köcher, "Bloodhounds or Missionaries." See also Donsbach, "Journalists' Conception of their Roles."

28. Hallin and Mancini, *Comparing Media Systems*, 145.

29. W. Lance Bennett, "Toward a Theory of Press-State Relations," *Journal of Communication* 40 (1990): 103–125; Robert M. Entman, *Projections of Power: Framing News, Public Opinion, and Foreign Policy* (Chicago: University of Chicago Press, 2004).

30. S. Robert Lichter, and R. E. Noyes, *Good Intentions Make Bad News*, rev. ed. (Lanham, Md.: Rowman and Littlefield, 1997).

31. Markus Prior, "Liberated Viewers, Polarized Voters: The Implications of Increased Media Choice for Democratic Politics," *The Good Society* 11 (2002): 17–25.

32. Thomas E. Patterson, *Out of Order* (New York: Knopf, 1993).

33. Jurgen Westerstähl, and Folke Johansson, "News Ideologies as Molders of Domestic News," *European Journal of Communication* 1 (1986): 137.

34. Catherine A. Steele and Kevin G. Barnhurst, *The Growing Dominance of Opinionated Journalism in U.S. Presidential Campaign Television Coverage, 1968 and 1988.* Paper presented at International Communication Association Annual Convention, 1995, Albuquerque, N.M., 16.

35. Larry Sabato, *Feeding Frenzy: How Attack Journalism Has Transformed American Politics* (New York: Free Press, 1991).

36. Westerstähl and Johansson, "News Ideologies," 141.

37. Ibid., 146–147.

38. Ibid.

39. Hallin and Mancini, *Comparing Media Systems*, 123.

40. Bernard Cecil Cohen, *The Press and Foreign Policy* (Princeton, N.J.: Princeton University Press, 1963).

41. John Johnstone, Edward Slawski, and William Bowman, *The News People: A Sociological Portrait of American Journalists and Their Work* (Urbana: University of Illinois Press, 1976).

42. David H. Weaver and G. Cleveland Wilhoit, *The American Journalist: A Portrait of U.S. News People and Their Work* (Bloomington: Indiana University Press, 1986).

43. Köcher, "Bloodhounds or Missionaries."

44. Janowitz, "Professional Models in Journalism."

45. Hallin and Mancini, *Comparing Media Systems*.

2 Icon-Anchors and Russian Television Viewers

Ellen Mickiewicz

One of the most visible, effective—and courageous—of the groups to challenge Soviet power, when it was still dangerous to do so, were reformist journalists. They were not organized; they earned little money; and they were scrutinized from above. When a crack in the unity of the Politburo created an opportunity, television journalists could seek the patronage of reformers or hard-liners, and several went to the former. It was an unsteady patronage; new programs and formats were frequently canceled by the apex of the Politburo, but then different programs would start. Many of these risk-taking, on-screen journalists were young, brash, and, perhaps, arrogant, possessing the utter conviction of youth that they could conquer anything, even the Soviet system.

They became the heroes of the time of Mikhail Gorbachev, the last phase of the Soviet Union. The head of the State Television's Youth Department, Eduard Sagalaev, wanted "rebels, a new mentality." [1] Viewers were immediately attracted, even when these kinds of news and talk programs were relegated to time slots very late at night. One of them, *Vzglyad* (Viewpoint or Glance) became the most popular show in the country within one and a half years. Some of the young journalists used their new fame to run for parliament in the partially competitive elections of 1989, and the voters supported them. With their dual jobs of journalist and deputy, they secured parliamentary immunity and the protections that went with it. The most famous of them became producers, noted anchors, or political talk show hosts in post-Soviet Russia. The media covered their personal and professional lives, and they became a combination of public intellectual and celebrity. Over the course of this transformation, the iconic anchors became rich.

This chapter finds from the discourse of ordinary Russians that in the viewers' minds each of these famous icon-anchors has had a trajectory over time, but the contrail of the past has disappeared for some. This change in attitude raises some questions: To what degree have people's feelings changed and why is more than the usual then/now dichotomy in evidence? What is the perception of these viewers about the news and the techniques the icon-anchors purvey at the present time? What causes the disturbing notes of bigotry punctuating the discussion? Basically, although the post-Soviet viewers have little real memory of the exploits of the icon-anchors before the fall of the Soviet Union (except in one notable case of a memory burned by emotion into the mind of a young woman), older, university-educated viewers show in their conversation that the analogies they use and the conclusions they draw embed the icon-anchors in the surrounding reality, which at present is rife with corruption. As part of that truth, the goals and behavior of these journalists are congruent with the rest of the environment. In the environment of the past—in the last phase of communism and the beginning of the Russian Federation—they were the heroes, performing acts of singular importance and at great risk. Those images are unavailable to most of the viewers in our focus groups, partly because the images have merged with the larger reality and partly because the anchors themselves did not do enough to manage their images (and behavior) across the transition, although their transgressions of style or petty favor were minuscule compared to the scale of greed and grabbing at the time. Thus, there emerge almost two distinct personae for each anchor but little sense of continuity, and the viewers are deprived of an ally in their arduous processing of the news.

The Media Landscape in Russia

Post-Soviet Russia is a useful laboratory for this study. Russia is a nation of television viewers, and just about every home has at least one television set, except for a few far-flung rural dwellings in Siberia. The sudden collapse of the Soviet Union and the introduction of a post-Soviet reality happened very quickly, for everybody, and across the whole country. Whatever the arguments about the importation of democracy, no one today would suggest that the habits of democracy seen in advanced Western countries were or could be simply imprinted on a blank slate. There is no blank slate in human affairs and no clarity about what exactly democracy means to Russians.

In 1993 the Soviet-style, state-owned and state-operated television system became a limited market in which, for the first time, the state competed with commercially run networks. By 2002 the television landscape was dominated by four Moscow-based networks: Channel One, a public-private hybrid with the greatest penetration and ratings; Channel Two, directly owned and operated by the state; NTV, the largest commercial network; and TV-6, another commercial, less widely received station. In 2000 NTV was taken over by force by its largest stockholder, the natural gas industry, an ally of Russia's president. Many of NTV's staff went over to TV-6, then under the control of tycoon Boris Berezovsky, and TV-6 became the transplanted opposition side of television news. It, too, was crushed by presidential disapproval, hasty court decisions, bankruptcy, and closure. Months later, TVS emerged with the same leader and familiar on-screen personalities, but also with a set of quarreling investor-directors, a hugely reduced audience, and perilously low advertising revenue. By summer 2003, after TVS had closed down, all that was left of national network television news were Channels One and Two, and NTV, all owned either wholly or in part by the state or large energy companies close to the state. When this study was in the field, Russia still had four networks, and it was still possible for viewers to access external diversity in the news.

Most Russians have lived through a period called transition to democracy, which began when the Soviet Union collapsed at the end of 1991. This period has been characterized by startling contradictions: the relaxation of control of the economy, speech, ownership, opportunities to travel, and job choice, but also by food shortages and financial collapse, public health catastrophes, corruption and crime, and old people on fixed pensions of pennies under the new inflation sometimes committing suicide out of hunger and often tricked or threatened out of their former state-owned apartments.

The dominance of the national networks for news consumption has remained remarkable. Eighty-five percent of the national prime-time television audience in Russia is tuned in to one of the Moscow-based networks, and in time of crisis it is overwhelmingly the national television networks to which Russians turn. One reason is the weakness and limited penetration of the newspaper market, which has contributed to the mass audience's dependence on television for news and information.[2]

The media landscape would not be complete without some sense of the legal culture in which it is found. For the media to function effectively as producers of news and public affairs, legal protections and the legal culture that supports them should be in place. At its most developed point, diversity of viewpoints on Russian television news came in the form of external diversity: each channel had its own political agenda. Beyond that, some news is bought and paid for or shaded or planted by interested parties.[3] The payments may be made for attention to something advantageous (covering the opening of a commercial plant or a press conference during an electoral campaign) and spinning an event in favor of the sponsor, or disadvantageous, such as killing a story or failing to cover a candidate. During election campaigns, rate sheets describe the prices the various media outlets charge not only for ads but also for news coverage.[4]

Speech protections are included in Russia's laws governing the press, but they exist in a nascent, uneven legal culture in which enforcement is neither predictable nor uniform, and interpretation is far more variable than one would hope. The media sector cannot depend either on the weak judiciary or on effective government regulatory structures, and the media market is left without rules that are applied impartially across the country. This weakness affects reporters' access to information, war reporters' access to war zones, slander and libel cases, the protection of investigative journalists and their work, as well as the granting of broadcast licenses.[5]

Focus Group Methods

One hundred fifty-eight participants were invited to participate in focus groups in four cities: Rostov, Volgograd, Nizhny Novgorod, and Moscow. Each of the four cities represents a different political profile and media market.[6]

Moscow is by far the best-educated region of the four. Residents can access a large number of television stations: over-the-air, cable, and direct broadcast satellite. In this, it exceeds by an order of magnitude any of the other three cities. At the time of the focus groups, Volgograd had the narrowest range of nonstate television choices of the cities outside Moscow. Nizhny Novgorod had eight commercial channel choices; Rostov, seven; and Volgograd, only two and a half.[7] All of the cities except Moscow are situated within a large and populous area (home to 37 percent of Russia's population) of the adjacent Volga and Southern Federal Districts, thus reducing confounding differences that more dissimilar population points would produce. The focus groups were differentiated by college and secondary education, a pattern shown by pilot studies to enhance participation. There were twice as many college-educated groups, reflecting their current and future centrality to the political and economic development of Russia.

To address the generational question—will Soviet-era information processing patterns be lost, altered, or continue?—we created one "post-Soviet" group in each city. The participants were too young to have watched the typical Soviet (pre-Gorbachev) news. The average post-Soviet participant was born in 1980; old-style Soviet television began to change markedly in 1985. We cannot know if any differences are related to youth as a stage of life or to a genuine generational change; it is a first cut at the question.

It should also be noted that the post-Soviet groups in this study had mixed educational experiences: some were studying at university full time; some were part-time students with part-time jobs; some had chosen the vocational route and were working in white-collar semispecialist jobs; some were housewives, usually bringing up children full time. They were all members of the same generation, however, with no older people contributing to the discourse. This discourse was laid back, sarcastic, yet quick to become passionate, particularly in negative judgments, and attuned to a particular set of referents. It is also true that many ages and kinds of training were mixed in with the other groups; people in their twenties were in the high school groups and in the university-educated groups, as well. I do not label these young people as post-Soviet in the terms of this study, because being only with one's peers is a different experience. The post-Soviet groups had actually experienced little of full-blown communism, but their elders certainly had done so. To limit variability of context, a single experienced specialist from the Public Opinion Foundation, a Russian survey organization headquartered in Moscow, conducted all the focus groups.

As is customary in focus groups, everything was done to make the discussion among ten strangers (with nametags showing only a first name, but not the real one) as casual and comfortable as possible. Discussions went on for two hours and tended to be very lively. Before each session, the participants filled out a short questionnaire asking age, employment, education, media use, and a summary attitudinal question about the market economy and about tolerance. The form contained two factual questions to find out something about participants' political knowledge.

In response to the criticism that focus group members discuss topics animatedly but may not think them important when surveyed, Peter Lunt and Sonia Livingstone note that "people do not talk at length or with interest about an issue on which they have nothing to say."[8] Doris Graber writes about mass surveys: "In the ordinary interview situation, where closed-ended questions predominate, people's thought processes are guided only in a limited number of directions. The few cues that are provided to assist in memory searches may not resonate at all with the respondents' memory structure."[9] In contradistinction, focus groups show that the typical interpretation of responses to pivotal survey questions—for example, trust in state television and the desire for positive news—is quite flawed and that respondents intend virtually the reverse.[10]

This study was conducted in Russia in January 2002, the last period in which external diversity in television news was clearly present on a national scale. It was also a relatively normal time, chosen deliberately, without national election campaigns going on or about to begin and without an immediate crisis looming. To see how and which cognitive methods were employed, we wanted the potential distractions and divisiveness of exogenous claims on participants' attention to be reduced as far as possible.

Activist Anchors

During the period of Soviet rule, there were, strictly speaking, no anchors. Instead, there were newsreaders, who read scripts placed in front of them. Although this arrangement might seem sterile and uninteresting for some viewers, a good number of older viewers thought the newsreader brought into the living room the highest form of Russian speech, an advantage over the star anchors who came later. Looking back from the perspective of a wholly new television culture, members of the focus groups, especially the well educated, frequently displayed their appreciation of a practice long gone: the newsreaders' devotion to a standard of Russian that had disappeared. In Rostov, Irina [age 49, white-collar employee] says, "The newsreaders were clear and crisp; magnificent language." She is not alone. In Nizhny Novgorod, Nikolai [45, general director], thinking about what he liked about Soviet television, replies, "For me, to this day, these newsreaders, the quality of language." When I spoke to the most famous of all newsreaders, Igor Kirillov, he said that he considered himself a guest entering millions of living rooms; it was his obligation to display the highest form of civility and fidelity to language.

To emphasize the break with the Soviet past, anchors and correspondents no longer recited long, abstract versions of static news. For the first time, new, mainly young, good-looking anchors took over, and they did their job the way ordinary Russians, especially the new generation, recognized as their own. They spoke rapidly and used colloquialisms and slang. With this dramatic change, the anchor as star, it was tempting for television anchors to run for office in the first partially competitive parliamentary elections in 1989. While campaigning, they retained their jobs in front of the camera, a practice that violated the ethics of most news systems. That situation would not be repeated. The ability of journalist-candidates to use the medium to put themselves forward initiated controversy about ethics, and later electoral campaigns did not permit it. The journalists were by no means politically unified. Some of the leading journalists of the Soviet period were also just as eager to keep and improve their status in the new system.

"Removal of the reformist journalists from their media pulpits would, as many knew, be the ethical thing to do, but this was an argument mainly advanced by those who wished to close down the pulpit and nullify the advantages the minority reform group could exploit against hostile institutions."[11] There was also the plum of parliamentary immunity available to the successful deputies. The newly minted journalists and rising young journalists covered that legislature unevenly and, perhaps, unfairly. They concentrated their interviews on the new reformist deputies who knew how to look, talk, and keep up the tempo during their interviews. When rapped on the knuckles for this clear imbalance, the journalists said it was not their fault that the old Communist Party stalwarts were wooden figures speaking bureaucratese. They were habituated for many years to speaking without challenge at some length and to speak in the abstract, virtually incomprehensible, terms of Party language. The reporters argued that talking to the reformists and activists simply made better television. The constitution adopted in 1993 made parliament a distinctly less powerful organ and therefore less attractive to liberal journalists, and the political climate there did not favor their reform-minded agendas. [12]

The famous anchors, the "stars," were able to forge a connection with viewers in the early days of the renewed Russian Federation. They showed empathy and shared the emotion of the new time. Recall that the old regime had only newsreaders—emotionless, pleasantly impersonal communicators. It was a break with the past, even before the collapse of the Soviet Union, that new, younger anchors deliberately injected emotion and subjectivism into their stories, thus signaling a wholly different weltanschauung.

Today's young adult viewers have little first-hand knowledge of how the anchors rose to fame. This "next generation" group, averaging about age twenty-two, were very young children or toddlers before Gorbachev partially changed the medium. It is intriguing to ask members of the new generation about their relationship to the great and pioneering icons of television news. Is a new discourse forming and why? Is a generation gap also a gap in values? We will focus on anchors Evgeny Kiselev, Tatyana Mitkova, and Vladimir Pozner.[13] Kiselev, bluff, florid, and smart, was one of the partners who began NTV, the first private television news station with majority, but incomplete, national penetration. When NTV was closed down, he went to lead TV-6, a Berezovsky private property. When that was closed down, after a short interim trying to found still another television station, Kiselev went on to edit Moscow News. When that organization lost money and coherence, he left.

In January 1991 Tatyana Mitkova, a strikingly attractive woman, was at State Television in Moscow when government troops marched into Vilnius, Lithuania, and took the chief branch of State Television by force. Lithuanians were killed. By this time, national feelings in the Baltics had developed with surprising speed, and the State Television branch in Vilnius was in the hands of the secessionists and had become their strategic asset. Gorbachev, in one of the ill-considered moves of that period, tried to curb reform and reinstitute controls, but it was already too late. Mitkova was to anchor the news from Moscow while the coercive operation was in full swing. The duty officer, the deputy director of State Television in Moscow, wrote out some hastily conceived "news" for her to announce. According to her, it was gibberish that said the Lithuanians had called in the help of Soviet troops to quell an attack by a group of extreme nationalists. When she categorically refused to say it on the air, she was threatened. She then came on the air, looking pale and very grave. She said there was news from Lithuania, but another reporter would deliver it. A female newsreader read from the pencil-scribbled page. When she was finished, Mitkova came on again, saying this "was all we were allowed to say." She was fired immediately. When the Soviet Union dissolved, she was on NTV as a leading anchor.

Finally, an undoubted star with long staying power, which in itself displays considerable tightrope-walking-skills is Vladimir Pozner. He was born in Paris; his father was a Jewish Communist emigré, who was in the movie business. The family moved to New York and had a comfortable life. Pozner went to high school in New York, and then, as he tells it, Sen. Joe McCarthy rose to prominence, and the family went to East Germany, after which Pozner landed in Moscow as secretary to a famous children's author. From there it was to the foreign service of Moscow Radio and then to television. Along the way, he was not allowed to leave the country for bringing up the war in Afghanistan in critical terms; when that ban was lifted, he continued his rise. He was by far the eldest and most erudite of the anchors; his slight American accent and subtle, diplomatic, nonconfrontational conversation with the guests on his talk show set him apart from the others.

Today's Assessments of Yesterday's Media Freedom Heroes: Positive Features and Nationalism

Through what prism do the young post-Soviet viewers understand these icons and what distinguishes them in terms of positive—and negative—talents?

In all the cities, many participants call one of the three, but primarily one of the two men, "smart" and "professional." Sometimes the descriptors have a positive meaning, something that should not be in question, as when the adjectives describe Vladimir Pozner. Dima [24, university student, Rostov] calls him a "luminary"; all chime in that he is "very smart." Sergei [23, secondary education, unemployed, Rostov] says that although "he's remote from me in everything, he has a kind of individuality and he very frankly talks about himself . . . he speaks about his point of view . . . for me he's very honest. That's how I see him, like honesty."

Perhaps that is why these attributes are so powerfully negative when attached to an intent to deceive. In the Moscow post-Soviet group, Pozner's very skill at acting professional and his intelligence in appearing sincere and spontaneous elicit opposite views, such as the following:

Andrei [23, secondary school, economist]: "Simply if I speak honestly about him, I don't like something about him. He's generally a vile guy who was in cahoots already with the Soviets. As anchor I don't like him . . . such awful antipathy, such awful negative energy, a feeling that this is the other side of a person . . . insincere, unnatural. I don't like him 100 percent . . . he is an actor and anchor 100 percent."

Ivan [24, university student]: "I don't know. In the aggregate of all the subjective factors, he elicits a negative impression, at least with me. And that's why when Pozner comes on, I switch stations immediately."

Because there was a generalized allusion to history, another participant wants to restore the balance to get at the truth:

Nastya [25, secondary school, housewife]: "They said how much they had to toler-ate under communism, how much they were persecuted, hounded, and Pozner anchored those space bridges with America.[14] How he was given them [the pro-grams]; how he was fired; how many proposals he had [to make] the programs he was able to do. That is the person who gives himself to his work. . . . He achieved and maintains his situation. Let's say Kiselev achieved his situation. He lost him-self, and soured, but Pozner attained; he found it in himself and he stays."

These young people were so emotionally at odds over their judgments of an old-hand anchor that they could have been discussing a rock star. At least one underlying variable that surfaces with some participants and acts as a power-ful stimulus to emotional responses. In one Moscow group, budding lawyer Ivan [21, student in jurisprudence faculty] does not intervene very much. Tall, lanky, blond, wearing glasses, he sits and watches and listens. Then, when he has something to contribute he does so. These interventions are mini-lessons, going on at some length, never interrupted, and spoken in a firm, yet modulated voice. What he has to say about Pozner introduces what has not been articulated before in this or any other group: arguments about the titular and nontitular ethnic minorities in Russia. Titular minorities constitute the majority or a large concentration in the regions where they live, and the region is given their name. Other minorities are nontitular.

Ivan: "He [Pozner] has high professional skills. He could irritate if he were less professional. A good journalist, probably the most experienced on our television. And therefore those moments. He could irritate if he were less professional. I'm not talking here about myself, but about our television viewers. In this given case, his membership in the Jewish Diaspora is exactly the same as [anchor Nikolai] Svanidze is a representative of a nontitular ethnicity, which usually can have the potential to be a factor that irritates our television viewers. And Pozner could also irritate, but it's fully compensated for by his high professionalism."

Facilitator: "How does titular differ from nontitular? Why do you know that the majority of viewers can be irritated by this?"

Ivan: "It's just that I have a specific circle of friends I know that it irritates. And then this is in general and according to sociological data I have, simply research, that it is really so, and in general you don't have to go far, they present us history and psychology that is really us versus others. It's the typical attitude of the majority to the minority. It's self-identification when people do not identify themselves purely externally, purely emotionally. And stylistic differences are more important than ideological differences because the first encompasses a wider aspect of life from the manner of blowing your nose to the manner of thinking."

Facilitator: "What are you saying about Pozner?"

Ivan: "That he's a very smart, very professional person. There are only positive emotions to him."

Viktor and Maxim agree or, as Maxim puts it, "I sign on to what Ivan said." Smart and professional and not one of us. If he had not been so charming, cultured, and educated, would he have drawn close to the others in these viewers' minds?

Ivan's almost bureaucratic disquisition on the "other" in what is supposed to be a multiethnic country is extremely mild compared to some of the same sentiments voiced by his elders in focus groups for the college-educated. Different ages are mixed together in them, so that there is no prevailing "youth culture." Some are full of praise: Vlad [40, higher education, engineer, Rostov] calls him "a classic"; Olga [37, higher education, teacher] gushes that he is "professional, wonderful." Vika [41, higher education, biologist]: "I think he's attractive. . . . I find him attractive and I give preference to his intelligence."

Although not the majority of the observations, the anti-Pozner Russian nationalism surfaces unpleasantly: it appears to these generally older, but university-educated, focus group members that to be clearly *for* Russia is essential for anchors, as if the vulnerability of an earlier time is still present. Economically (they said in another context that they or their region are not beneficiaries of oil) and politically they have lost so much power and status, that some think of Russia as a vassal of the United States. Nizhny Novgorod participants begin talking about Pozner, when the facilitator asks Sergei [28, higher education, work unknown] if he knows about whom the group is talking? Sergei answers, "Yes, about a Soviet spy." Sergei continues:

"He [Pozner] is a person who does completely pro-Western agitation on the territory of the Russian Federation. He's a person who absolutely doesn't look at what's happened in the East. The East does not mean the Arab world and everything except Japan. There are still large countries, like China and so on. A lot of our money is sitting there. We can make so much money there for the Russian Federation that we won't need, there won't be any credits. But [he's] constantly looking back at the West, the West this, the West that."

In the south, Rostov, the anti-Pozner sentiment has the same general tone.

Vladimir [59, higher education, unemployed]: "Let's not talk about a toothache. . . . I dislike him very much. Because you watch and analyze his show. He selects without fail that person he wants to hear. If somebody starts to say something else, he instantly stops you or takes away the microphone or something, but without fail turns away. He's literate and well educated and performs the role they gave him."
    Kolya [45, higher education, general director]: "He's a professional, Vladimir—he is a professional. You really have to give it to him, his professionalism. . . ."
    Alesha [52, higher education, teacher]: "From the time of the famous space bridges. It seems to me that in his tirades he very often permitted lapses and it seems to me that he doesn't know our life deeply enough. He just doesn't know it, because he didn't live it. But he lived a lot there, well some part, abroad. He does know it but really he takes on himself the responsibility to speak for our life."

In Volgograd, where the media market is the most limited and the politics have something of the Soviet days, some college-educated participants repeated the sense of alienation they feel from the admittedly intelligent and professional anchor.

Sasha [35, higher education, distributor]: "Smart, yes, but those times when he led space bridges [mainly with the United States] differ cardinally from those he now leads. . . . In level, yes. There he connected with people and here he simply erects barriers with people. He became very irritable; he doesn't accept the opinions of people who go against what should go on in his program. He cuts them off. . . ."

Vitaly [24, higher education, job unknown]: "I don't like him because he presses his opinion. There are professional people who do it in a way that you don't think about it. But he does it so unattractively and unethically that you don't even want to watch."

Andrei [42, higher education, entrepreneur]: "Still his first programs were interesting to watch [back then]."

Viktor [60, higher education, pensioner]: "His long life in America has left its mark and although he tries to pass for a Russian, but. . . ."

Vitaly: "He doesn't succeed."

A consensus among all the groups that Vladimir Pozner has learning and professional presence leads some—the post-Soviets less than older participants—to tie these accomplishments to a will to mislead or misinform to the detriment of Russia's national interests. Had another anchor with similar gifts, but not the same biography and ethnic background been the subject of discussion, would the same reactions have surfaced?

Today's Assessments of Yesterday's Media Freedom Heroes:
Success and the Pursuit of Money

When the three anchors were struggling to keep their deeply indebted stations going and at the same time sending reporters to danger zones where the government's stories looked artificial by comparison, the viewer saw a good deal of military equipment, outfits, and smoke from bombs and rockets. By the time the post-Soviets were watching television, the anchors had finally achieved a fragile stabilization of their programs and, along the way, got a piece of the good life after so many drab generations. Evgeny Kiselev traveled and ate. His taste in wine was reputed to be excellent, and his widening girth showed his appetite. A florid man, he looked like a caricature of a supremely successful boss. And why not? A piece of what had been denied was irresistible. His weekly show *Itogi* [Results] had the highest ratings in the country of households receiving NTV signals. It was a cross between a magazine and a news show, with a good deal of Kiselev's commentary and provocative questions and daring plans—always finding what the government preferred to remain in the shadows.

To some post-Soviets his very appearance represented consumption, money, and greed, and, because he led his weekly show as a maestro with the camera centered on him much of the time, he frequently injected himself and his comments. The post-Soviets talked about this contemporary "insincere" style of his and spoke with contempt.

Lena [24, translator, higher education, Moscow]: "If you compare Kiselev with some animal, I'd liken him to such a fat, satisfied cat."

Olya [24, college student]: "Yes, he's narcissistic. . . ."

Viktor [22, higher education, manager/tour company]: "He sold [out]; ambitious. In a word, a complete bastard. I don't like him. Throw him out; send him to jail."

Julia [20, secondary education, student]: "I think he's too self-assured in his point of view . . . arrogance."

To Oksana, a twenty-year-old student in Rostov, he is "willful and proud," but she finds what he says compelling. She also calls it "subjective," by which she means that he gives his own differing view on what he is covering. "Differing" in this case means a view that challenges government policy, that goes against the official grain, and that, she says, is an enormous contribution the viewer gets nowhere else—certainly not on state stations. She went on:

Willful and proud . . . everything he says: this is interesting; this is a sensation; this is interesting for everybody. But this is still a little subjective. You feel that although interesting, subjective. But that's also necessary. Because a different approach, different points of view, so that the person can define it himself. A person [*i.e.*, viewer] can't choose himself if he has nothing to choose from, because in principle, it's necessary to speak out, know different points of view.[15] But what relates to Kiselev himself, I'd say that he's a bit proud, this man.

One would expect the university-educated groups to connect today's successful Kiselev with all that went before, but that does not often happen. Three women in Moscow take note of his personal courage and his constant challenges of government policy.

Katya [31, higher education, secretary]: "I'm still amazed that he hasn't been killed yet. He gives his views too intensely and openly; he's bold."

Sveta [36, higher education, teacher]: "A little arrogant, pretentious. . . ."

Lena [29, higher education, teacher]: "I always watch him; I like how he does the show . . . he presents the material so interestingly, that you listen and you can't tear yourself away. I like him."

Kiselev appears to be much less skilled than Pozner at connecting his challenging behavior in Soviet times to the current times of relative prosperity. For one thing, it is nearly impossible for Kiselev to appear to suffer deprivation of any kind. The issue here, the reason why the tested and heroic icon-anchors of the past have so little currency with the post-Soviets, is their common reaction to success and the successful. Success in the new post-Soviet system called capitalism is the sign of having sold yourself. The more money you appear to display, the more unworthy and cheap you are as a person. It is the opposite of the shoe-shine boy rising to be the head of the company. In Russia, all his neighbors would consider that former shoe-shine boy corrupt.

This is the kind of conversation that takes place:

Liuda [52, higher education, physician, Nizhny Novgorod]: "He [Kiselev] depends financially and politically on some people, and he does struggle all the time, maybe not only for truth as much as for his own welfare."

Vladimir [50, higher education, unemployed, Moscow]: "Kiselev knows well to whom you can sell yourself and to whom not. And he won't sell himself cheaply."

Andrei [35, higher education, engineer/programmer]: "Well, what do you want? Capitalism is the ability to sell yourself."

Olga [47, higher education, bookkeeper]: "Yes, yes. Any person can be bought; it's only necessary to know the price."

Kolya [45, higher education, general director]: "Everybody sells himself, unfortunately. We all sell ourselves . . . it depends on how much money. . . ."

Is wealth the visible mark of a life of toil? Or is it a sure sign of corruption, cronyism, ill-gotten gains? Although the post-Soviet groups were not as emotional about or convinced of the answer, most of the others brook no disagreement. The very fact of being rich is the unimpeachable evidence of guilt.

Aleksei [22, higher education, work unknown, Rostov] made the point in his group that he respects someone who has made something of his life, while Andrei [43, higher education, military] says the opposite: "You know, in our time, I don't respect people who earn money by any means whatever: with the use of filth. [How] is not important." Kiselev, they say, is a professional, but that working hard and advancing through the ranks was not the source of his wealth, they believe. They are speaking of the conferral of significant wealth that comes with, as Olga, the forty-seven-year-old bookkeeper put it, selling yourself.

Tatyana Mitkova, the third anchor, had a courageous past and a responsible position as director of news for NTV (staying on after the takeover). Actually, very little is said about Mitkova in the post-Soviet groups, even though she still anchors the news. She is called "soft and fluffy" by someone who does not like that quality. *Five* women in a group in Rostov called Mitkova "pleasant." Lena, a translator of twenty-four, finds Mitkova a "snake . . . so pushy, aggressive" and yet later says that she delivers the news with dignity: "Here's a really good brain." Reactions are superficial and tied to her appearance. Some stress her powerful personality, recognizing that she had to push her way through the male establishment. Only one of the post-Soviet participants, Ira, a twenty-year-old university student in Rostov, remembers and honors Mitkova:

I remember her very well when we had that putsch and when they anchored one program [the rest had been commandeered by the putsch committee], and it was perfectly clear what condition she was in and still she anchored at that channel. They stayed there just the same as though nothing was happening and how hard it was for her and without makeup, without anything, she conducted that program. She didn't think about herself; she thought about the people, that they had to know.

Conclusions: Changed Publics and Deteriorating Icons

Very few of the post-Soviet viewers deeply understand the risky path the three anchors took in a hostile Soviet land. What they see now—if they see them at all—comes in the form of aging rebels. Tatyana Mitkova, especially, comes in for ridicule for her hardened features. "Courage" is not a word one hears among the post-Soviets, but "out-of-touch" is. Evgeny Kiselev is dubbed old-fashioned, unschooled in today's slang. The post-Soviets look no further back.

Some memory of the anchors as they were in the past is attached to Vladimir Pozner, especially for the space bridges. The post-Soviets in our focus groups, however, remembered little of the content of those events. They observed their parents' intense interest and mobilization readying for an historic event. The children were there too and recalled their parents' behavior.

Pozner became known for his interest in and access to the American way of life. But because the post-Soviets did not analyze the content, some of which was critical of the United States, they assume that these programs were an American platform of entry. In this connection, the post-Soviets and their elders add another dimension to the understanding of the icon-anchors and their disappearing past heroism. Nationalism surfaces among some as a requirement for anchors. Finally, the icon-anchors cue some of the ultrana-tionalism and bigotry of viewers. Comments of this sort are by no means the majority, but when they are made, they are made with no hesitation, no contingencies, and with every conviction that they are right. Pozner, with his long-standing American ties and Jewish parent—although Pozner professes no religion—is the chief magnet of these comments. Ivan, the twenty-one-year-old Moscow law student, calls him a "member of the Jewish Diaspora . . . a representative of a nontitular ethnicity, which usually can have the potential to be a factor that irritates our television viewers." Fortunately for Pozner, his consummate professionalism offsets what could be a negative consequence. It is not only Pozner, but other nonconforming types who are questioned about how Slavic they really are. Post-Soviet Maxim, twenty-three, a history teacher in Moscow, says about Mitkova, "Clearly she does not have a Slavic appearance." Although these kinds of observations are not the majority or even present in many of the groups, it is curious and disturbing that they are the kinds of bigoted observations that the speakers believe can be said without recriminations and in public (and expect no peer disapproval).

The second reason for the disappearance or mere ghost of the anchors' civic deeds is their financial success. They won, and they bought into their companies and got interest-free loans or downright gifts to buy apartments. After all those years of Soviet drabness and dour days, sour humiliations from bosses who often knew nothing at all about television or scripts, the anchors observed how American and other anchors dressed and copied them. They looked good and ate well.

To viewers who remembered the anchors in their old form, their change in life style was a betrayal. The anchors had prospered very visibly and could not be respected any more. They were now part of a different world, while viewers were scratching out a living.

Finally, discourse about the icon-anchors opens wide the relationship of the individual to the environment at large. They do not know what Adam Smith had in mind for a free market or Milton Friedman for capitalism. They do know that they are living in a system described as capitalism. To them, therefore, as for Marx, all you have to sell is your own person (and not so much what you can produce as a result of labor, but as a result of influence and fraud). Looking at the prosperity of the icon-anchors, viewers easily draw the conclusion that they have sold themselves and surely for a good price. How can images of the heroism of an earlier time survive the bright styles of the present? And it goes further.

The rapid, massive changes in the economy, the crony capitalism the few at the top invented, have rendered suspicious for our participants *any* obvious wealth. Recall the military man's remark [Andrei, 43, college-educated, Volgograd]: "You know, in our time, I don't respect people who earn money by any means whatever: with the use of filth. [How] is not important." It is not envy or greed, but vengeance and anger that provoke such comments. Many building projects in the provinces have been burned down because of these emotions. Marina Goldovskaya did a documentary film called *The Prince is Back*, in which a poor family with an old pedigree comes back to the crumbling, muddy family seat, determined to rebuild it and make a museum: Napoleon had stopped there. When it was nearly finished, under the most trying of conditions without running water or electricity, the neighbors burned it down. It was not envy of one rising above the others, but a determination to bring everyone down.

With corruption so pervasive at all levels in Russia, viewers take it for granted that many people and much of the "news" are "bought." The conversation between Andrei, the engineer from Nizhny Novgorod, and Olga, the bookkeeper, was illuminating. Andrei: "Capitalism is the ability to sell yourself." Olga: "Any person can be bought; it's only necessary to know the price." This is the present. The past, when the icon-anchors had no real money and displayed their altruism, has disappeared under the weight of contemporary massive corruption that has hit the media very hard.

One focus group member said that the bought or planted news was "commissioned, but objective." What he meant was that everyone knew what was going on; no one was fooled, even though the top officials kept thinking that the undifferentiated mass of viewers were too dull-witted to require a change in their strategy. By *objective* this viewer meant that all or most of what they see is planted in one way or another. Knowing this, it is the task of the viewer to extract whatever correct information is possible out of that item. By doing the same with other pieces, the reader can make up a reasonable picture of reality. That kernel or center of reality was there to be used if a highly literate viewer could do it. Naturally, the burden of time and energy on the viewer is considerable, but in the post-Soviet time, especially with independent voices disappearing under the pressure of the government, viewers are willing, indeed, determined to do their part of the work. Perhaps for that reason, viewers criticize the icon-anchors quite sharply for sitting at their desks in the studio and no longer going out in the field to dig up the truth and bring it back.

Perhaps these anchors are no longer of real interest, and perhaps it is because they made their reputations by their exploits on behalf of freedom of speech, on behalf of Russians in general. That standing has not weathered the years very well; granted, the intervening years were turbulent. The new environment of illegally gained wealth has tarred all who seem to have reached it, even though these anchors are not in the same league as the oil industry chiefs.

If the officials controlling Russian television plan to exercise what they think of as more influence by removing dissent, the anchors, old and new, are not likely to bring with them a new credibility.

Appendix A

The Public Opinion Foundation recruits focus group participants in two stages. The first—and basic—stage involves selecting people from the "respondent pool" constructed in cities in which the foundation conducts its mass random surveys. As part of these regular, representative surveys, information is collected on the respondents' sociodemographic profile (age, sex, education, occupation, and so on) to facilitate quality control of interviewers and validation studies. When a focus group is needed, respondents from this pool are invited to participate, given a supplementary questionnaire, and told the time and date of the group meeting. If additional participants are needed, their numbers are supplemented by snowball methods. Participants in focus groups are given a small stipend and are not eligible to participate in another focus group for one year.

Appendix B

Focus Group Participants: Sixteen groups were convened in a total of four cities, differentiated by political and media market profiles. One group in each city was limited to post-Soviet (*i.e.,* participants who were too young to be fully aware of pre-perestroika [Gorbachev] television). Two groups in each city were reserved for participants with higher education. (*N* = 158, from four cities: Rostov, Volgograd, Nizhny Novgorod, and Moscow).

Sex
    Women: 53 percent
    Men: 47 percent

Age
    30 and under: 50 percent (includes post-Soviet groups, which are 25 percent of the total)
    31 to 45: 25 percent
    Over 45: 25 percent

Education

(This category excludes the four post-Soviet groups, who are still mainly in the educational system and did not indicate their intended terminal point.) Thus, for the percentages below, $N = 118$.

Higher education: 66 percent

Secondary education: 33 percent

(Given the importance of educated individuals as opinion leaders and the salience of education in post-Soviet Russia, twice as many higher education groups were convened.)

Focus Groups' News Sources

News Consumption

Daily: 51 percent

3–4 times a week: 29 percent

1–2 times a week: 20 percent

(Heavy viewing = 80 percent: that is, those who watched daily plus those who watched 3 to 4 times a week)

Moscow-based networks: 85 percent.

Notes

1. Interview with Eduard Sagalaev, January 1995.

2. Ellen Mickiewicz, *Changing Channels: Television and the Struggle for Power in Russia,* exp. and rev. ed. (Durham, N.C.: Duke University Press, 1999).

3. T. Tsyba, " 'Cherny Yashchik' TV, ili chto mozhno uvidet za degni." *Argumenty i fakty,* January 1993, 6, 30; O. Dobrodeyev, "Otkrytoe pismo Olega Dobrodeyeva Evgeniu Kiselevu," *Izvestia,* September 4, 2001, 1.

4. ABC's *Nightline* program spent a week in Moscow and broadcast pictures of rate sheets and both the producer, Jay Lamonica, and the show itself found evidence of the practice. The same information came from the author's conversation with the head of public relations for the Yabloko political party, a "Western-style" liberal political party.

5. Yana Sklyarova, "The Russian system of licensing of television and radio broadcasting," 2002, www.obs.coe.int/online_publication/reports/ru.

6. I thank Danielle Lussier for her very knowledgeable comments on these regional features and Robert Orttung for his expert assistance.

7. I count as commercial channels those that broadcast entirely on a channel or share the broadcast time with another channel and whose audiences are large enough to ensure ratings.

8. Peter Lunt and Sonia Livingstone, "Rethinking the Focus Group in Media Communications Research," *Journal of Communication* 46 (1996): 79–98.

9. Doris Graber, *Processing Politics: Learning from Television in the Internet Age* (Chicago: University of Chicago Press, 2001), 50–51.

10. Ellen Mickiewicz, "Does 'Trust' Mean Attention, Comprehension and Acceptance? Paradoxes of Russian Viewers' News Processing," *Mass Media and Political Communication in New Democracies*, ed. Katrin Voltmer (London; New York: Routledge, 2006).

11. Mickiewicz, *Changing Channels*, 86.

12. Ibid., 149.

13. Much of the material provided below comes from conversations and from the media literature and programs. They are documented fully in the author's book, *Changing Channels*.

14. The "space bridges" were people-to-people talks conducted by Vladimir Pozner, mainly, though not only, with the United States. Large studio audiences in each country could talk directly to their counterparts in the other country, with Pozner in the Soviet Union and an American, such as Phil Donahue or Peter Jennings, in the U.S. studio.

15. The question of viewpoint diversity in the immediate aftermath of the dissolution of the Soviet Union came up immediately. For the first time private news channels were permitted (two national ones). It was a system of external diversity, but more accurately, dueling advocacy. Still, President Vladimir Putin and his allies in the natural resources industries drove both of them bankrupt. One of them, NTV, was reconstructed with entirely new personnel and became, as our focus group members noticed, increasingly similar to the two state-owned or state-controlled stations. The other, TV-6, went out of existence.

3 Guidelines for Journalism Professionals: A Broadcast Journalist's Views

Jim Lehrer

I am delighted about receiving the 2006 Goldsmith Career Award for Excellence in Journalism. It is not false modesty when I say I accept it in the names of the hundreds of people past and present, who have worked on *The NewsHour*. Journalism, broadcast journalism in particular, is the ultimate collaborative medium. It takes eighteen people just to make it possible for me to look out at a red light every evening and say: "Good evening, I am Jim Lehrer." So I accept this award for those eighteen people and the hundreds of others I have worked with in these now almost thirty years.

The MacNeil/Lehrer Report started in 1975. When it began, it was called *The Robert MacNeil Report.* Can you imagine a worse title for a television program! After six months, they consulted my mother and changed the name to *The MacNeil/Lehrer Report.* Many wise people at the time said "this program is a crazy idea" because we did one story a night, for thirty minutes. They said "that's ridiculous; nobody is going to sit in front of their television set and watch a report on only one story."

We persevered, we hung in there, and in 1983 we went to one hour. It prompted one idiot TV critic to say, "Oh my God, I thought they already were an hour long." But anyhow, we persevered and we are still there. And we are there mostly and primarily and always because of the hard work and talent of a group of very classy, important professional journalists. But there are some basics that underlie our operation. Several years ago I was asked by a journalism seminar in Aspen if I had any guidelines that I used personally in the prac-

Editors' Note: This essay is an edited version of Jim Lehrer's remarks at the awards ceremony. The editors thank Harvard University's Joan Shorenstein Center on the Press, Politics, and Public Policy at the John F. Kennedy School of Government for sponsoring the event and encouraging us to include Lehrer's speech in this volume. Lehrer is executive editor and anchor of *The NewsHour,* a nightly Public Broadcasting Service offering.

tice of journalism. If I did, would I mind sharing them. Well, here is part of what I sent them.

- Do nothing I cannot defend.
- Cover right and present every story with a care I would want if the story were about me.
- Assume there is at least one other side or version to every story.
- Assume the viewer is as smart and as caring and as good a person as I am.
- Assume the same about all people on whom I report.
- Assume personal lives are a private matter until a legitimate turn in the story absolutely mandates otherwise.
- Carefully separate opinion and analysis from straight news stories and clearly label everything.
- Do not use anonymous sources or blind quotes, except on rare and monumental occasions. No one should ever be allowed to attack another anonymously.
- And finally, I am not in the entertainment business.

Those are our guidelines. And that is the scripture from whence my brief message will come tonight. I believe several of them touch on some of the critical issues of our practice of journalism at the moment, a moment that in many ways is a moment of absolute panic.

Newspaper circulation and profits are down; so are the ratings of the nightly news programs. Sound the alarms! Cable news and Internet bloggers, the satellite and other radio talk shouters, and the late night comedians are teaming up with things called Yahoos and Googles and iPods and MP3 players and other strange things to put us out of business.

I say to you tonight, sounding such alarms is absolute nonsense. As somebody said before this, I think the only thing we have to fear is fear itself. I think we need to look at a few basics. The bloggers are talkers and commentators, *NOT* reporters. The talk show hosts are reactors and commentators, *NOT* reporters. The comedians are entertainers and commentators, *NOT* reporters. The search engines search, they do *NOT* report. The iPods and MP3 are mere machines, as are cable television and satellite radio.

All of them, every single one of them has to have the news first to exist, to thrive, or, to put it in another way, first there must be the news. David Letterman tells a joke about Dubai and the ports; nobody is going to laugh if they don't already know about Dubai and the ports. Nobody is going to laugh. Jon Stewart reports a made up news story about Danish cartoons; nobody is going to get it unless they know about the real news story concerning Danish cartoons. A blogger or a radio talker comes unglued about a shotgun accident or somebody named Michael Brown or Jack Abramoff or Barry Bonds or Donald Rumsfeld or Howard Dean or Governor Taft or Duke Cunningham. They and their varied readers and listeners have to know who these people are and what the fuss is all about or it isn't going to work. Whatever the route it may travel to the blogger, the screamer, the comedian, the search engine, the whatever, it has to start with one of us, one of us in the real news business. Real news reporting always begins with one of us straight reporters, one of us journalists who was there, as Nick [*New York Times* op-ed columnist Nicholas D. Kristoff] was there in Darfur, or one who read the original document, as many award-winning journalists have done, or the persons who did the original interview and did whatever it took to make it news in the first place, to bring it to the attention of all others in the information and reaction food chain. A recent report from the Project for Excellence in Journalism made this point dead on, saying that little if any original reporting is done by the bloggers or anybody else except the established news organizations.

What concerns me is a growing tendency among some of us to stray from these basic principles that make us unique from all the others. We go with stories before they are quite ready; we spice them up a bit with over-the-line commentary to raise the volume and, worst of all, we make entertaining people one of our purposes. I tell people all the time "if you want to be entertained, go to the circus, don't watch *The NewsHour*." I never want anybody to confuse the news with entertainment or me with the clowns.

There is even a very strong competitive reason for us to stick to our journalistic guns. We have the field all to ourselves; none of these others can tell a joke or shout anything unless we have been there first. Now that does not mean that we should not adjust to the new information environment. There are technology and cultural developments that are revolutionizing the way our good, solid, needed news is delivered and distributed.

Most newspapers are sticking with their core mission to report the news. But many of them, some of them in desperation, others in quiet acknowledgment of reality, are trying bold things with the Internet and other technologies to amortize their news collecting costs and spread their reach beyond the traditional ink on paper newspaper delivered to the front door. Television networks and news programs, including ours, are making our segments on demand for iPods and all other kinds of pods. Partnerships between and among various media delivery modes are proliferating; more and more are coming; and that is the way it must be.

My point is simply that in the rush to modernize, to innovate, to survive in the new environments, that we don't lose sight of our purpose. Whatever the delivery system—the information platforms, as they are called now—we journalists are there to report and cover the news in a straight and professional way. Whether the news consumer is ultimately an old fogey reading the newspaper in a library in front of the fireplace, or a fourteen-year-old getting the latest on a pink iPod with her name engraved on the case, the story, the first story, the straight news story, the investigative story from which all commentary streams and jokes flow, that story originates in the eyes, ears, judgments, and presentations of people who report the news for a living, if not a calling.

It is not only just about our reporting. There is also evidence that the job of the news gatekeeper is not only not going away, it is coming back big time. The news noise and noise about the news is increasing out there in the blogosphere, on the satellite, the iPod, and other spheres. Because people are busy, they want some professional, unbiased, disinterested assistance in sorting through it all, to determine what is and is not important. They want that help before they read the editorial page or listen to the commentators or are shouted at or entertained. Journalists have always given that help. There is no question that the nature, the machinery, and certainly the looks of the gatekeepers must change. But like it or not, there will always be a need for the likes of television anchors who present the end result of the story sorting. They probably won't always be, or they may never be just old white men like me anymore.

A major problem we mainstream gatekeepers have now is a loss of the substantial credibility and trust that it takes to do our work effectively. Our arrogance, among other things, has gotten in the way. That is fixable, all of it is fixable. I happen to believe that there is nothing wrong with the basic practice of journalism in America today that a little humility and a lot of professionalism and transparency couldn't cure—the very traits we want others that we report on to bring to the table.

Humility, professionalism, and transparency have to come along with the realization or re-realization that journalism is still about the story. Newspaper owners and network executives and Wall Street financiers must be in on it as well. They too must remember that Thomas Jefferson said our democratic society is dependent on an informed electorate. That means that the health of democracy depends on us, the journalists, who report the information from which opinions and informed votes flow. It also may mean leaving the huge profits to the search engines, as well as the shouting to the shouters and the entertaining to the clowns. Again, I am delighted to be here to accept this award for excellent professional journalism on behalf of my colleagues at *The NewsHour* and wherever else professional journalists practice their calling. Thank you very much.

Excerpts from the Question and Answer Period

QUESTION: I have one question about the business pressures facing the industry and how that might affect the quality of journalism. You said that it's possible to get the quality back and all it takes is humility. But in the face of such tremendous business pressures, is that really possible at this current junction?

ANSWER: Well, I probably oversimplified, as one tends to do. I just happen to believe there is a business case to be made for good journalism because the clowns are going to beat us if we try to compete as entertainers. The shouters are going to beat us if we try to become shouters. I think it makes good economic sense to stick to our guns and stay in the journalism business where we are needed. All these other things are spin-offs of us. I do believe that the business case needs to be made. I know it's hard to make the case that good journalism is good business, particularly when you have corporations that are not satisfied with 10 percent profit. They want 20 percent; if they get 20, they want 25. Nonetheless, a business case can be made. That's the only point I'm trying to make.

QUESTION: What is the most difficult part of your job?

ANSWER: I will quote my best friend and former partner Robert MacNeil. When he was asked this question, he said "the worst thing about my job is that it forces you sometimes to take seriously people you wouldn't otherwise take seriously."

QUESTION: Very few people are currently getting their news from in-depth reports; more and more people are starting to get their news from superficial reports. My question is how do we get more people to watch programs like *The NewsHour*? How do we get more people to care about in-depth reporting?

ANSWER: Serious news is not only essential to democracy; there is also a competitive advantage in presenting serious news. You can go out and sell the point that people should go to the original source. When people say they get their news from the bloggers, they must realize that only 1 percent of the blogs do any kind of original reporting at all.

Instead of backing off from the business of delivering serious news, we must emphasize that we are in a business that counts. There are a lot of folks in the journalism business that say "no, no, no, we've got to emphasize other things." I'm saying don't do that!

QUESTION: I want to ask you about the Democratic and Republican national conventions. Arguably they've changed significantly in the past fifty years. Some news organizations have argued that there is actually less news content, that the American people don't want to follow the conventions unlike previous generations who were very interested. What do you think needs to happen so that the public and news organizations feel that covering these conventions is worthwhile?

ANSWER: By their headline and by their reporting, journalists tell their audiences what is really important. That means something to the audience. When NBC, CBS, and ABC feature one hour of condensed reporting of the Democratic and Republican conventions, they are saying to audiences all over the United States, "We don't think this is a big deal." Yes, the nature of conventions has changed, there's no question about it. But it's still a major story. It's just a different kind of story, requiring different resources. You have to offer interpretive information rather than the old-fashioned cop shop things, that's all. I think if we did that and if the networks and everybody else took the position that the conventions were important, as important as I think they are, I think the public would come around.

QUESTION: How did you feel, as a news anchor, when a majority of Americans believed Saddam Hussein was linked to al-Qaeda and the attacks on 9/11? Could you speak a little bit about the news media's role?

ANSWER: Well, there is nothing more frustrating for somebody in our line of work than to see polls that show the American people believe something that you know as a reporter is not so, based on the best thing you read. All I ever do when that happens is just feel terribly frustrated and realize we have to do a better job. Keep in mind that for every reporter who is out there trying to get it right, there are thirty people out there trying to get it spun. They are trying to spin the reporters; they're trying to spin the editors; they're trying to spin the executive producers; they're trying to spin the anchor people—it's all part of the process. Read Nick's column about Darfur. He is angry because of the very points you're making. Why isn't the United States of America—forget about the rest of the world—up in arms about the genocide in Darfur? Nick is doing everything he can, and he is upset because everybody else isn't doing what they can, and because people don't get it yet; they still don't get it. That is just the frustration of being in our line of work.

QUESTION: Am I correct in thinking that the BBC enjoys a deeper international trust and credibility than American media? If so, what can the American industry do to enhance trust and credibility on the international scene?

ANSWER: Trust and credibility overseas flows from trust and credibility at home. We have had a lot of difficult times in journalism recently. Sure there have been the Jayson Blairs and the Jack Kellys and other stories about falsified reporting. There has also been a terrible deterioration of local news coverage, and people no longer identify with their newspaper.

Trust and credibility is something you don't just one day wake up and get. If you lose it, and a lot of them have lost it, they have to rebuild it. The way you rebuild it is by doing stories about things that people care about. You may have to tell them they care about it. As a journalist that is your responsibility. You tell people what you think is important and lead the paper with important stories. That is part of serious professional journalism. But I am less concerned about our credibility as journalists overseas than I am at home right now.

QUESTION: What effect does the lack of racial diversity among reporters have on the news that's reported, and what steps need to be taken to improve the situation?

ANSWER: A news organization, I think, should have every kind of person there is, racially and otherwise. Race is just one of the types of differences that should be represented in a newsroom, not because you want black people to cover black news and white people to cover white news. Quite the contrary, diversity is mainly important because people who come from varied backgrounds differ in their orientations.

That is why we rigidly adhere to a policy of diversity at *The NewsHour*. The worst problem we have in assuring diversity is not so much in our personnel. You can control that pretty easily if you just work at it. But it is far more difficult to assure diversity among our guests, the people we bring on the air. There are gaps along racial and gender lines in various expertise areas.

We are always balancing diversity concerns against the need to bring the best minds to bear on the subject. Well, the best minds have been mostly white males. I remember that was particularly the case when the Balkan war was going on. Everybody who ever studied the Balkans, I'm convinced, was a forty-nine-year-old white male.

You touched on something that is extremely important to me and extremely important to us at *The NewsHour*. I'm not saying we do a perfect job, because we do not. But we are conscious of it, and I try to practice what I preach.

QUESTION: My question is about your role in the presidential debates. What debates do you feel went well? And which ones perhaps didn't go as well as you wanted?

ANSWER: I look upon the debates as things that I survive and escape from intact. It's not like doing a television program. In the unlikely event I screw up on a television program, I can look out at the red light and say "sorry, I'll try to do better tomorrow night." If you screw up a presidential debate you can affect who is going to be the next president of the United States. I am conscious of that all the time.

When I finish a presidential debate, my hope and my prayer is that nobody is talking about me, that nobody is talking about any question I asked, nobody is talking about how tough I was or how this or that I was. Instead, people are talking about the answers of the candidates because the debate is between them—it's not about me. I'm not even functioning in a journalistic way; I'm not there to ask questions and follow up. My role is to try to get them to debate each other and engage.

No one debate comes to mind as going especially well or poorly. They all come together in one excruciatingly difficult way.

Section II   Political Actors

4 Government News Management: Institutional Approaches and Strategies in Three Western Democracies Reconsidered

Barbara Pfetsch

Many contemporary Western countries have been described as media democracies.[1] The main characteristics of such democracies are that the media have taken over some of the vital functions of political parties and moved into the center of the political system.[2] As a result, the institutions and practices of politics and government have adapted themselves to the central role of mass media, particularly television.[3] This development is held responsible for deficits in mass politics.[4] It is also charged with changes in institutions, styles, and strategic behaviors in political communication, such as the growth of press operations and the professionalization of political public relations.[5] As Hugh Heclo notes, "The pervasiveness of political marketing means that all national politics takes place in a context of permanent, professionally managed, and adversarial campaigning to win the support of those publics upon whom the survival of the political client depends." [6] In the context of politics as a permanent campaign, chief executives seem to assume that to govern successfully, they must proactively be controlling the media agenda.[7] News management therefore appears as one of the practical solutions for governments and other political actors to communicate their messages strategically and use the media to further their political and policy goals.

This chapter explores government news management in modern mass democracies from a number of angles. What is news management? Does news management matter and, if it does, how is it related to the political process? What is the difference between governments and other political actors who try to manage the news? How is news management organized, and how does it vary across different countries? These questions are pressing because public information strategies in politics have changed from the traditional press release practice—based on interpersonal exchanges between politicians and journalists—to a professionalized and specialized process of strategic communication controlling the flow of news. Moreover, news management has grown in sophistication as new information and communication technologies have advanced and penetrated all forms of political communications in every Western country. Internet technology, with all its possibilities of information processing and targeted communication, has pushed the further professionalization of government communication.

Although the general objectives of news management and its technological means might converge across governments and countries, the institutional setting of political public relations—the media system and the political system environment of its practice—is subject to variation. Our assumption is that news management styles and outcomes across different political systems depend on a series of contextual factors, originating in the political system, the media system, and the media culture. This chapter therefore aims not only to conceptualize news management, but also to compare the context in which it occurs in three countries: the United States, the United Kingdom, and Germany.

These countries were selected for two reasons. All are highly developed Western democracies. The environment of government communication varies, however, due to different political systems (presidential and parliamentary), the makeup and role of the executive (single party government and multiparty government), and the formal and informal institutions of government communication. These countries also differ in terms of media institutions and journalism culture. The central argument proposed in this chapter is that news management of the U.S. government is closest to being driven by the logic and prerogatives of the mass media, while German news management is subject to party politics. And in the United Kingdom government news management for various reasons may range between these opposite approaches of news management style.

Communication Strategies and Action Repertoire of News Management

The modern technology of media communication combined with the modern political publicity process has changed the way news is made. Political marketing methods and strategic communication planning have replaced the formerly close personal ties between press secretaries and journalists.[8] The professionalization implies not only the use of communication specialists but also the introduction of a general set of rules and knowledge derived from political marketing.[9] Jarol Manheim describes the essential professional dynamic that powers the strategic management of communication as an iterative process in which messages are shaped, tested, evaluated, and revised until they encourage the desired effects.[10] In this process the professionals seek (1) to establish objectives and communication options; (2) to sense the environment; (3) to select and implement the communication option most likely to achieve the desired objective; and (4) to assess the effectiveness of the communication.

Although it seems easy to define the general political goals of news management, it is more difficult to find an encompassing pattern as regards the choice of communication options for governments when managing the news. If, however, we look at public information policy as a "permanent campaign" and at government news management as a specific type of political message production, we are able to draw some parallels with campaign communication. Gianpietro Mazzoleni identifies two basic patterns of political message production.[11] The *"media* logic" is guided by the "values and formats through which . . . events and issues are focused on, treated, and given meaning" by journalists and media organizations. The goal is to promote a particular kind of presentation and understanding compatible with media formats, news values, and the logistics of news organizations. The *"party* logic" draws on the structural and cultural assets that govern the communication and the objectives of the political parties. The goal is to strengthen the parties as institutions and to mobilize and integrate the voters within their subcultural ties. For government communication, however, the message production is determined by the aim of informing the public, legitimizing decisions, mobilizing public and political support, creating trust in its performance, and by the executive's need to make its message compatible with the public opinion and the institutional prerequisites of the political process. Within this framework, the main purpose is to retain political power.[12]

Media-Centered Versus Political News Management

If we apply Mazzoleni's dichotomy to patterns of message production in news management, we are able to differentiate between *media-centered* news management and *political* or *party-centered* news management as two general types of strategic communication. In political news management the genuine political objectives are in the center of the strategy, and the media are the means but not the ends of the action. Political news management aims at orchestrating the "political game" among the political elites and concerns the political competition within the government system. The practical task of such news management is to shape the message according to the political objectives of the executive vis-à-vis the other political parties and to maximize the political

Figure 4.1 Typology of news management and action repertoire

Object of the message	Strategy of news management	
	Media-centered	Political (party)
Person is the message	Image management visualization	Political attacks Negativism
Issue is the message	Pseudoevents Drama and action	Dethematization Framing/spin control

aspects in message production while minimizing the adaptation to the media. By contrast, media-centered news management focuses directly and only on creating positive news coverage and popular support for which the media audience is a surrogate. "The new media logic [uses] the techniques of political marketing. It is oriented toward strategic target groups, perceives voters as consumers, and is eager to offer a symbolic product, which is constructed and marketed on the basis of the empirical knowledge of the opinions, diffuse emotions, and the moody and changeable electorate." [13] The practical task of this variant of news management is to subject any political message to the formats, news values, and logistics of the media to maximize the chances of (positive) news coverage, while the substance of the message is secondary.[14]

A second distinction we can adopt from campaign studies is that communication varies depending on whether the object of the message is a candidate or an issue. Even though a sharp distinction is quite artificial and hard to draw, the differentiation of messages as to its central object is a useful heuristic tool that also structures the communication options of government news management. We can distinguish the personalization of politics by setting apart those messages that focus on the *person* of the chief executive or other leading government personnel, such as cabinet ministers, from those messages that focus on the *issue* or policy that is to be communicated. These distinctions produce a typology of news management shown in Figure 4.1.

Action Repertoire

Much of governments' news management takes place during the day-to-day institutional and personal exchanges between public information workers and journalists. Regular press conferences, briefings, and social events provide fertile ground for stabilizing the "working relationship," even if both groups have a critical relationship as regards their professional norms and political objectives. These routine contacts are supported by the new information and communication technologies that enable instant contact between political communicators and journalists. Moreover, the permanent contact is enhanced by regular mailing lists and instant provision of briefing documents. The policy of permanent availability of communication personnel and materials provides the portfolio for the proactive measures of news management that stimulates positive news coverage of national leaders or governments. In the political message production, a number of rhetorical and symbolic actions might help launch an issue. Although we have no encompassing list of the proactive behaviors in news management, Fritz Plasser and his colleagues point to a number of activities that are intended to serve the projected aims: (1) image management or the personalization of politics; (2) pseudoevents or the dramatization of politics; (3) political attacks and negativism; and (4) framing, spin control, and dethematization.[15]

If we look at this action repertoire in terms of our two dimensions of news management—strategy of news management and object of the message—we can categorize those behaviors in their strategic context (see Figure 4.1). The media-centered strategy, which focuses on individual government members, fosters practices that stress the personalization of politics and leadership. This technique draws on the media format of visualization and the fact that people are easier to visualize than complicated policy proposals. Moreover, the exploitation of personality features caters to the human interest dimension of news reporting. Very often in such a strategy the head of the government is portrayed as a political star, and politics is seen as a game between individuals instead of a political competition.

The second media-centered technique of news management focuses on issues and includes the staging of pseudoevents. Daniel Boorstin coined this term for synthetic events that are staged only to stimulate media reporting.[16] The timing and location of the event, the logistics, and the presentation can be designed according to the formats, the selection criteria, and the logistics of news reporting. Pseudoevents "turn into managed and manufactured news. Their acceptance, however, makes their occurrence no less real than the spot news of an assassination attempt or a declaration of war. What makes them real or urgent is their surfacing in the public consciousness." [17] Pseudoevents are frequently used to achieve political goals by stimulating positive images and public support in the permanent campaign of a government. Critics point to the pervasiveness of orchestrated events in politics, which they say transform public affairs "into a twenty-four-hour campaign cycle of pseudoevents for citizen consumption." [18]

Very often, the distinction between personalization and pseudoevents blur, as news managers try to combine both image management with some sort of action or pseudoevent. Such occasions can be symbolically loaded, as political leaders use public appearances to show their connection with "the people."[19]

Examples include bill signings, the greeting of foreign guests, the honoring of a group or individual, and the commemoration of a historical or seasonal event. Some of these appearances border on the trivial, for example, when a president congratulates the baseball team winning the World Series. But they demonstrate the importance of the president's role as chief of state domestically, just as foreign travel demonstrates it abroad. These appearances offer presidents the opportunity to project an image of caring and concern to the nation as a whole through television and newspaper coverage.[20]

The political strategy of news management concerning individuals sometimes coincides with the media's preference for negative news.[21] News managers use this inclination to launch messages that attack the political opponent or put the opponent into a negative light. Such a strategy might occur more often in parliamentary systems than in presidential systems. In the United Kingdom and Germany, the political process includes direct confrontations of ministers and opposition leaders in parliamentary sessions and committees. These occasions are often used to criticize the performance of the opponent publicly. But negative evaluations also can be spread by off-the-record statements or leaks.

The political strategy of news management concerning issues refers to the control not only of the salience of issues but also their definition. As Robert Denton and Gary Woodward note: "Political contests are really contests of competing definitions of situations. Winners are those who successfully articulate the definition of situation held by the majority or those who successfully create a potent definition of situation held by the majority of voters."[22] Defining the issues is one step in the processes of framing in order to mobilize public consensus and of spin control to influence the media coverage. If it is not possible to control the message, news managers may resort to another technique, dethematization, a diversionary tactic that tries to divert attention from substantial issues.[23]

Framing refers to a structure of meaning and significance of a political message, while spin control aims at shaping the version of the story politicians prefer to give to the media. Framing includes the interpretation of the issue, the exposition of its cause, and the depiction of those responsible for the problem solution. It is geared toward the general political discourse of a society, thereby achieving "consensus mobilization."[24] For an executive, therefore, it is particularly important to demonstrate performance and (actual or symbolic) leadership in problem solution. Very often, governments use their position to point out and define only those problems for which they have already developed a ready solution.[25]

Spin control refers to the depiction of an issue in the interaction of news managers and journalists.[26] A practitioner defines spin control as "a flexible technique that can be used not only to 'fix' the results of happenings (or interviews, debates, and so on) after the event, but also to manage expectations of an event yet to take place."[27] Spin control includes the simple pattern of stressing the importance of features that are most attractive to target publics or target media and avoiding the features that are deemed to be undesirable from the point of view of the government.[28] Attempts to spin can be regularly observed after major political developments, when journalists are often desperate to speak to authoritative sources capable of giving them an instant interpretation of what has happened.[29] Finally, the competition of spin doctors for attention has become a news issue in itself.[30]

While framing and spinning deal with the interpretation and depiction of issues, dethematization tries to avoid communication about the core issue. This technique is an attempt to shift from substantial issues to other aspects of the problem. Communication about the substance of the topic is replaced by the discussion of political strategies, coalition building, the style and the rhetoric of the leader, and media performance.

Governments as News Managers

All actors in the political sphere compete for favorable media attention. These include executives, political parties, parliamentary factions, interest and advocacy groups, social movements, individual politicians, and political entrepreneurs. The chances of achieving media attention depend on the actors' positions, their resources, and their objectives. Compared to parties, interest groups, and the opposition, the government always has a better chance for its messages to pass the media filter. The most obvious reason for the government's success is the executive branch's role as a powerful decision-making body.[31] Administrations are active in setting national priorities and proposing policy innovations, taking collectively binding decisions, and implementing them in their programs. As to the politics aspect, governments constantly work on legislative and political coalition building. Finally, the leadership function is expressed in the executive's role of crisis management, in maintaining international commitments, and carrying on foreign relations, if not proclaiming war.

Another reason for the government's favorable starting position in news management is the availability of state resources and institutions for public information. As every government is obliged to inform the citizens, modern executives are in command of institutions that prepare and disseminate official information. These official publicity agencies are filled with civil servants and public information specialists who work in intelligence, media communication, and policy consulting.[32] Although most public information offices are obliged to be nonpartisan and pursue their information task in a politically neutral way, they are news management's most precious resource.

The leading position of the executive compared to the legislative branch and the judicial branch in media attention is well documented by Doris Graber, who has been analyzing the television news coverage of the major U.S. networks for many years.[33] The figures for evening network news broadcasts in 2003 and 2004 show that ABC, CBS, and NBC ran an average of forty-five stories per month about the president. The numbers for Congress and the Supreme Court were considerably lower, with a monthly average of thirty-five Congress stories and twelve Supreme Court stories. All in all, the majority of stories and network air time of all ABC, CBS, and NBC news stories about the three government branches are devoted to the executive. Even though the presence of the government on network television has suffered a long-term decline since the early 1980s, the bias still favors the president.[34] This lead in media attention gives the government in office a huge potential to determine overall communications. Other actors, such as the parties in opposition, find it difficult to compensate for the advantageous status of the administration. Although they might also draw on financial and human resources such as pollsters and communication experts, they usually do not have access to the same amount of official public information resources. In terms of media attention, the legislative parties must compensate for the disadvantages by an extraordinary message, outstanding personnel, or spectacular actions.

Environmental Factors Affecting News Management

The political communication literature suggests fairly general objectives and action repertoires of news management. Despite common general characteristics of public information approaches, their meaning might differ in various political systems. For example, in campaign communication, the existence of common practices of campaigning in different countries, such as the use of campaign professionals and big international marketing firms, has long been interpreted as a general trend toward the "Americanization" of political communication. Yet it is also widely agreed that political communication processes are not uniform but highly culture sensitive and largely affected by environmental factors across and within different systems.[35]

From all the potential factors affecting news management, we shall discuss three aspects of the political environment that might contribute to different styles of political communication and as a consequence have an impact on the prevalent type of news management. Concerning government communication we first discuss the role of the executive and compare the presidential system with the parliamentary system. We might assume that the greater the independence of the chief executive from the parliament, the more personalized and media-driven is his or her public information strategy. The second set of factors that might be responsible for different meanings of news management is the nature of the media system. The third set of factors is the political communication culture.

Following the typology developed by Daniel Hallin and Paolo Mancini, we can differentiate between the North Atlantic or liberal model and the Northern Europe or democratic corporatist model.[36] The models are different as regards the development of the media market, the links between media and political parties, journalistic professionalism, and the potential of state intervention in the media system. According to the Hallin and Mancini framework, the three countries can be located therein with Germany as a democratic corporatist media system on one pole and the United States as a liberal media system on the other.[37] The United Kingdom is located somewhere in between these poles with a tendency toward the liberal type of media system. We might assume that in the democratic corporatist model of the media system, the political type of news management prevails due to the political parallelism of media and politics. In the more liberal system, which is characterized by high commercialization, competition in the media is expected to coincide with a media-centered type of news management.

Finally, the last context variable refers to the political communication culture that shapes the interaction and relationship between political actors and the news media.[38] Political news management should occur more frequently in systems characterized by consensual roles between journalists and politicians, and media-centered news management might be more common in adversarial media cultures.

Political System Factors: Presidential Versus Parliamentary Systems

When we compare political communication in the United States with Britain and Germany, we see that government communication in a presidential system with low party cohesion in the legislature, as in the United States, is focused on the chief executive. Because the president is elected independently from the legislature and stays in office for a fixed term, the White House government information policy does not depend on the support of the legislative factions. Instead, the administration is geared toward creating favorable public opinion. In this situation, the government most likely draws on the strategy of "going public" to replace the negotiations between the executive and Congress.[39] Aiming at mobilizing the general public, this approach is a proactive strategy of reaching out to the electorate by determining the media agenda.[40] If maintaining public support is the modern president's strategic instrumental goal, it follows that the chief executive must actively engage in "the politics of prestige."[41]

The task of promoting the president is assigned to the White House communications operations, which draws on a group of communication specialists who manage the president's image in line with the issues on the political agenda at stake. Observers of George W. Bush's administration report a remarkably high level of professional division of labor and specialization in the White House communication apparatus. "Once those at the strategic level decide what the themes are they want to communicate," writes Martha Joynt Kumar, "the operations people decide how the event will be structured, and the implementers work at setting up the event and the pictures to carry out what the planners want to get across."[42]

Such reports reveal that the creation of pseudoevents around the issues of legislation and national security characterize the main features of the news management of U.S. presidents. In fact, various sources document a remarkable number of public appearances by the president that are symbolic events made available to the national media.[43] Symbolic public events have become a common means of government communication in the contemporary United States. When the president meets with a particular community to commemorate a local event, addresses civic groups, or surveys damage caused by natural disasters, those events are made available to the media and appear on the evening news.[44] The number of such events has increased from 461 for Lyndon Johnson in 1964 to 1,455 for Ronald Reagan in 1984, 1,930 for George H. W. Bush in 1992, and 2,419 for Bill Clinton in 1996.[45] The accounts for the George W. Bush White House also document that the communication machine adheres to the politics of staging favorable media events.[46] The most remarkable media event took place May 2, 2003, when President Bush in a flight suit declared victory in the second Iraq war on the deck of the USS *Abraham Lincoln* in front of a "Mission Accomplished" banner. This event was but one in a series of public appearances fully controlled by the White House not only in terms of the message but also the visual needs of the media.

By contrast to the presidential system in the United States, the institutional arrangements in parliamentary systems tend to support communication strategies that aim at orchestrating the debate between the parties and in the parliament. In Germany, where two or more parties form a coalition government depending on the support of the parliamentary factions, the efforts of the chancellor to set the media agenda clearly aim at positioning his administration as political leader within the coalition government and vis-à-vis the opposition parties. This general constellation became even more complex during the chancellorships of Gerhard Schröder and Angela Merkel, who have always been confronted with strong oppositional voices from within their own party.

Against this background, the executive's communication strategy is not only designed to control the media agenda; it must also respond to the political rivalries within and across the coalition parties.[47] Internal rivalries in the cabinet usually mean that the coalition parties in the government want to appear independent and need to develop their own version of public information contents and strategies.[48] Externally, the logic in the political contest between the government and the opposition parties defines the strategies of news management. The constellation of strong parties under high competition provokes public information approaches that focus on political issues. The major activities, therefore, are thematization and dethematization, framing, and spin control. In Germany, it is not so much the immediate response to public opinion data or the creation of highly visible pseudoevents that govern news management. Instead, the political response to the statements of the coalition partner and the political opponents vis-à-vis the media is the crucial characteristic of strategic communication. In this constellation the media are used as vehicles to influence the debate within the government system. The use of the media for stirring up political issues became essential during the Schröder chancellorship. Because Schröder's party backing was weak to begin with, he developed a sophisticated and highly professional strategy of public leadership in which the government's policies were sold to his own party and the coalition partners via the mass media.[49] In contrast to his predecessor, Helmut Kohl, who had heavily relied on his party and tried to ignore the media,

Schröder focused his communication efforts on the mass media. He concentrated all responsibilities of public relations and news management in the federal government's press office and installed a highly effective machinery of media relations to make up for the neglect of traditional party management and leadership as a basis of government.

The news management of the British executive includes features of both strategies. On the one hand, news management in the United Kingdom as well as in Germany consists of making sure that all the ministers speak with one voice.[50] British scholar Bob Franklin observed, however, that the spin of New Labour has not always been homogenous, as "members of the Cabinet continue to brief against each other."[51] Despite these internal rivalries among cabinet ministers, the prime minister's leadership in agenda-setting and political communication is usually not contested, which also means that political messages and the public information policy are organized in a politically coherent way around the prime minister. In fact, the New Labour government under Prime Minister Tony Blair has established a communication machinery at No. 10 Downing Street of unprecedented size and a reputation for "control freakery in its media relations."[52] News management in such a situation is designed to be extremely political and tightly focused on the issues of the governing party. New Labour has indeed enhanced the system of spin control and professional media and issue management that allowed No. 10 to control the agenda over many years. Blair's government communication machine has been managed by the director of communications, Alastair Campbell, and an ever-increasing number of special advisers working on press relations and the promotion of government policy. At the same time, the leadership role of the prime minister as performed by Blair has enhanced the personalization of politics.[53] Recent analyses of the British government process show that the system is moving toward a "presidentialisation" of politics that stresses the prime minister's role and his inclination to speak from the bully pulpit more often.[54] In this context, the press secretary and the communication experts around the PM are orchestrating and coordinating various news management activities that include all measures of the political strategy such as attacking the opponent, defining the agenda of public information, and spin control. In its communication activities the Blair government was able to build on the legacy of the former Conservative administrations and perfect them. Campbell was successful in creating a highly centralized system of tight message control and spin.[55] In 2002, however, Blair in a public announcement rejected the politics of news management and spin. This statement was rather surprising as the

Labour government had established a strong reputation for its media image creations, its rigorous and tight approach toward journalists, and its professionalism in news management. No one, therefore, should be surprised that observers interpreted the commitment to openness and the rejection of news management not as the end of spin but as the launch of a "no spin is the new spin" strategy.[56]

Communication Roles and Institutions of Government News Management

Looking at the institutions and communication roles of news management in all three countries, we find a division of labor regarding the day-to-day relations of government spokespeople and the media and the more strategic and political aspects. The press secretary occupies the most prominent position in official government communication. As Seymour-Ure points out, modern press secretaries perform at least four communication roles: spokesperson, adviser on media relations, agent, and manager.[57] When we compare the three democracies, we see that the interpretation of the press secretary's role and the forum for informal and interpersonal exchanges between government spokespeople and the media vary in each country. But the structures are also similar in basic ways. The formal and informal roles of strategic communication are usually held by a circle of advisers who decide on the strategy of news management and the reactions to the issues and opinions raised in the media. Those positions are located at the heart of the executive office (the White House Office of Communications in Washington, the chancellor's office in Berlin, and No. 10 Downing Street in London).

The communication function in the White House is a highly centralized and specialized task entrusted to the White House chief of staff. Under this official's oversight the functions are further divided between the Press Office and the Office of Communication.[58] Other communication tasks are assigned to the Office of Media Affairs and Speechwriting.[59] The principal objective of all these offices is to manage the information flow about the president and to design messages that most effectively resonate with voters, especially targeted subgroups.[60] Over the years the number of staff working in a framework of highly centralized decision making about communications has increased to about fifty people.[61]

The press secretary's role is to place the president and his message in the national media on a daily basis. During the Reagan administration, journalists' access to the president was quite restricted, which meant that the press secretary was highly visible. George W. Bush has employed a similar strategy; he seems to be quite reluctant to hold solo press conferences but prefers to appear jointly with other U.S. officials or foreign leaders.[62] As a result the press secretaries, Tony Snow and predecessors Ari Fleischer and Scott McClellan, play an immensely important role as brokers between the administration and the press. The press secretary appears at least twice daily in front of the media, so the chances for getting the message across are favorable to begin with, because his interaction with journalists is frequent and close.[63] The accredited correspondents practically cohabit the White House, so they are at the disposal of the press office for briefings, announcements, and freshly breaking information any time.[64]

When the Office of Communication was established, it signaled the growing trend toward tighter control of White House communication through a centralized approach to information management.[65] Today, the office is in charge of managing the presidential agenda through long-term public relations planning and strategizing. The staff is "responsible for creating the focus for the day, organizing the planning up to four months out, and coordinating with White House and administration personnel."[66] It works on managerial and proactive tasks such as designing strategies for presidential policy announcements, long-term image building, and creating popular support. By using new satellite techniques and other direct communication channels, the Office of Communication is able to set up self-produced news stories from the White House and interviews with officials for local news stations. The Office of Media Affairs also deals with the regional and local press and with radio stations outside the Washington news scene, while Speechwriting prepares the text of public remarks. Although the institutional settings of government news management have been pretty stable over time, the perceptions of the performance in government communication and its success vary in each administration. The Bush White House has taken "a strikingly disciplined and systematic approach" to handling the press and a tight structure to controlling the information flow.[67]

In contrast to the White House press secretary, this position in Germany underwent a severe fluctuation of personnel, and until the 1990s none of the government spokesmen gained public visibility or political significance. Officially, the press secretary to the chancellor has two functions. He officially speaks for the coalition government by answering to the national press corps three times a week. And he is the head of the Federal Press and Information Office, which is a rather bureaucratic operation for official public information and government intelligence. Because of its size (seven hundred civil servants) and bureaucratic nature, the agency is somewhat ineffective regarding the development and planning of a proactive political communication strategy. The powerful positions of government communications have traditionally been located in the chancellor's office where a small group of communication advisers, political analysts, and speechwriters monitors the findings of opinion polls, works on framing political issues, and decides on the communication strategies toward the media.[68] The press secretary has the responsibility of implementing these decisions on a daily basis. During Kohl's chancellorship, the division of labor between the political and the information functions prevailed, which also meant that the press secretary was a weak and secondary political actor. In the late 1990s, the Schröder administration introduced a policy of communication that tried to integrate and concentrate the political and media-oriented aspects of news management. The result was that during Schröder's two terms, the press secretary became a powerful political figure who advised the chancellor in all political and communications issues. Moreover, the structures and strategies in the press office were changed so that the communication apparatus would operate under modern public management rules and quality management principles. The Schröder administration also tried to adopt the information strategies of corporate public relations which meant dividing the office into units that specialize on certain media products and target groups.[69] Angela Merkel, the current chancellor, has kept the institutional and managerial innovations, but her political approach to government communication resembles Kohl's more than Schröder's.

The tasks of the press secretary to the prime minister in Britain are managerial, and news management is defined as "ensuring that nothing is allowed to get in the way of the story the Government wants to get over."[70] Since Margaret Thatcher's era, government communication is highly centralized in the PM's office and integrated through a system of internal reporting to ensure that No. 10 is fully abreast of all important developments within the government. Bernard Ingram described his job as press secretary as coordinating the timing and the coherence of government messages.[71] The British case shows that news management must be seen as only one option in an encompassing communication strategy whose measures extend beyond the simple news operation of the executive. During the Thatcher years, the Government Information and Communication Services, whose purpose was to explain government policy and to communicate information of genuine public interest, was transformed "from relatively restrained government publicity"[72] into a marketing machine for the promotion of controversial policies. The New Labour government continued to enlarge the Government Information and Communication Services to about twelve hundred civil servants. Among them are eighty-one special advisers who are not duty bound—like the other staff—to impartiality, working instead in clearly political roles of news management. These advisers' jobs are to oversee and control the message production while the civil service press officers deal with the more routine matters of government information and communication.[73] Eventually, the Blair government also boosted commercial political marketing. Under Thatcher, the government had become one of the biggest advertisers in the country, with expenditures for publicity increasing from £60 million to £225 million.[74] The New Labour government followed up by boosting the expenditure to the unprecedented amount of £295 million. News management in the UK was therefore facilitated by implementing marketing techniques and accompanied by huge paid campaigns for particularly controversial issues. With the large scale use of professional political marketing, the government's efforts to manage the news profited not only from the material resources but also from the expertise of external marketing professionals.

While the press offices and public information agencies must be seen as formal institutions of government communication, another method of news management is the use of interpersonal networks that develop between government officials and journalists. Those communication networks are venues of steady interaction and contact that contribute to the formation of trust among the actors and eventually to the emergence of common cultures of political communication where information is exchanged for publicity. We have seen that the interaction between journalists and press officers is quite close in Washington because the press corps is always present in the White House. Functional equivalents to this availability are the Parliamentary Lobby at Westminster and the background circles in Berlin.

In Britain the most important arrangement for the managed disclosure of news and information was the Lobby, about 220 selected journalists who had privileged access to Westminster, received briefings from the prime minister's press secretary twice a day, and socialized on a regular basis with government officials. The Lobby's central principle is the nonattribution of sources, making it a useful tool for political management of the news. The exchange of information and agenda-setting were facilitated because the reporters could claim to present information from high-level sources or sources close to Downing Street without attributing it to a specific person.[75] Another function of the Lobby was to impart information and offer journalists "guidance" as to additional background or the interpretation of the message.[76] This system has been praised for its value as an information stock exchange, but criticized for its alleged secrecy. In the early 2000s the Lobby's character changed when access was broadened to all journalists and London-based correspondents.[77] In addition, briefing contents are distributed on the Internet and television. Finally, some newspapers undermined the Lobby's previous code of secrecy by introducing stricter policies to avoid the anonymity of sources. As a result, however, new venues where journalists and politicians meet for informal information exchange have come up.

The German functional equivalent to the Lobby in Whitehall are the so-called Hintergrundkreise, which were a characteristic feature of the Federal Republic before unification. Against all odds, after the government moved to Berlin, the Hintergrundkreise still prevail. The neutral label as "background circle" pretends that the purpose of those clubs of journalists who regularly invite politicians or their spokespersons is the exchange of background information, but they also provide useful opportunities for strategic news management. The circles are divided along the journalists' party political lines, or represent a certain type of media, or constitute a selection of regional outlets. They are not only important as a platform of continuous exchange and a possibility of socializing in a less official form but also helpful for infusing issues and opinions into clearly defined target media without giving the information an official label. Government officials often use these circles as a way to test new issues by launching the information and waiting for the reaction of journalists.

Media Cultures

In each country we have discussed, government communication clearly reacts to and reflects the national media culture. For example, political actors in the United States have no choice but to account for the commercial nature of the press and television. Judging from the degree of the commercialization of the media system and the competition among the media, it is clear that strategic communication follows the orientation of the media system. It is most likely, then, that the dominant pattern of government news management in commercial systems is the media-centered approach. By contrast, the UK and Germany maintain a pillar of strong public service broadcasting and, in the press system, a parallelism between the political parties and newspapers' editorial lines. Against this background, media cultures—defined as subcultures of the national political culture—provide the framework for the reporting of politics and the context in which the relationship between political actors and journalists emerges.[78] Two dimensions of the media culture are essential to influence news management: (1) the role definition of journalists as newsmakers in the political arena and (2) the orientations of journalists toward political institutions. The role definition of journalists is influenced not only by the media they work for but also by the socially and culturally defined expectations that dominate in a national news system.[79] Professional roles can range from neutral transmitter of polities to interpretative or even openly adversarial styles of news reporting. Jay Blumler and Michael Gurevitch contend that "journalists react to all special groups and institutions, not only via news-value criteria, but also according to the degree of respect (or lack of it) to which they are regarded as entitled by the dominant value system."[80] The orientations of newsmakers toward the political system can vary from respect and appreciation for the political system to cynicism and distrust.

The way in which media professionals define their role and how they react to news management influences the political actors' communication behaviors. The assumption is that the higher the cynicism and distrust in the media, the more political actors have to engage in media-centered news management. The higher the risks and contingencies of news reporting from the point of view of political actors, the more they have to adapt their messages to the media logic simply to maximize their potential control of the media agenda. On the other hand, the more journalists respect the political institutions and comply with traditional professional norms of impartiality and neutral description, the more political actors may trust political news management to be effective.

Comparing the orientations toward political institutions of U.S., British, and German newsmakers, we find the Americans and Germans at opposing poles and the British journalists somewhere in between. In the United States, Thomas Patterson finds that news reporting during the past few decades has changed from the traditional descriptive style to an interpretive style.[81] (See Chapter 1 of this volume for Patterson's discussion of this point.) This approach to news reporting is filled with a profound negativism toward political institutions and incumbents. The study shows that American journalism could be characterized by a general anti-politics bias that applies to all institutions of government including the president. The media use interpretative styles of reporting that stress the journalist's role as a political analyst. This style goes hand in hand with attack journalism and adversarial, arrogant attitudes toward political institutions.[82] Journalists constantly question politicians' motives, methods, and effectiveness. This type of reporting looks like watchdog journalism, but it is not. It is ideological in its premise: politicians are assumed to act out of self-interest rather than from political conviction. Journalists routinely claim that politicians make promises they do not intend to keep or could not keep even if they tried.[83]

The American media culture has been characterized by a journalism that has grown markedly negative in its coverage of Congress and the president.[84] Patterson maintains that the media's constant antipolitics messages have weakened the government.[85] From this perspective, it is no surprise that political actors in general, and the executive in particular, try hard and invest huge resources and intelligence in media-centered styles of news management.

The British and German media cultures differ quite substantially from the U.S. model; at least Americanization does not seem to be a straightforward positive model in Europe. The British media culture does not reveal the same features of antipolitics bias as the American. Regarding the British media's attitudes toward political institutions, Blumler and Gurevitch found that in the past the central institutions of the state and government used to receive an almost reverential treatment.[86] But the "sacerdotal orientation towards institutions *qua* institutions," which might attract the respect they are entitled to "by virtue of their symbolic embodiment of the value system of society" does not preclude a critical, even hostile, media stance toward the policies and personalities of such institutions.[87] Concerning their orientations vis-à-vis political institutions, British journalists seem to be pretty respectful and follow the cues that come from political actors. Since the mid-1990s, however, observers have noticed tendencies toward a more independent critical force and evidence of declining respect, particularly in the UK press.[88] Wolfgang Donsbach and Thomas Patterson find a split in the British media culture between the press and broadcasting, and they speak of the clear gap between the "partisan-tinged world of British newspapers" and the "air of neutrality that pervades British broadcasting."[89] Today the British press seems to embody the highly partisan type of journalism, while broadcast journalism stands for neutral reporting and being a common carrier of information for the public. Moreover, the social responsibility tradition of broadcasters as actors for the public is still prevalent. It is generally argued, however, that several scandals involving the New Labour government have contributed to considerable mistrust between political journalists and the government's press office, as journalists felt they were misled during the briefings.[90]

The attitudes toward political institutions among German journalists, who basically view themselves as actively involved in the political discourse, are twofold. On the one hand, journalists are obedient vis-à-vis state institutions and the government. Observers even criticize political journalism as obsequious to government announcements and official statements. Moreover, journalists seek close social contact with politicians who then expect to be rewarded by favorable coverage.[91] On the other hand, German journalists tend to take a political position insofar as they emphasize the political conflicts within and between the political parties and take sides for one or the other actor. The political role interpretation of journalists means that it is legitimate for them to advocate their own political values and ideas, side openly with one of the political parties, or infuse their convictions in the political debate.

From our insight into the three national media cultures, we would expect political strategies of news management to prevail in the United Kingdom and Germany, although for different reasons. In Germany, journalists would be expected to actively side with or oppose the government's messages but not cast doubt about their appropriateness or legitimacy. In Britain, by contrast, we would expect political strategies of news management to prevail as it targets broadcast journalism, which is still characterized by high professional standards of impartiality, respect for political institutions, high quality discussion of political problems, and civic-minded journalism.[92] Because the British media culture is divided, we would also expect media-oriented styles of news management to coexist with the political styles of government information policies. Judging from the media culture dimension, we also can infer that the media-oriented patterns of news management found in the United States are closely linked to the orientations of journalists to whom the messages of the government are targeted.[93]

Conclusion

From the discussion of government news management we can draw two general conclusions. First, news management can be conceptualized as a strategic variant of public information whereby governments manage communication in order to influence public opinion by controlling the news media agenda. It is a top-down process of communication in which the media are the means as well as the targets, and the strategies are determined by the political objectives of the specific actor. For government, the practices of news management aim at both informing the public about its policies and legitimating its decisions. The prime motive, however, is the executive's desire to accomplish goals in the political competition and to create the popular consent that determines the chances of retaining or—even more desirable—increasing political power.

Given this general framework, in the countries reviewed in this chapter, we find quite similar agencies and communication roles that engage in feeding the media and managing the government's press relations, public relations, and political marketing. We also find the same kinds of experts devising political strategies to frame issues and set the media agenda. The discussion shows that the formal and informal structures and institutions of government news management are functionally equivalent in the United States, the United Kingdom, and Germany. Revisiting public information approaches in the three countries since the late 1990s revealed that the practical solutions taken by governments have come to resemble each other despite the variation of political systems and media systems. The enhancement of strategic political management and marketing, the higher levels of professionalization and specialization of government information, and the fact that media savvy political leaders came into power in all three countries may be interpreted as convergent tendencies.

Second, the essential argument of this chapter refers to the political systems and media contexts that allegedly accounted for different approaches, strategies, and objectives of news management. Even though we find that the media-centered strategy of news management continues to prevail in the United States, while the political strategy seems to be more obvious in the German and British executives' approach to public information, these differences have become smaller since the late 1990s. The assumption that the political and media environments determine the meaning and effects of strategic communication must lead us to closely scrutinize these factors for the diagnosis of future political communication. Political systems as well as media systems in Europe and the United States have been undergoing profound changes. Due to (post)modernization, political systems have witnessed the weakening of political ties, increasing volatility, and the public's growing dissatisfaction with political actors, all of which tend to undermine the formerly central role of party organizations and other political intermediaries. This change also seems to coincide with the advent of political leaders who are sensitive to the media and aware of the power of communication for public appearance and political success. Media systems in Europe and the United States cope with the consequences of profound technological changes, which have introduced new venues of communication. They also face the growth of commercialization and competition between the outlets, leading to fragmented audiences. Moreover, technology has boosted and speeded up the timing and networking of information and provided individual leaders and collective actors with immense resources for communication as well as the power to abuse it. We may understand from this radical change that the environment of government news management is becoming more and more conducive to the media-centered styles of communication. In addition, this approach may also have gained significance because social science and humanities scholarship has continuously produced the information resources and knowledge for refining and perfecting news management techniques and effects. Changing contexts, information technology, knowledge, and resources of strategic communication may contribute to changes of news management styles and affect the broader meaning of political communication in modern Western democracies. They also may produce completely different styles not only of communication but of the processes and outcome of politics itself.

Notes

1. Gary R. Orren, "Thinking about the Press and Government," in *Impact: How the Press Affects Federal Policymaking*, ed. Martin Linsky (New York: W. W. Norton, 1986), 9. For other labels, see Jay G. Blumler and Michael Gurevitch, *The Crisis of Public Communication* (London; New York: Routledge, 1995), 3.

2. Jack McLeod, Gerald Kosicki, and Douglas M. McLeod, "The Expanding Boundaries of Political Communication Effects," in *Media Effects: Advances in Theory and Research*, ed. Jennings Bryant and Dolf Zillmann (Hillsdale, N.J.: Lawrence Erlbaum, 1994), 123–162.

3. Michael Gurevitch and Jay G. Blumler, "Comparative Research: The Extending Frontier," in *New Directions in Political Communication*, ed. David L. Swanson and Dan Nimmo (Newbury Park, Calif.: Sage), 305–328.

4. For a discussion, see Gianpietro Mazzoleni and Winfried Schulz, "Mediatization of Politics: A Challenge for Democracy?" *Political Communication* 16 (1999): 247–261. Examples of the consequences of media democracy for mass politics are "the decay of politics" (Entman 1989, Fallows 1997, Sabato 1991); the decline in social trust (Putnam 1995); and changes in the political and electoral process at large. For the various aspects, see the chapters in Ornstein and Mann (2000). The works referred to are: Robert Entman, *Democracy Without Citizens: Media and the Decay of American Politics* (New York: Oxford University Press, 1989); James Fallows, *Breaking the News: How the Media Undermine American Democracy* (New York: Vintage Books, 1997); Larry J. Sabato, *Feeding Frenzy: How Attack Journalism Has Transformed American Politics* (New York: Free Press, 1991); Robert Putnam, "Tuning In, Tuning Out: The Strange Disappearance of Social Capital," in *American Political Science and Politics* 27 (1995): 664–683; and Norman J. Ornstein and Thomas E. Mann, eds., *The Permanent Campaign and its Future* (Washington, D.C.: American Enterprise Institute and Brookings Institution, 2000), 1–37.

5. Orren, "Thinking about the Press and Government," 3.

6. Hugh Heclo, "Campaigning and Governing: A Conspectus," in *The Permanent Campaign and its Future*, 3.

7. See *Impact: How the Press Affects Federal Policymaking*.

8. Historical examples of a public information operation based on close personal ties between press secretaries and journalists are the Roosevelt presidency in the United

States. See Richard W. Steele, *Propaganda in an Open Society: The Roosevelt Administration and the Media, 1933–1941* (Westport: Conn.; London: Greenwood Press, 1985). Good relations with the press were also observed for the Kennedy and Reagan presidencies. See Lori Cox Han, *Governing from Center Stage: White House Communication Strategies During the Television Age of Politics* (Cresskill, N.J.: Hampton Press, 2001). For Germany the early period of the Adenauer government was characterized by a cooperative relationship between government and the press. See Johannes J. Hoffmann, *Adenauer: "Vorsicht keine Indiskretionen!" Zur Informationspolitik und öffentlichkeitsarbeit der Bundesregierung, 1949–1955* (Aachen: Shaker, 1992).

9. For example, Bruce I. Newman, *The Mass Marketing of Politics: Democracy in an Age of Manufactured Images* (Thousand Oaks, Calif.: Sage, 1999).

10. Jarol Manheim, "Strategische Kommunikation und eine Strategie für die Kommunikationsforschung," *Publizistik* 1 (1997): 42, 62–72.

11. Gianpietro Mazzoleni, "Media Logic and Party Logic in Campaign Coverage: The Italian General Election 1983," *European Journal of Communication* (1987): 2, 85.

12. Lawrence Jacobs notes that for the American presidency in particular the communication is constrained by the tension between advertising the promotion of national interests while maintaining the support of critical political subgroups. See Lawrence R. Jacobs, "Communicating from the White House: Presidential Narrowcasting and the National Interest," in *The Executive Branch*, ed. Joel D. Aberbach and Mark A. Peterson (Oxford; New York: Oxford University Press, 2005), 175–177.

13. Fritz Plasser, Franz Sommer, and Christian Scheucher, "Medienlogik: Themenmanagement und Politikvermittlung im Wahlkampf," in *Wahlkampf und Wählerentscheidung: Analysen zur Nationalratswahl*, ed. Fritz Plasser, Peter A. Ulram, and Günther Ogris (Vienna: Signum, 1996), 86.

14. In the meantime, there are abundant reference manuals about the methods and techniques of public relations as applied to politics; see, for example, Newman, *The Mass Marketing of Politics*.

15. Plasser, Sommer, and Scheucher, "Medienlogik," 90.

16. Daniel J. Boorstin, *The Image, or What Happened to the American Dream* (New York: Atheneum, 1962).

17. Robert E. Denton Jr. and Gary C. Woodward, *Political Communication in America*, 2nd ed. (Westport, Conn.: Praeger 1990), 152.

18. Heclo, "Campaigning and Governing," 30.

19. Lyn Ragsdale, *Vital Statistics on the Presidency: Washington to Clinton* (Washington, D.C.: CQ Press, 1996). See also Han, *Governing from Center Stage;* and Lori Cox Han, "The Rose Garden Strategy Revisited: How Presidents Use Public Activities," in *In the Public Domain: Presidents and the Challenges of Public Leadership*, ed. Lori Cox Han and Dianne J. Heith (Albany: State University of New York Press, 2005), 163–177.

20. Ragsdale, *Vital Statistics on the Presidency*, 151.

21. Thomas Patterson, "Bad News, Bad Governance," *Annals of the American Academy of Political and Social Science* (July 1996): 97–108.

22. Denton and Woodward, *Political Communication in America*, 42.

23. See Plasser, Sommer, and Scheucher, "Medienlogik."

24. Robert Entman, "Framing: Toward Clarification of a Fractured Paradigm," *Journal of Communication* 43 (1993): 51–58.

25. John Kingdon, *Agendas, Alternatives, and Public Policies* (Boston; Toronto: Little, Brown, 1984), 98.

26. Nicholas Jones, *Soundbites and Spin Doctors. How Politicians Manipulate the Media and Vice Versa* (London: Indigo, 1996).

27. Brendan Bruce, *Images of Power* (London: Kogan Page, 1992), 141.

28. Denton and Woodward, *Political Communication in America*, 92.

29. Jones, *Soundbites and Spin Doctors*, 123.

30. Frank Esser, Carsten Reinemann, and David Fan, "Spin Doctors in the United States, Great Britain, and Germany: Metacommunication about Media Manipulation," *Harvard International Journal of Press/Politics* 6, no. 1 (2001): 16–45.

31. Jacobs, "Communicating from the White House," 190.

32. For a general discussion, see Kingdon, *Agendas, Alternatives, and Public Policies*. For an assessment of the Bush White House, see Martha Joynt Kumar, "The Contemporary Presidency: Communications Operations in the White House of President George W. Bush: Making News on His Terms," *Presidential Studies Quarterly* 33 (2003): 366–393.

33. Doris Graber, *Mass Media and American Politics*, 7th ed. (Washington, D.C.: CQ Press, 2006), 251.

34. Stephen J. Farnsworth and S. Robert Lichter, *Mediated Presidency: Television News and Presidential Governance* (Lanham, Md.: Rowman and Littlefield, 2006), 31–40, show the considerable variation over time in the presence of the executive branch on network news and a general declining trend of the amount of coverage of the legislative branch. The drop in the amount of legislative coverage reflects not only the networks' shifting news agenda but also a decline in the total news hole (the time allotted to news) of the broadcasts. Despite the decline, the study still documents a huge bias in favor of the president in the coverage of the executive branch and a bias in favor of the executive branch of all government branches.

35. David L. Swanson, "Transnational Trends in Political Communication: Conventional Views and New Realities," in *Comparing Political Communication. Theories, Cases, and Challenges*, ed. Frank Esser and Barbara Pfetsch (Cambridge: Cambridge University Press, 2004), 45–63. See also Barbara Pfetsch and Frank Esser, "Comparing Political Communication: Reorientations in a Changing World," in *Comparing Political Communication*, 3–24.

36. Daniel Hallin and Paolo Mancini, *Comparing Media Systems: Three Models of Media and Politics* (Cambridge: Cambridge University Press, 2004).

37. Ibid., 70.

38. Barbara Pfetsch, "From Political Culture to Political Communications Culture: A Theoretical Approach to Comparative Analysis," in *Comparing Political Communication*, 344–365.

39. Samuel Kernell, *Going Public: New Strategies of Presidential Leadership*, 4th ed. (Washington, D.C.: CQ Press, 2006).

40. Hanspeter Kriesi, "Strategic Political Communication: Mobilizing Public Opinion in Audience Democracies," in *Comparing Political Communication*, 184–212.

41. Denton and Woodward, *Political Communication in America*, 198.

42. Ken Auletta, "Fortress Bush," *New Yorker*, January 19, 2004, 53–65; Kumar, "The Contemporary Presidency," 385.

43. Ragsdale, *Vital Statistics on the Presidency*. See also Han, *Governing from Center Stage*; and Han, "The Rose Garden Strategy Revisited." For details on the Bush White House, see Martha Joynt Kumar, "Source Material: The White House and the Press: News Organizations as a Presidential Resource and as a Source of Pressure," *Presidential Studies Quarterly* 33, no. 3 (2003): 669–683.

44. Ragsdale, *Vital Statistics on the Presidency*, 151.

45. Han, "The Rose Garden Strategy Revisited," 170–171.

46. See Auletta, "Fortress Bush."

47. Wolfgang Reineke, "Regierung ohne Kommunikationskonzept," *prmagazin*, April 1988, 30.

48. Stefan Reker, "Maulkorb vom Chef: Helmut Kohl will die Bonner Ministerien mit strengeren Benimmregeln an die Leine legen," *Focus* 25 (1995): 104.

49. Ludger Helms, *Presidents, Prime Ministers, and Chancellors: Executive Leadership in Western Democracies* (Houndmills; New York: Palgrave Macmillan, 2005), 217–222.

50. Bernard Ingram, *Kill the Messenger* (London: Harper Collins, 1991).

51. Bob Franklin, "A Damascene Conversion? New Labour and Media Relations," in *Governing as New Labour: Policy and Politics under Blair*, ed. Steve Ludlam and Martin J. Smith (Houndmills; New York: Palgrave Macmillan, 2004), 105.

52. Ibid.

53. Colin Seymour-Ure, "Prime Ministers and Presidents' News Operations: What Effects on the Job?" in *Media Power, Professionals, and Policy*, ed. Howard Tumber (London; New York: Routledge, 2000).

54. Richard Heffernan and Paul Webb, "The British Prime Minister: Much More Than First Among Equals," in *The Presidentialization of Politics: A Comparative Study of Modern Democracies*, ed. Thomas Poguntke and Paul Webb (Oxford; New York: Oxford University Press, 2005), 26–62.

55. Franklin, "A Damascene Conversion," 91.

56. Ibid., 89.

57. Colin Seymour-Ure, "The Role of Press Secretaries on Chief Executive Staffs in Anglo-American Systems," in *Executive Leadership in Anglo-American Systems*, ed. Colin Campbell and Margaret Wyszomirski (Pittsburgh: University of Pittsburgh Press, 1991), 383.

58. For detailed descriptions of the institutions of White House communications, see Kathryn Dunn Tenpas, "The American Presidency: Surviving and Thriving Amidst the Permanent Campaign," in *The Permanent Campaign and its Future*, ed. Norman J. Ornstein and Thomas E. Mann (Washington, D.C.: American Enterprise Institute and Brookings Institution, 2000), 108–133. See Jacobs, "Communicating from the White House"; Auletta, "Fortress Bush"; Kumar, "The Contemporary Presidency"; and Kumar, "Source Material."

59. Under the circumstances of the war on terrorism, the Coalition Information Center and the Office of Global Communication were added to the traditional structure of government communication of the Bush White House. See Kumar, "The Contemporary Presidency," 368.

60. See Jacobs, "Communicating from the White House," 190.

61. See Kumar, "The Contemporary Presidency," 379.

62. According to Ken Auletta in "Fortress Bush," by January 1, 2004, George W. Bush had held just eleven solo press conferences, far fewer than his predecessors at the same point in their presidencies: Reagan (twenty-one), Clinton (thirty-eight), and G. H. W. Bush (seventy-one). See also Kumar, "Source Material."

63. Michael McCurry, "The Background on Background," *Harvard International Journal for Press/Politics* 1, no. 4 (1996): 4–9.

64. Auletta, "Fortress Bush."

65. The office was established during the Watergate affair because President Nixon felt the national press corps was not treating him fairly. See John Anthony Maltese, *Spin*

Control: The White House Office of Communications and the Management of Presidential News (Chapel Hill; London: University of North Carolina Press, 1992), 26.

66. See Kumar, "The Contemporary Presidency," 379.

67. Jacobs, "Communicating from the White House," 194.

68. Dieter Fuchs and Barbara Pfetsch, "The Observation of Public Opinion by the Governmental System," *Research Paper Series, Berlin Science Center for Social Research,* FS 96-105, Berlin, December 1996.

69. Barbara Pfetsch, "Regierung als Markenprodukt. Moderne Regierungskommunikation auf dem Prüfstand," in *Machtdarstellung und Darstellungsmacht,* ed. Ulrich Sarcinelli and Jens Tenscher (Baden-Baden: Nomos, 2003), 23–32.

70. Ingram, *Kill the Messenger,* 188.

71. Ibid.

72. Margaret Scammell, *Designer Politics: How Elections Are Won* (New York: St. Martin's Press, 1995), 230.

73. Bob Franklin reports on the debates over whether this arrangement violates the fine line between promotion of government policy and the promotion of the ruling party's policies or between government information and political propaganda. See Franklin, "A Damascene Conversion."

74. The issue accounting for most of the growth in spending was the funding of television advertising and marketing of the government's privatization measures. See Scammell, *Designer Politics,* 204–207.

75. Jones, *Soundbites and Spin Doctors.*

76. David G. Boyce, "Government and the News Media: The British Experience," in *Government and the News Media: Comparative Dimensions,* ed. Dan Nimmo and Michael W. Mansfield (Waco, Texas: Baylor University Press, 1982), 90.

77. Bob Franklin, Martin Hamer, Mark Hanna, Marie Kinsey, and John E. Richardson, *Key Concepts in Journalism Studies* (London; Thousand Oaks; New Delhi: Sage, 2005), 133–134.

78. Holli A. Semetko, "Political Balance on Television: Campaigns in the United States, Britain, and Germany," *Harvard International Journal of Press/Politics* 1 (1996): 52.

79. Wolfgang Donsbach and Thomas E. Patterson, "Political News Journalists: Partisanship, Professionalism, and Political Roles in Five Countries," in *Comparing Political Communication: Theories, Cases, and Challenges,* ed. Frank Esser and Barbara Pfetsch (Cambridge; New York: Cambridge University Press, 2004), 251–270.

80. Jay G. Blumler and Michael Gurevitch, "Journalists' Orientations to Political Institutions: The Case of Parliamentary Broadcasting," in *Communicating Politics: Mass Communications and the Political Process,* ed. Peter Golding, Graham Murdock, and Philip Schlesinger (Leicester: Leicester University Press, 1986), 89.

81. Patterson, "Bad News, Bad Governance," 102.

82. Sabato, *Feeding Frenzy.*

83. Patterson, "Bad News, Bad Governance," 103.

84. This general trend was interrupted briefly after the September 11 attacks and in the early period of President Bush's war against terrorism. Moreover, as studies on foreign policy and war reporting by W. Lance Bennett and David Paletz show, U.S. media are quite obedient to the administration's message in foreign policy and in wartime. See *Taken by Storm—The Media, Public Opinion, and U.S. Foreign Policy in the Gulf War* (Chicago; London: University of Chicago Press, 1994).

85. Patterson, "Bad News, Bad Governance."

86. Blumler and Gurevitch, "Journalists' Orientations," 89.

87. Ibid.

88. Jay G. Blumler, Dennis Kavanagh, and T. J. Nossiter, "Modern Communications Versus Traditional Politics in Britain: Unstable Marriage of Convenience," in *Politics, Media, and Modern Democracy: An International Study of Innovations in Electoral Campaigning and Their Consequences*, ed. David L: Swanson and Paolo Mancini (Westport, Conn.: Praeger, 1996), 66.

89. Donsbach and Patterson, "Political News Journalists," 266.

90. See Franklin, "A Damascene Conversion," 104.

91. See Barbara Pfetsch, *Politische Kommunikationskultur. Politische Sprecher und Journalisten in der Bundesrepublik und den USA im Vergleich* (Wiesbaden: Westdeutscher Verlag, 2003), 127–148.

92. Blumler, Kavanagh, and Nossiter, "Modern Communications Versus Traditional Politics."

93. Pfetsch, *Politische Kommunikationskultur.*

5 The News Shapers: Strategic Communication as a Third Force in Newsmaking

Jarol B. Manheim

The favored status of journalism in our society, like that of any other social institution, depends on public acceptance of a myth structure—a widely accepted set of beliefs that lead people to accord credence, authority, and value to its role in national life, its actions, and their results. People grant journalists and news organizations a special place—and special protections—because they believe, and because they want to believe, that doing so makes them better informed citizens, which in the process enhances democracy. Given those stakes and given our widespread dependence on the media for the waves of news and information that stream through daily political life, it is worth asking: What are the essential elements of that journalistic mythology?

The Underlying Mythology of Journalism

The traditional mythology of journalism holds, in effect, that news is a naturally occurring product of two factors: the elements of the political environment that exist at any given time and the visible content of events or actions that develop within that environment. News grows plant-like on the surface of the political system. Under the most basic form of journalism, the "assignment" system, the task of the journalist is to recognize the outcrops of protonews that are scattered about, pick them, sort the grain from the chaff, and blend them into a finished product—the story. Let us characterize this as the hunter-gatherer form of news.

The myth structure also incorporates a more affirmative and systematic form of journalism, the "beat" system, in which reporters actually plow the surface to some depth, and water and fertilize their sources, in the expectation of producing additional and more orderly growths of protonews that can be converted into stories, add texture and allure to stories, and perhaps even con-

Table 5.1 Typology of journalism forms

Form of journalism	Basic	Enriched
Hunter-gatherer	Fact-centered; assignment-driven	Investigative; explanatory
Cultivation	Source-centered; beat-driven	Enterprise; reporter-defined

tribute a deeper level of understanding. Let us characterize this as the cultivation form of news; indeed, it is common to hear journalists speak of "cultivating" sources. It produces a more even and predictable story flow.

Both of these core forms can be enriched through two variants, known respectively as "investigative" and "enterprise" journalism. Investigative journalism is that in which a reporter pursues the apparent causes, effects, or correlates of an action or event—seeking out the story behind the story. Enterprise journalism carries this activity a step further. The journalist may actually be the source of the idea for the story. Investigative and enterprise journalism vary from the first two forms primarily in the amount of resources—time, money, staffing, and editorial latitude—they are afforded, and from one another by the degree of ingenuity or intellectual capital that the journalist and/or the news organization is prepared, and permitted, to invest. Table 5.1 summarizes these diverse story forms.

Investigative and enterprise journalism, with their connotations of initiative and, for the audience, vicarious participation in political events (through the agency of the journalist), are central to the myth structure of the profession. The fact that they are separately identified and labeled, however, is ample testimony to their relative rarity. Moreover, for a variety of reasons tracing to media economics, the sociology of the newsroom, and the professional training of journalists, all of which are common to all forms of reporting, investigative and enterprise journalism share with their lesser cousins (1) the same basic assumption that news occurs naturally, and (2) the same dependency on action and environment. For purposes of the present discussion, then, any distinction between basic and enriched journalism is a distinction without meaning.

Within the myth structure of journalism, the principal difference between the hunter-gatherer form and the cultivation form is the relative weight each assigns to the two news-making forces: action and environment. The assignment-driven hunter-gatherer form is both acutely and superficially action-oriented, while the beat-managed cultivation form is far more dependent on environmental considerations. The principal similarity between the two is that both are clearly bounded and defined by those forces. The enriched forms of journalism differ from the basic forms, not with respect to their essential character, but in the resources and entrepreneurial effort that are added to the mix.

A final component of the myth structure of journalism is objectivity—the notion that a journalist is, in some meaningful sense, a neutral and objective observer and chronicler of political actions and the political environment.[1] For present purposes, the most interesting aspect of this component is the presumption that events are what they seem and that by conveying their content to an audience, the journalist is portraying reality. Although the profession allows for interpretation, it does so only grudgingly, taking care to distinguish observation from opinion or at least appearing to do so.[2] It is at this point that the assumed natural occurrence of news is closest to the heart of journalism's mythology, for the only reality that can exist under the myth of objectivity is the one true reality that can be observed.

Journalism's dependence on the observation of this one true naturally occurring reality—shaped by the individual and institutional norms of the profession—has left journalists, and the public that depends upon them for its understanding of political reality, susceptible to manipulation. The reason is that news is not necessarily a naturally occurring phenomenon; rather, some news is purposefully formulated and shaped with skill and effectiveness to take advantage of the needs and interests of reporters and news organizations, even as they serve the interests of other parties altogether. It is not the reporters or the news organizations that do the shaping. It is the news sources themselves, or more correctly, the strategic advisers whose recommendations guide and form their public actions. These strategic communicators, or news shapers, constitute a third force in newsmaking.[3] They strive systematically to ensure, insofar as is possible, that the work product of journalism reflects events and an environment, and creates a reality, which they, not the journalists, define. Their purpose is not to question or undermine the credibility or esteem that our society attaches to journalism. To the contrary, their purpose is to capture and exploit it for their own benefit.

That newsmakers should have an interest in influencing stories relating to them or their interests is hardly a new idea. What is new is the sophistication with which they are now able to affect the news, the considerable and growing extent of their success, and the expanding body of newsmaker types who are employing such methods. The breadth and depth of this trend—and, as a result, the gap between the myth and the reality of news—are now sufficient to con-

Table 5.2 Journalism: Myth and reality

The myth	The reality
News occurs naturally.	News is manufactured.
News is a form of inquiry and explication.	News is a form of storytelling.
News organizations seek to find and expose the truth.	News organizations seek to maximize profits.
Journalists are independent-thinking professionals.	Journalists are bureaucrats whose job is to fill time or space in a cost-effective, audience-pleasing manner.
Journalists are deep-earth miners who will move mountains to find the truth.	Journalists are hunter-gatherers who skim the surface for the most readily available material.
News content is a product of objective observation.	News content is a product of manipulation.

stitute a genuine threat to the viability of journalism as we have come to know it. Table 5.2 summarizes some dimensions of the myth-reality gap.

The Traditional View of News and Politics

The traditional view of news and politics descends directly from the so-called "basic model of communication." This model comprises three components—sender, message, and receiver—and one action—the issuance of the message by the sender to the receiver—as the essence of communication. Scholars recognized early on that this model was overly simple, especially when applied to mass communication, and they began to modify it. The results have included notions such as the following:

gatekeeping—editorial or other criteria are used to select from among the huge number of available stories or messages those that would actually be transmitted;

the two-step flow hypothesis—component groups among the receivers process and modify the meaning of the message;

diffusion theory—institutions and social interactions create channels and barriers that facilitate or impede the effective dissemination of various types of information;

framing—the visual and linguistic elements of a message interact with existing audience "storylines" to shape its interpretation and effects; and cognitive theory—the cognitive processing of information by the receiver affects the meaning and functional utility of the message.[4]

Recent scholarship has also emphasized factors such as the social networks within which communicators and audiences function and the impact on communication of the changing technologies and social processes by which it is accomplished.[5]

As time has passed and theory has evolved, we have learned a great deal about the multiple filters through which information passes between sender and receiver, about the degree and significance of differentiation in both audience and message, and about the psychological and sociological processes that refine news and other information and give it meaning. As a result, our view of journalism as an expression of the basic model has been greatly enhanced.

What has not changed in most writing about news and politics, however, is our treatment of the core assumption that news is a naturally occurring phenomenon, and that news stories are merely the stochastic outcomes of a system of interactions between journalists and the two main forces of newsmaking—environment and actions.

The role of the journalist in the basic model is essentially that of the sender. Leaving aside the considerable physical importance of the medium itself, it is the journalist (or the news organization) who selects, packages, and distributes information to the audience. But this basic model is iterative: it operates in a recurring sequential manner. In other words, before becoming a sender of information, the journalist first functions as a receiver. And before deciding what constitutes the news and disseminating it to a larger audience, the journalist is influenced by many factors that make the coverage of a given story more or less likely, more or less accurate, and more or less complete, and that shape the verbal and visual imagery that will give it meaning. It is these pre-journalism factors that are increasingly manipulated in ways, and with a purposefulness and effectiveness, that undermine the classical assumption of naturally occurring news.

Questioning the Assumption of Contextual Neutrality

The notion that journalism is, or can be, independent of political and other pressures and that news itself exists in a similar motivational vacuum is distinctly American in origin and distinctly a product of the latter half of the twentieth century. It is the product of the confluence of two forces: (1) the creation, for the first time in history, of a genuinely mass audience and genuinely mass media, and (2) the rise of both an institutionalized pluralism in American politics and a sustaining ideology to support it. The audience came first, born in the cauldron of yellow journalism, cheap pulp-based papers, mechanical typography, and compulsory education that intermingled in the first two decades of the last century and was later nurtured by the spread of radio and television. The political structure came only slightly afterward, born of the New Deal coalition, rationalized in the work of political scientist Robert Dahl and others, and sustained by survey research, database management, and direct mail. These social technologies allowed political leaders to identify, target, and mobilize potential constituencies.[6]

Today many Americans accept without question the core idea of so-called pluralist democracy, which holds that although the U.S. political system is too large and complex to permit governance by the citizenry in its purest form— one person, one vote on every issue—the democratic principle is preserved through a series of intermediary structures—interest groups, political parties, and the like. In this view the news media serve as one of the intermediary structures, and an especially important one, sufficient to be singled out in the Constitution for protection. Their role is to inform the citizenry of what the government and the other mediating institutions are doing, presumably in the citizenry's behalf. That information is presumed to be important because it will lead, eventually, to outcomes that are in some meaningful sense representative of the net needs or preferences of the public.

Stripped of its rhetoric, the foundation of pluralism rests on a bedrock belief: through an interplay of the apparent self-interests of a multiplicity of groups in the society, decisions are made that serve some collective "public" interest. Pluralists believe that this interplay is at once important, appropriate, and definitive. This bedrock belief sustains the mythology of contemporary journalism, for it is to this belief that the assumption of naturally occurring news and of its genuine significance can be traced. The public interplay of the visible participants in pluralist democratic institutions and processes defines and legitimizes the news. The myth of objective and informative political journalism works and has meaning because it exists in a context of pluralist democracy.

Pluralism, however, has not always been the leading political ideology, even in the United States. It is not the only explanatory framework available today, and it may well provide an inadequate—even misleading—characterization of the workings of the American political system. Thomas Dye, among others, has long argued that to be the case.[7] Dye believes that latent interactions among lesser-known and seldom-observed economic, social, and political institutions, such as corporate boards of directors, university research centers, private foundations, and public policy think tanks, are far more influential than the institutions of pluralist democracy. Moreover, he believes that the institutions of pluralist democracy are more important for the appearance of public influence and purpose they epitomize than for any genuine influence.[8]

If that is true, even in some limited degree, then along with the ideology of pluralist democracy, the myth of objective and meaningful journalism must come into question. For if Dye and his like-minded colleagues are correct, pluralist ideology and journalistic myth both constitute a form of disinformation whose effect and, in the most conspiratorial view, whose purpose, is to obscure the true centers of power, not to reveal them. But one need not go that far to appreciate the genuine vulnerability of journalism to manipulation.

In its dealings with the external world of news objects—the people, institutions, and events that have the potential to become subjects of the news—journalism claims a measure of pro-activity—of exercising the initiative in identifying, defining, and portraying the news—that simply does not square with reality. Investigation and enterprise may drive the myth structure, but they do not predominate in the newsroom. In fact, most journalism is reactive. Some event has occurred or some news source has said or done something that is judged worthy of time or space on a given day, and as a result an act of journalism is committed. Environmental considerations enter the decision matrix as well. They help to identify the absolute significance of the day's events (how well they meet the general criteria of newsworthiness such as conflict, drama, or prominence), and they help to sort out the relative significance of those events compared with others occurring the same day. Depending on the interplay of actions and environments, what is news today might or might not be news if it happens tomorrow.

Journalists routinely assert that they do not make the news, they merely report it. By this they mean, in effect, that they scan the horizon in search of events and settings that meet the established criteria of newsworthiness, then convert those that best match into the day's news. As an expression of professional beliefs, this statement makes clear the inherently reactive orientation of its practitioners. But it does much more. For when viewed from the perspective of the news shapers, the assertion defines the targets of opportunity for news-directed communication strategies. If events and settings can be effectively managed by an interested elite—whether economic, political, social, cultural, informational, or merely functional—if events can be staged and settings structured in ways that will lead reporters down predictable and preferred paths, then the news itself will be effectively managed.

In its dealings with the internal world of the news organization—job pressures and preferences, editorial discretion, marketing, and other business considerations—journalism asserts a measure of independence—of the ability to render judgments on the selection, development, and presentation of news stories—that similarly fails to square with reality. As Edward Jay Epstein, Leon Sigal, Herbert Gans, Pamela Shoemaker and Stephen Reese, and W. Lance Bennett have long and ably argued, news is far more a product of internal behaviors and values, of the institutional needs of the newsroom, than it is a daily response to the unknown and unpredictable.[9] News organizations, like other commercial enterprises in the United States, live in a risk-reward environment. Because predictability reduces risk, daybooks, rolodexes, and news routines are far more important in shaping political coverage than are investigation and original discovery. Because news that features prominent personalities and simplified conflict builds audiences, it provides rewards. From this perspective, events and actions are important less in their own right than for the ways they fit the institutional needs of the news organization. Because these institutional forces operate across virtually all media and at all times, they lend predictability to journalistic behavior. That predictability, in turn, if it can be effectively managed by an interested elite, can provide yet another avenue through which to influence and shape the ultimate journalistic product—the news.

In fact, not only may such an elite exist, but its emergence within a context of ostensibly pluralist democratic politics may well be a product of the ability to manage news and information with ever-greater effect. That is to say, precisely because the media that lay at the very heart of pluralist democracy could be manipulated, an elite has emerged based on the skill set that is most effective at this task. And as a result, the institutions of pluralism have been altered through their interaction with journalism and the news in ways that further separate the appearance of democracy from the reality of what we might term neopluralism, a system in which the identity of the groups that sponsor political initiatives and their motives in doing so are obscured, even as such group efforts become more efficient, and in which political information becomes available only in more and more specialized and targeted forms, even as it becomes greatly more available. In such a system, competing views challenge one another and are judged, not on the merits of their substantive positions, but on the strength of their communication management skills.[10]

If such an elite (or set of elites) does exist, and if it does exercise such influence in any significant degree, then the underlying assumption of contemporary journalistic mythology—that news is a naturally occurring phenomenon and its reporting a stochastic process—must be questioned. In its place, we must consider the alternative: news is in some measure an artificial—some would say manufactured—product determined in some measure by factors that remain out of view of the journalists upon whom they operate. Whether that is the case would seem a question well worth posing.

In the balance of this chapter, I limit my analysis to two aspects of this question. First, by what strategies and tactics might one or more elites successfully shape the news and the behavior of journalists to advantage? Second, are there players on the contemporary political scene who are systematically employing these strategies and others like them?

Strategy and Tactics

In fact, the development of a social technology of influence has been well and widely documented.[11] Its adoption in the form of "strategic political communication" is quite advanced.[12] Elsewhere, I have defined this form of communication as "the use of sophisticated knowledge of such attributes of human behavior as attitude and preference structures, cultural tendencies, and media use patterns—and such relevant organizational behaviors as how news organizations make decisions regarding news content and how congressional committees schedule and structure hearings—to shape and target messages so as to maximize their desired impact while minimizing undesired collateral effects."[13] It is, in sum, an applied science of persuasive political communication. Among the common elements of this science are the identification of stakeholders and their respective interests and points of susceptibility to influence, the creation of positions, the forging of alliances, and the definition and promulgation of a persuasive and goal-supporting political reality.

Identifying Stakeholders

Every political institution and every political issue is associated with a set of stakeholders—individuals, groups, or organizations with some interest in its advancement. Typically, the principal stakeholders of a policy or agency are the beneficiaries of its implementation or actions or those whose positions could be put at risk through the same. For example, the stakeholders in health care policy would include health care providers, health care workers, insurers, employers who offer health care benefits to their workers, the public, and various levels of governments. Stakeholders in the Environmental Protection Agency would include the regulated industries, private contractors who work on EPA projects, and environmental interest groups, among others. Each of these stakeholders has a set of interests, and each has ways in which it is susceptible to influence. The strategic communicator typically initiates a persuasive effort by inventorying the range of stakeholders involved in a particular policy or agency, specifying insofar as possible the nature of their respective interests, delineating their respective susceptibilities to influence, and identifying those points around which some form of common interest or alliance might be established that could bring about the desired objective. The idea is not to get any stakeholder to act against its own interests, but to cause it to act selectively in its own interest in ways that help advance the goals of the communicator.

Building Positions

With this cluster of targets in mind, the strategic communicator next begins to develop, test, refine, and roll out issue positions in such a way that two objectives are achieved. First, the positions must serve—either explicitly or indirectly—the communicator's underlying goals. Second, the positions must be framed so as to maximize the chances of building a sufficiently powerful alliance to make their achievement likely. There are many ways to build such positions, ranging from selecting particular aspects of a given issue to highlight or obscure, to choosing specific language and visual images through which to portray them. Typically, when making these choices, strategists employ social science research—surveys, focus groups, content analysis, and even physiological experimentation—to evaluate specific formulations with representative audiences.[14] Then, as selections are made and implemented, they are tested through further research until the optimal strategy becomes clear.

Building Alliances

Having identified the relevant stakeholders and designed and tested the themes to be used to influence them, the communication strategist builds political alliances. Alliance building can have several purposes. The most obvious is to enhance the likelihood of obtaining the desired outcome. But other, less obvious, purposes can be at least as important. For example, a group that knows itself to be politically unpopular can, through strategic communication, generate an alliance of other groups without itself joining or even being identified with that alliance. It thereby stands to benefit, not merely from the achievements of the alliance it has fostered, but from the greater popularity of the participants.

Defining Realities

With a message and an alliance in place or in prospect, the communication strategist next sets out to exercise political influence—to advance the substantive cause. This is the point at which the greatest incentive exists to manage—manipulate—news outcomes.

For any individual or group or institution, reality is a social construct.[15] It is the product of (1) judgments made about the meaning of (2) the information that is available at any given time. The judgments themselves are driven by many well-entrenched internal dynamics—psychological, sociological, and other factors. The judgments are generally not highly susceptible to influence, but the same cannot be said of the flow of information upon which these judgments are to be based. In greater or lesser measure, that flow can be conditioned through political action in ways that will bend perceptions of reality in one direction or another. In politics and public policy, even in the age of blogs, Blackberries, and instant messaging, the principal form in which information flows is as news. Therefore, through effective management of the news, "reality" can be shaped and influence achieved.

News management can take many forms. Knowing, for example, the predilection of editors for particular types of stories, such as those with distinct elements of human pathos, communication strategists can literally create stories of those types, then bring them to the attention of editors. Similarly, knowing the preference of television editors, in particular, for stories that incorporate graphic video imagery, stories can be crafted to incorporate such imagery, then "shopped" to those most likely to pursue them. Knowing that reporters like to document their stories with quotations from authorities, strategists can provide to those reporters lists of authorities whom they know (but the reporter may not) will support their view, or they can even deliver the quotations themselves. Knowing that the media gravitate toward simple language and visual imagery to represent complex stories, communication strategists can devise a verbal and visual lexicon that at once meets the journalists' needs and benefits their own positions. Through these and many other devices, news can be—is—managed with some effect.[16]

The Players: Who Would Do Such a Thing?

Such behaviors might seem to lie beyond the pale in the context of a normative discussion of democratic practice, but they are, in fact, commonplace.

Their existence is an empirical fact. Strategic communication is employed by an astonishingly wide range of players in the U.S. political system, and its use continues to grow.

Political Parties and Candidates

Not surprisingly, the techniques of influence I have described were first developed in the electoral arena, where today they are not only assumed to operate, but are actually afforded some measure of legitimacy. After all, people expect their politicians to attempt to influence them, and are not surprised when others, such as the so-called "527 groups" that were active in the 2004 presidential campaign, try to sway their votes. Sophisticated efforts to employ social technologies for this purpose have their roots earlier, but are probably best traced to the presidential campaign of John F. Kennedy in 1960, when a computer simulation was used to shape a communication strategy.[17] Succeeding years saw the rapid development of sophisticated message-testing methodologies and rather explicit strategies for taking advantage of the journalistic myth.[18] Though perhaps the most prolific, these electoral efforts at persuasion are in many ways the least interesting and the least significant in the political system for the simple reason that they are widely recognized, a factor that automatically minimizes their effectiveness. Strategic communication is most effective when it is least visible, and least effective when it is revealed.[19]

Policy Interests in Nonelectoral Settings

By 1981, when Ronald Reagan became president, strategic communication was a fully integrated component of the policy-making process. Reagan's advisers knew that the centerpiece of his legislative agenda, a massive tax cut, would be dead-on-arrival in the Democratic Congress, so they set out to resuscitate it through an orchestrated campaign of grassroots organizing, coalition building, issue framing, and media managing. By the time they had finished, they had not only made adoption of a relatively radical policy inevitable, but they had also demonstrated for all to see the potency of strategic communication.[20] In the major public policy battles that followed—perhaps most notably in the battle over health care policy in the first Clinton administration and in the contest to shape public understanding of the U.S. role in Iraq after the overthrow of Saddam Hussein—communication strategists have been employed by industry, interest groups, and others to create and generate support for versions of reality supporting their respective goals.

Foreign Governments

One area where journalists and news organizations are especially susceptible to manipulation is foreign policy making. With the exception of the occasional high profile crisis or conflict, and even in the wake of the September 11, 2001, attacks, the American public has relatively little knowledge of, or interest in, foreign affairs and makes few demands on the news media for extensive and informed coverage. The media therefore have little incentive to devote their resources to covering routine international news. The high cost of providing such coverage is a further disincentive. As a result, very little international news reaches Americans.[21] Most of what does reach Americans is oriented toward events more than toward explanations of events and is filtered through a relatively small number of originating news organizations. The combination of low interest and limited information translates into news organizations and citizens being vulnerable to manipulation. Over the years a number of governments have worked to exploit that vulnerability. One study has shown that by the mid-1980s more than five hundred foreign governments, political entities, and companies had hired American "agents" to assist them in the United States, and that number was growing. Many of these "agents" monitored and shaped media coverage expressly to influence U.S. foreign policy.[22]

Corporations

Corporations expend vast amounts of money every year for the purpose of shaping their images. The most obvious elements of this effort include advertising and public relations, but many other routine business activities—employee relations, marketing, customer service, policy positions, philanthropy and public service, and regulatory compliance—affect corporate images. Although most of this activity has a commercial rather than political intent, it cannot help but have an impact on a company's political positioning. Companies that are well regarded commercially are advantaged when their political interests are at stake, and those that are poorly regarded are disadvantaged.[23]

The mechanics of marketing or other corporate activities often take forms similar to those characterized here as strategic political communication, especially with respect to a company's efforts to manage its portrayal in the news, which can affect everything from its stock price to its ability to attract customers. It is only natural, then, that when a corporation sees that a political interest is at stake, it employs the same methods of influence in that arena as it does elsewhere. Examples of such behavior abound, but the clearest in recent years may be the efforts of Wal-Mart to defend itself against a series of allegations from organized labor, environmentalists, health care advocates, and antigrowth activists. Wal-Mart's strategy included recruiting experienced political operatives from the electoral arena to help the company formulate and articulate its positions.[24]

Labor Unions

For labor unions, particularly since the mid-1990s, strategic communication has supplanted the strike as a weapon of choice in dealing with the managements of unionized companies and has played a primary role in efforts to organize workers at nonunion companies. The unions use "corporate campaigns," which are primarily strategic communication campaigns—generally negative in character—that are designed to attack the reputation and essential stakeholder relationships of a company to pressure management to accede to a union demand. These campaigns incorporate all of the principal elements identified earlier—stakeholder identification, message development and targeting, image framing, and media manipulation. The unions have become sophisticated practitioners of this approach, which they have directed at a growing number of companies.[25] In 1995, when John Sweeney was elected president of the AFL-CIO, then the nation's premier labor federation, he publicly committed the federation to increased corporate campaign activity and pledged tens of millions of dollars to the effort.[26] In 2005 the federation split roughly in half, with the newly formed Change to Win Federation committing itself to even greater reliance on corporate campaign activities.

Social Interests

The core elements of corporate campaigns were first identified, not by the labor movement, but by New Left political activists in the 1960s. These activists, and their successors who now constitute the contemporary Progressive Left, did not lead in the full-scale development of this form of activism. But they have rediscovered it, particularly as an element of the environmental, human rights, and similar social movements. The result is a growing number of campaigns, primarily directed against corporations, but also against governments, that seek to mobilize stakeholders as a force for change. One of the most interesting and potentially far-reaching of these efforts is the social responsibility investment movement, which, in concert with union and public employee pension funds and other allies, has been working to leverage the influence of institutional shareholders (banks, pension funds, mutual funds, insurance companies, and the like, which hold millions of shares in publicly traded companies) to change corporate governance structures and social policies.[27]

Litigants

"Litigation journalism"—the systematic manipulation of the media by parties to a lawsuit—is another application of these techniques that came of age in the 1980s.[28] The objective of litigation journalism is to shape public opinion, either at large or among a specified pool of prospective jurors, in such a way that one side in a trial or the other defines the reality of the case. For example, it was only in the context of a civil trial alleging harm from the use of a cellular telephone that the public "learned" that the use of cell phones may be associated with an increased incidence of certain brain cancers.[29] There is some reason to doubt that association, but the fact that it entered the public discourse as an assertion of fact at a critical time in the litigation framed the trial in a whole new way.[30] In a similar way, it is now commonplace for corporations, other organizations, and even individual litigants to engage in media framing when they are involved in major litigation.

Outcomes

The presence of so many players in the game of strategic political communication seems to suggest pluralism at work. After all, if corporations and unions, governments and social activists, litigants and others are all playing the same game, is it not likely that a reasonable balance of some sort will emerge? That is the obvious question, but it misses the point.

To begin with, the ability of so many different kinds of political interests to manipulate the communication system to their respective advantage hardly constitutes a ringing endorsement of the system itself. To the contrary, it suggests that the information being distributed through news organizations and other channels is, in some broadly systemic sense, not what it appears. Moreover, because the information in question has, as a central feature of the strategic communication process, been systematically reduced to its lowest common denominator of audience appeal, the apparent quality of the information provided by the aforementioned political actors and through the news media is a mere façade.[31] In point of fact, much of that information has been stripped of its substantive content and packaged in verbal and visual symbols.

Added to that is an essential fact of strategic communication: negatives trump positives. For a variety of reasons ranging from their inherent appeal to journalists to their prurient appeal to the public and their memorability, negative messages carry more weight than positive messages, and those on the attack generally have the advantage over those on the defensive. Therefore, the labor union attacking a company's reputation in a corporate campaign holds the advantage, as does the litigant making broad damage claims against another, and so forth. The likely consequences of this rising tide of negativism are greater public cynicism and less public confidence in social institutions. Both trends can be observed in the United States today.

Finally, the pluralist presumption of offsetting interests carries an implicit assumption that all of the interests in question—or some set of relevant competing clusters or alliance structures—share equally in the skills, experience, and resources that can be brought to the contest. When one considers the range of players now employing these techniques, the pairs in which they might compete, and the constraints under which they operate, that assumption is not on its face valid.

For the society subjected to the substantial and growing degree of this strategizing and implementing, the net outcome is a diminution of the quality of political dialogue in direct proportion to the degree and effectiveness of the manipulation that occurs. To the extent that political dialogue guides and limits policy making and other political behaviors, and that such guides and limitations preserve the values of the society, the political life of that society is impaired.

In contemporary democratic polities, journalists have been widely accepted as the principal gatekeepers for and interpreters of political information. But the same professional myth structure of neutrality and independence that has raised their profile above the horizon has marked journalists as potential targets of opportunity for would-be image managers. As distinct from the myth, the reality of the profession, with its genuine and predictable internal pressures, its regularities, and its dependence on the most superficial forms of information gathering, renders journalists truly vulnerable. The increasing sophistication of the image managers and their growing record of success bring together the means and the incentive for them to exercise their influence. In this way, these news shapers have emerged as a third force in the news-politics relationship. The result is that political "news" is surely not what the public believes it to be, and, to the extent that they subscribe to the popular mythology, it may well not conform to the beliefs of journalists themselves.

Notes

1. For an alternative, but generally compatible, treatment of objectivity to that presented here, see Richard L. Kaplan, "The News About New Institutionalism: Journalism's Ethic of Objectivity and Its Political Origins," *Political Communication* 23 (July 2006): 173–185.

2. W. Russell Neuman, Marion R. Just, and Ann N. Crigler, *Common Knowledge: News and the Construction of Political Meaning* (Chicago: University of Chicago Press, 1992), esp. 70.

3. The term *news shaper* was coined by Lawrence Soley. See *The News Shapers: The Sources Who Explain the News* (New York: Praeger, 1992). Soley applied it to the community of "experts" whose comments are routinely solicited by journalists. Here the term is applied to actors at a far earlier stage of the newsmaking process.

4. On gatekeeping, see David M. White, "The 'Gatekeeper': A Case Study in the Selection of News," *Journalism Quarterly* 27 (1950): 383–390; on the two-step flow hypothesis, see Elihu Katz and Paul F. Lazarsfeld, *Personal Influence: The Part Played by People in Mass Communication* (Glencoe, Ill.: Free Press, 1955); on diffusion theory, see Everett M. Rogers, *Diffusion of Information*, 3rd ed. (New York: Free Press, 1983); on framing, see William A. Gamson, and Andre Modigliani, "Media Discourse and Public Opinion on Nuclear Power: A Constructionist Approach," *American Journal of Sociology* 95 (1989):1–37; and on cognitive theory, see Doris A. Graber, *Processing Politics: Learning from Television in the Internet Age* (Chicago: University of Chicago Press, 2000).

5. On social network effects, see Manuel Castells, *The Rise of the Network Society*, 2nd ed. (Oxford: Blackwell, 2000); on the transformation of communication technologies and social processes, see W. Lance Bennett and Jarol B. Manheim, "The One-Step Flow of Communication," *The Annals of Political and Social Science* 608 (November 2006): 213–232.

6. Robert Dahl, *A Preface to Democratic Theory* (Chicago: University of Chicago Press, 1956). See also Robert Dahl, *Dilemmas of Pluralist Democracy* (New Haven: Yale University Press, 1982).

7. Thomas R. Dye, *Who's Running America? The Bush Restoration*, 7th ed. (Upper Saddle River, N.J.: Prentice Hall, 2002).

8. Jarol B. Manheim, *Biz-War and the Out-of-Power Elite: Anti-Corporate Activism and the Attack on the Corporation* (Mahwah, N.J.: Lawrence Erlbaum Associates, 2004), argues that the recent rebirth of the progressive left is based on a reverse engineering of this view of the hidden power structure.

9. Edward Jay Epstein, *News from Nowhere: Television and the News* (New York: Random House, 1973); Leon V. Sigal, *Reporters and Officials: The Organization and Politics of Newsmaking* (Lexington, Mass.: D.C. Heath, 1973); Herbert J. Gans, *Deciding What's News* (New York: Random House, 1979); Pamela J. Shoemaker and Stephen D. Reese, *Mediating the Message: Theories of Influences on Mass Media Content*, 2nd ed. (New York: Allyn and Bacon, 1995); W. Lance Bennett, *News: The Politics of Illusion*, 6th ed. (New York: Longman, 2004); and Timothy E. Cook, *Governing with the News: The News Media as a Political Institution* (Chicago: University of Chicago Press, 1998). *Political Communication* 23 (2006): 135–230, is an entire issue devoted to the value of viewing news itself as an institution in the context of developments in organizational theory within the discipline of sociology.

10. W. Lance Bennett and Jarol B. Manheim, "The Big Spin: Strategic Communication and the Transformation of Pluralism Democracy," in *Mediated Politics: Communication in the Future of Democracy*, ed. W. Lance Bennett and Robert M. Entman (New York: Cambridge University Press, 2001), 279–298.

11. Gary Mauser, *Political Marketing: An Approach to Campaign Strategy* (New York: Praeger, 1983); Nicholas J. O'Shaughnessy, *The Phenomenon of Political Marketing* (New

York: St. Martin's, 1990); and Philippe J. Maarek, *Political Marketing and Communication* (London: John Libbey, 1995).

12. Jarol B. Manheim, *All of the People, All the Time: Strategic Communication in American Politics* (Armonk, N.Y.: M. E. Sharpe, 1991); and Bennett and Manheim, "The Big Spin."

13. Jarol B. Manheim, *Strategic Public Diplomacy and American Foreign Policy: The Evolution of Influence* (New York: Oxford University Press, 1994), 7.

14. For an example, see Liana Winett, "Advocates Guide to Developing Framing Memos," in *Do the Media Govern?* ed. Shanto Iyengar and Richard Reeves (Thousand Oaks, Calif.: Sage, 1997), 420–427.

15. For the definitive statement of this notion, see Peter L. Berger and Thomas Luckman, *The Social Construction of Reality: A Treatise in the Sociology of Knowledge* (New York: Doubleday, 1966).

16. For an example of this sort of analysis as applied by so-called "progressive activists," see Michael Pertschuk, "Putting Media Effects Research to Work: Lessons for Community Groups Who Would Be Heard," in *Do the Media Govern,* 391–400. To see why the term "progressive activists" is itself a demonstration of the art, see Manheim, *Biz-War,* esp. 82–88.

17. For a review of this early model, see Ithiel de Sola Pool, Robert P. Abelson, and Samuel L. Popkin, *Candidates, Issues and Strategies: A Computer Simulation of the 1960 Presidential Election* (Cambridge: MIT Press, 1964).

18. Jarol B. Manheim, "Communication Strategies in the 1996 Campaign," in *America's Choice: The Election of 1996,* ed. William Crotty and Jerome M. Mileur (Guilford, Conn.: Dushkin/McGraw Hill, 1997), 52–59.

19. Manheim, *Strategic Public Diplomacy,* 139–142.

20. Manheim, *All of the People,* 69–73.

21. Stephen Hess makes this point in *International News and Foreign Correspondents* (Washington, D.C.: Brookings Institution, 1996), 85–104.

22. Manheim, *Strategic Public Diplomacy,* 160–162.

23. For a discussion of corporate public affairs in general, and of the factors affecting a company's political positioning in particular, see Otto Lerbinger, *Corporate Public Affairs: Interacting with Interest Groups, Media and Government* (Mahwah, N.J.: Lawrence Erlbaum Associates, 2006).

24. For example, see "Wal-Mart Fight Turns More Political," Associated Press, April 24, 2006. As noted there, the company's antagonists have similarly employed political professionals to assist in framing their messages. One such effort is summarized in Celinda Lake, David Mermin, and Nancy Wiefek, "Re-Branding Wal-Mart," in *Social Policy* (Fall 2005), accessed January 31, 2006, at *www.socialpolicy.org/index.php?id=1575.*

25. Jarol B. Manheim, *The Death of a Thousand Cuts: Corporate Campaigns and the Attack on the Corporation* (Mahwah, N.J.: Lawrence Erlbaum Associates, 2001). An annotated list of approximately two hundred such efforts from their inception through 1999 is found on pages 311–339.

26. James Worsham, "Labor's New Assault," *Nation's Business* (June 1997): 16.

27. See Manheim, *Biz-War,* esp. 169–173; and Jarol B. Manheim, *Power Failure, Power Surge: Union Pension Fund Activism and the Publicly Held Corporation* (Washington, D.C.: HR Policy Association, 2005).

28. Carole Gorney, "Litigation Journalism Is a Scourge," *New York Times,* February 15, 1993, A15.

29. Carla Lazzareschi, "Suit over Cellular Radiation Raises Hazard Questions," *Los Angeles Times,* January 23, 1993, D1.

30. As recently as June 2006, scientists, who were still unable to resolve this question, joined with tumor victims for a conference sponsored by the National Brain Tumor Foundation. See "Brain Cancer and the Environment: What's the Connection? First-Ever Conference to Take Place in San Francisco," *PR Newswire,* June 21, 2006.

31. Manheim, *All of the People.*

6 Unmasking Deception: The Function and Failures of the Press

Kathleen Hall Jamieson and Bruce W. Hardy

Although scholars see various roles for political information in civic life, most agree that if citizens rely on misleading or false information when they make their political decisions, the results would be harmful to democracy.[1] Assessing citizens' capacity to recognize deceptive claims creates a stringent test of the extent to which the press informs the public. At its base, our question here is: Does the press provide the tools to enable citizens to discern truth from deception in presidential elections?

Our answer is this: although it is difficult to override the influence of often-repeated deceptions, the press has the capacity to do so. In 2004, reading the newspaper or viewing cable news corresponded with a heightened ability to distinguish factual from inaccurate general election presidential campaign claims. Overall, however, the press is neither disposed to delineate deception nor to make comparative judgments about the relative levels of deception in presidential campaigns. We offer reasons for this aversion and then suggest that voters who are deceived about candidate positions may vote differently from how they would if they were fully and, more important, accurately informed.

In short, this chapter considers whether news coverage is successful at overriding the influence of misleading political advertisements to ensure that the public has an accurate sense of the background and proposals of presidential candidates. Instead of concentrating on the accumulation of facts about political workings and current events in the United States, we focus on whether citizens can adequately recognize which 2004 campaign claims were truthful and which misleading.

To answer our question we analyze results from two separate surveys: one of the American public and one of professional journalists. Employing a battery of questions measuring the public's ability to discriminate true from false campaign claims is advantageous because it enables us to examine the relationship between news consumption and holding accurate campaign information. A survey of journalists permits us to assess the likelihood that they will report that one campaign is more deceptive than another.

The Role of the Information

In modern democracies citizens elect or appoint others to represent them. If constituents are ignorant, political actors may be in a position to betray the interests of those they represent. Avoiding this outcome does not mean that complete information is necessary to produce appropriate votes. Citizens are capable of making rational choices with limited informational resources.[2] Indeed, average citizens are able to make rational vote decisions based on past experience and heuristics.[3] Despite their disagreements about how much the public needs to know, most scholars agree that regardless of the net level of accurate information it holds, if the citizenry makes decisions based on misleading information, such a process would be detrimental to democratic society. Rule-of-thumb reasoning based on misinformation could produce even more negative consequences than those often outlined in the literature indicting low levels of political information held by the general public.[4]

The Press as the Custodian of Facts

If the press is acting as the custodian of facts, we would expect that citizens who consume high levels of news will be more likely to distinguish true from false statements in a presidential campaign. To determine whether that is the case, we turn to data from a postelection survey of 3,400 respondents conducted as part of the 2004 National Annenberg Election Survey (NAES) to answer two questions: Are high news consumers more likely to think that both campaigns are equally deceptive? And is news exposure related to increased command of facts in arenas in which ads are deceiving?

For this chapter, we look at forty-one claims made by the major party campaigns in 2004. All were offered in the course of the campaign. Most were fact checked by FactCheck.org, a project of the Annenberg Public Policy Center, which Kathleen Hall Jamieson and Brooks Jackson direct.[5] These questions were cumulated to construct an overall index of respondents' knowledge of the claims (see appendix for exact question wording and coding). The higher a respondent scored on this scale, the more claims he or she correctly identified as true or false.[6] The overall level of knowledge of the truthfulness of the campaign claims is moderate. On average, respondents correctly identified roughly

Table 6.1 Regression model predicting correct identification of the truthfulness of 2004 campaign claims

	Unstandardized B	Standard error	Beta
Female	−.732	.099	−.137**
Age	.002	.003	.011
Education	.116	.023	.107**
Income	.113	.026	.092**
Republican	−.418	.125	−.073**
Democrat	−.032	.120	−.006
Ideology (conservative coded high)	−.212	.056	−.078**
National broadcast television news	.024	.022	.024
Newspaper	.056	.018	.062**
24-hour cable news channels	.108	.019	.115**
Fox News[a]	−.061	.130	−.010
Local television news	−.040	.020	−.042*
R^2 (%)	14.1		

Notes: The "unstandardized B" is the regression coefficient representing the relationship of any independent variable and the dependent variable holding all of the other independent variables constant. The "standard error" is error of the regression coefficient and is used for significance testing. The "beta" is a standardized coefficient representing what the regression coefficient would be if the regression model were fitted to standardized data. The "beta" allows for comparisons among relationships.

**$p < .01$ *$p < .05$

[a] Fox News is included in the model because of the possible differential influence between Fox and other cable news channels. The 24-hour cable news channels measure also includes those who use Fox. Therefore, Fox viewers theoretically are entered into the model twice. Our biggest concern would be collinearity between these two measures, which could inflate standard errors and produce unstable coefficients. Although the two variables are moderately correlated ($r = .36$), collinearity statistics for the model do not suggest there is a problem. Additionally, the variables in question were measured in separate questions on the survey using different scales. The cable news channel variable was measured days per week. The Fox variable was a nominal variable that asked respondents which channel they watched the most. A regression model without Fox did not show any significant differences in the coefficients reported in the model here. Cable news produced a standardized beta of .112 in the model without Fox. As can be seen above, in the model that included Fox the beta for cable news was .115.

half of the claims.[7] Their scores, as we show in this chapter, are probably a reflection of political orientation. Citizens are more likely to believe their candidate than the opponent and more likely to hear about and believe the inaccuracies a favored candidate puts forward.

The results from a regression model predicting respondents' correct identification of the truthfulness of campaign claims permit us to examine the effects of news consumption (Table 6.1). We find detectable influence—some positive and some negative. Reading the newspaper and watching 24-hour cable news are both positively and significantly related to the respondent's ability to distinguish truthful from deceptive claims. This finding is true above and beyond the impact of sociodemographic and political orientation variables such as education or party identification and suggests that some news media are providing the tools that enable citizens to see through the deception in presidential campaigns. National television broadcast news was not related to respondents' ability to discern truthful claims from deception.

Local television news viewing is negatively related to distinguishing misleading from legitimate claims. This finding is consistent with past research showing that local television news consumption was negatively related to political knowledge.[8] An explanation for this relationship remains elusive. The finding could be, in part, a result of differences in content driven by local news' role as a "good neighbor," not as a watchdog. A 2006 study by Paula Poindexter, Don Heider, and Max McCombs found evidence that the public *expects* the local newspaper to be a good neighbor instead of a watchdog.[9] Although here we are looking at local television not the local newspaper that Poindexter and her colleagues studied, the same good neighbor role still applies: local television spends significant air time on local crime, local school sports, weather, and human interest and community stories.

What is problematic about this explanation is that it would forecast no relationship between local news consumption and accuracy, not a negative one. A possible explanation for this negative relationship is that the deceptions in the ads that run adjacent to local news are not scrutinized in local news the way they more often are in the national news that follows in most markets. As a result those who see the ads in local news may accept their distortions as fact, but those who rely on the national news and see ads there are more likely to hear an occasional correction. These occasional corrections were not, however, enough to produce a significant relationship in our analyses as national broadcast television news was not related to our dependent variable.

At a first glance, there seems to be some evidence that the press may be acting as the custodian of facts. We did find statistically significant positive relationships between some forms of news use and discerning truthful campaign claims from false ones. This finding does not justify unbridled optimism. Recall that the average number of claims correctly identified is around 50 percent. Additionally, this 50 percent can be explained, in part at least, by the fact that citizens believe their own candidate and not the opponent. People are pretty good at unmasking deception by a candidate they oppose but less adept at seeing through the deception of their favored candidate. For example, Table 6.2 shows the distribution of perceived truthfulness of some campaign claims by those who identify themselves as either Democrat or Republican.[10] As can be seen, individuals' perception of truth is highly dependent on their party identification. Although the influence of news may show up in our statistical model, the press's corrective power is not overwhelming.

What these analyses suggest is that partisans simply embrace claims consistent with their voting preference and in the process stubbornly reject correc-

Table 6.2 Perceived truthfulness of campaign claims, by party identification

Claim: George W. Bush's tax cuts reduced taxes for everyone who pays taxes. (False)

	Democrat (%)	Republican (%)
Very truthful	11.2	42.5
Somewhat truthful	17.9	27.5
Not too truthful	16.0	10.2
Not at all truthful	52.0	15.0
Don't know (volunteered)	2.8	4.8

Claim: John Kerry's health plan would have provided health insurance to all Americans. (False)

Very truthful	30.4	9.4
Somewhat truthful	41.5	23.5
Not too truthful	7.9	16.7
Not at all truthful	13.8	44.2
Don't know (volunteered)	6.3	6.2

Claim: Since George W. Bush became president, the economy has lost more jobs than at any time since the Great Depression. (True)

Very truthful	71.5	18.6
Somewhat truthful	17.2	23.0
Not too truthful	4.7	22.9
Not at all truthful	4.2	30.2
Don't know (volunteered)	2.1	5.0

Claim: John Kerry's health care plan would have taken medical decisions out of the hands of doctors and patients and put them under control of government bureaucrats. (False)

Very truthful	13.5	40.5
Somewhat truthful	16.7	28.4
Not too truthful	17.0	7.7
Not at all truthful	44.8	12.7
Don't know (volunteered)	7.9	10.7

tive claims and/or that the news media are failing to adequately put the claims of each side in a corrective context. On the bright side, we found some evidence that the press can provide the tools that help citizens make judgments on the truthfulness of campaign claims, as those who read the newspaper and watch 24-hour cable news are more likely to correctly identify the truthfulness of campaigns claims overall.

Also included in our survey was a question that asked respondents how difficult it is to figure out when the Democratic and Republican campaigns were telling the truth and when they were misleading (see appendix for exact question wording). Using the same independent variables as in the regression model above, we see somewhat similar relationships between news consumption and respondents saying that it is not difficult to figure out deception

Table 6.3 Regression model predicting respondents' perceived level of difficulty figuring out when the Democratic and Republican campaigns were telling the truth and when they were misleading

	Unstandardized B	Standard error	Beta
Female	.086	.030	.57**
Age	.000	.001	−.008
Education	−.005	.007	−.015
Income	−.015	.008	−.043
Republican	−.199	.037	−.123**
Democrat	−.385	.036	−.053*
Ideology (conservative coded high)	−.012	.017	−.016
National broadcast television news	−.007	.006	−.024
Newspaper	−.003	.005	−.013
24-hour cable news channels	−.020	.006	−.073**
Fox News	−.093	.039	−.051*
Local television news	.014	.006	.051*
R^2 (%)	4.0		

Note: **$p < .01$ *$p < .05$

Table 6.4 Perception of the amount of deception used by front-running candidates in the 2004 election

	How often do you think John Kerry told the truth about George W. Bush's record?	How often do you think George W. Bush told the truth about John Kerry's record?
None of the time	15.1%	17.8%
Some of the time	62.5	58.9
All of the time	16.9	17.6
Don't know (volunteered)	5.2	5.4
Refused (volunteered)	0.2	0.2

(Table 6.3). Cable news viewing, including Fox News, was significantly influential in this model. Those who are more likely to say that it was not difficult to figure out when campaigns were telling the truth were not significantly more likely to be able to correctly identify campaign claims ($r = −.027$, $p =$ n.s.). This finding is consistent with a body of research that suggests that humans are often unjustifiably confident in the accuracy of their beliefs.[11] And it is also consistent with rhetorician Roderick Hart's notion that exposure to deficient forms of news may increase the public's sense that it is knowledgeable without actually increasing knowledge.[12]

We also examined the public's perception of the truthfulness of the two front-running candidates in the 2004 election. Table 6.4 outlines the distribu-

Table 6.5 Regression model predicting perception of candidates telling the truth

	Standardized beta coefficients	
	How often do you think George W. Bush told the truth about John Kerry's record?	How often do you think John Kerry told the truth about George W. Bush's record?
Female	−.003	.005
Age	.031	−.048*
Education	−.015	.041*
Income	.019	−.015
Republican	.153**	−.133**
Democrat	−.140**	.191**
Ideology (conservative coded high)	.146**	−.094**
National broadcast television news	−.028	.071**
Newspaper	−.059**	−.013
24-hour cable news channels	.003	.048*
Fox News	.137**	−.101**
Local television news	−.025	−.004
R^2 (%)	15.1	15.1

tions of overall perception of level of deception the major party candidates employed. The perceived disparity between the two candidates is not huge: a large part of the public thinks that the candidates employ similar levels of deception. Without calibrating actual levels of deception, we have no basis for judging whether this belief is warranted.

The table reveals some reassuring news: a sizable majority thinks that the candidates tell the truth about their opponents at least some of the time. If the majority of the public believed that presidential candidates never told the truth, their perception of the link between campaigning and governance, a perception that creates a foundation for democracy, would be broken. More desirable still would be a finding that the public accurately perceives candidate claims and is therefore able to see the actual relationship between those promises and governance. Here we find public knowledge wanting.

Overall news use was not related to the perception that the candidates told the truth at least some of the time. However, different media channels had different effects on the perception of each individual candidate (Table 6.5). Not all that surprising is that reliance on Fox News produced the biggest divergence of all our media variables in the perception of the two candidates' claims. Fox News viewers were more likely to think George W. Bush told the truth about John F. Kerry's record and less likely to think the opposite. Other cable news viewers and those who watch national television news were more likely to think Kerry was truthful, and newspaper readers were less likely to think Bush was truthful. Nevertheless, the most influential predictors in this model were party identification and political ideology.

To see what press coverage contributes to the citizenry's ability to unmask deception, in the following pages we examine the effects of one campaign advertisement and its news coverage in the 2004 presidential campaign. We detail how the press covered the ad and examine the impact of the ad's claims on public opinion.

Kerry Would Throw Us To the Wolves

One of the misleading claims made during the campaign was based on Kerry's proposal to cut intelligence funding in 1994 and 1995. The Bush campaign painted a picture that implied that Kerry proposed these cuts after September 11, 2001. By indicting Kerry for the cuts, the ad obscured the fact that influential Republicans had supported them as well. The Bush campaign also implied that cuts proposed over five years would have occurred in a single year. (For a detailed analysis of the claims in the ad, visit FactCheck.org.)[13] Late in the campaign, the Bush camp encapsulated these notions in an advertisement titled "Wolves." This ad was made in spring 2004. When it was found to be highly effective in focus groups, the Bush camp waited until two weeks before election day to release the ad, which featured a pack of wolves in a forest eyeing the camera and preparing to attack:

Announcer: In an increasingly dangerous world. . . . Even after the first terrorist attack on America . . . John Kerry and the liberals in Congress voted to slash America's intelligence operations. By 6 billion dollars. . . . Cuts so deep they would have weakened America's defenses. And weakness attracts those who are waiting to do America harm.

Bush: I'm George W. Bush and I approved this message.[14]

"Wolves" was aired from October 22, 2004, until election day in thirty-nine media markets across fourteen states and on cable. According to TNS Media Intelligence/Campaign Media Analysis Group (CMAG) data, the 30-second spot aired a total of 9,128 times at an estimated cost of $8,065,215. Among the states where the airing was concentrated were the battleground states of Colorado, Florida, Iowa, Michigan, Minnesota, Missouri, Nevada, New Hampshire, New Mexico, Ohio, Oregon, Pennsylvania, Wisconsin, and West Virginia.[15]

Table 6.6 Perceived truthfulness of the claim that John Kerry voted to cut intelligence after September 11, 2001

	Democrat	Republican	Total sample
Very truthful	14.2%	43.6%	27.7%
Somewhat truthful	31.5	25.2	28.2
Not too truthful	15.1	7.1	10.8
Not at all truthful	20.6	8.2	14.6
Don't know (volunteered)	18.5	15.9	18.5
Refused (volunteered)	0.1	0	0.2

Table 6.7 Regression model predicting perceived truthfulness of the campaign claim that John Kerry voted to cut intelligence funding after September 11, 2001

	Unstandardized B	Standard error	Beta
Female	.100	.073	.036
Age	−.007	.002	−.082**
Education	−.016	.017	−.028
Income	.007	.020	.011
Republican	.386	.091	.130**
Democrat	−.252	.089	−.086**
Ideology (conservative)	.128	.041	.091**
National broadcast television news	−.013	.016	−.025
Newspaper	.010	.013	.020
24-hour cable news channels	.013	.014	.027
Fox News	.164	.096	.050
Local television	.019	.014	.039
Battleground state	.171	.071	.062*
R^2 (%)	8.3		

Notes: The "unstandardized B" is the regression coefficient representing the relationship of any independent variable and the dependent variable holding all of the other independent variables constant. The "standard error" is error of the regression coefficient and is used for significance testing. The "Beta" is a standardized coefficient representing what the regression coefficient would be if the regression model were fitted to standardized data. The "Beta" allows for comparisons among relationships.
$**p < .01$ $*p < .05$

Because ads air mostly in battleground states and national news coverage of them blankets the country, campaigns are "natural experiments" for researchers interested in campaign effects. This structure affords us the opportunity to see whether the press is doing its job as the custodian of facts. The postelection survey of 3,600 respondents of the NAES asked respondents to rate the truthfulness of the campaign claim "John Kerry voted for cuts in intelligence after September 11."[16] In our sample, only 25.4 percent of respondents rated this claim as not truthful (see Table 6.6).

A regression analysis predicting levels of perceived truthfulness of the claim shows us that those who live in the battleground states are more likely to believe it (see Table 6.7) when controlling for sociodemographic variables and political preferences. In other words, the advertisement or concurrent campaign claims in other campaign venues may have had an impact: people who lived in the states where the advertisement was aired were more likely to believe that Kerry voted to cut intelligence funding after September 11. It is no surprise that Republicans are likely to believe that the statement is true and Democrats that it is false. Because Republicans and Democrats rely on different news channels, it is possible that instead of correcting the claim, pro-Republican news channels underscored it. We do not, however, see this in the regression model.

Because we would expect the press to correct the mistaken impression regardless of the venue in which it was originally found, the possible conflation of ads with other campaign discourse is not problematic for our analysis.

Throughout this chapter we have argued that if the news media were acting as a custodian of facts, we would see a direct influence on the perception of truthfulness of misleading campaign claims. As seen in Table 6.7, none of the types of news use included in the model was significantly related to accurate assessment of the truthfulness of this specific claim. If the press was fulfilling its role, news consumers would be able to discern a false from a true claim. These news consumers should know that Kerry did not vote to cut intelligence funding after September 11. If this claim is the test, the press is not fulfilling its role as custodian of facts.

One reason that the claim was more likely to be believed in battleground states is that very little news coverage focused on the accuracy of the assertion. Where corrections occurred, ad exposure, or exposure from campaign sources in the battleground, overrode any effect the assessment in news may have had.

To determine how often news provides the public with corrective information, we used the terms *wolves* and *Bush* and searched the dates between October 21 and election day in the Lexis-Nexis database. This process located eighteen articles in major U.S. newspapers that discussed the advertisement. Although many outlets, including the Associated Press, carried information about the release of the ad, and many television news programs replayed the ad, through Lexis-Nexis we were able to find only six out of the fifty-three search results for television transcripts that commented on its content.

Most of that commentary was of little use to an audience interested in the factual accuracy of the claim about Kerry's record. The day this ad was released, Terry Moran on ABC's *World News Tonight with Peter Jennings* discussed it with advertising analyst Bob Garfield. Garfield commented that the ad "looks like a Halloween slasher flick. It's really spooky. It's really well done. I'm really afraid, and that's exactly what they're after." [17] In this segment, Moran mentioned, albeit briefly, that the ad contained some misleading claims: "As for the Bush ad's claims, while it is true Kerry proposed intelligence cuts in the 1990s, senior congressional Republicans did too. But Kerry's proposed cuts were larger and across the board." In this statement, Moran barely touched on the ways this ad could potentially mislead voters.

Much of the news coverage on this particular advertisement did not focus on the misleading claims. Of the eighteen newspaper articles only three mentioned that the ad was misleading. Even there, however, the identification of the misleading information was attributed to Kerry spokesman Phil Singer. For example, the *Houston Chronicle* noted, "Many congressional Republicans, including Porter Goss, whom Bush made CIA director this year, advocated deeper intelligence cuts than Kerry in the early 1990s as the Cold War was ending, *Kerry spokesman Phil Singer pointed out*" (emphasis added).[18] "Pointed out" hints that the reporter believes the partisan spokesman without making the journalist responsible for the conclusion. Using the partisan source makes it easier for Bush partisans to discount the correction as spin.

The October 22 Associated Press wire story focused mostly on the scare tactic used in the advertisement. The article quotes Kerry's running mate, John Edwards, saying that "Bush had 'stooped so low' that he was 'continuing to try to scare America in his speeches and ads in a despicable and contemptible way.'"[19] The press concentrated on the similarities between the "Wolves" ad and Ronald Reagan's "Soviet Bear" ad that was used during the 1984 campaign to counter Democrat Walter Mondale's attacks on Reagan's military spending.

Feeding much of the press's coverage of this advertisement was a response ad, released to the news media but not aired by the Kerry camp, that featured an eagle (to symbolize Kerry) and an ostrich (to symbolize Bush). This ad suggested that Kerry soars high and "knows when to change course" while Bush just sticks his head in the sand and stands in one place. The press picked up on the uses of wildlife in these ads. Headlines such as "Political Imagery Gets Wild in TV Ads," "A Zoo Out There: Wolves, Ostriches and Eagles Populate Presidential Ads," and "Candidates Use Animals in Campaign Ads," which opened with the sentence, "It's Animal Planet in the presidential advertising wars," populated discussion of the ads.[20]

Some news content did deal with the misleading claims in the Bush ad. Four days after Factcheck.org released its report on the "Wolves" ad, NBC's *Today Show with Matt Lauer and Katie Couric* featured a panel of undecided voters and their reactions to misleading claims found in "Wolves." Factcheck.org director Brooks Jackson also joined the show to explain why this ad is misleading.

Some of the panelists thought the ad was powerful. Panelist Anthony explained: "Just the way they portrayed the—deep music, trying to give a serious note to it. It kind of catches your attention. You're think [*sic*] where are the wolves coming in? And it's kind of putting you in a position where you don't want to be preyed on." Other panelists were not as moved. Panelist Steve commented, "All it does is ratchet up the fear in everybody, and sir, reminds them of all of the things that they need to worry about." [21]

Jackson points out that the ad refers to the first World Trade Center attack in 1993, that the cut was not $6 billion, and that it was less than 4 percent of intelligence spending at the time. Panelist Michael responds, "It's a slick marketing package. It happens real quick where they talk about—the $6 billion, but right away you think 9-11." [22]

The second half of this *Today* segment focused on the misleading claims found in the Kerry ad, "Middle Class Squeeze." Nowhere in the segment do the hosts, Lauer and Couric, put weight on either deception. They do not provide any relative statement, explicit or implicit, that one ad was more misleading than the other, thereby creating the sense that the two campaigns were involved in comparable levels of deception.

In this case the news media did on occasion provide the tools necessary for citizens to identify misleading claims. The debunking that occurred did not have much of an effect. We suspect that Bush's "Wolves" ad overrode any positive influence that the press may have because it enjoyed a wide airing in the battleground states.

This analysis of "Wolves" gives us insight into the media's lack of disposition to counter the misleading claims promoted in a heavily aired television advertisement in the battleground states.

Assessing Comparative Amounts of Deception

Misleading statements made during a presidential campaign are not all of equal weight and importance. Some claims made during the 2004 campaign, such as Kerry did not deserve his military decorations, or that Bush lied to the American public about the necessity to go to war with Iraq, are undoubtedly more consequential than other claims made during the campaign, including the debate about the number of times Kerry voted to raise taxes.

Knowing that a campaign claim is deceptive can buffer the voter from drawing false inferences from it. Moreover, when one campaign is more deceptive overall or more deceptive on topics of concern to the voter, the relative level of deception may become a factor in a voting decision by inviting the voter to penalize the offending campaign. Doing so requires knowing which campaign to blame. For reasons we outline below, the press is reluctant to conclude that one side in a campaign is more deceptive than the other.

The differences between two articles published in spring 2004 are illustrative. Each focused on the presidential campaigns' use of deception. One appeared in the *New York Times,* the other in the *Washington Post.* The *Times* article by Jim Rutenberg was titled "Campaign Ads Are under Fire for Inaccuracy," and the *Post* article by Dana Milbank and Jim VandeHei was called "From Bush, Unprecedented Negativity: Scholars Say Campaign Is Making History with Often-Misleading Attacks."[23]

Writing in his blog, *Press Think,* on June 4, media critic and New York University journalism professor Jay Rosen outlined the "world of difference" between them.[24] The Rutenberg article details the use of deception in advertisements by both campaigns in a fairly equal light. Rosen comments, "This makes Rutenberg a chronicler of the will to deceive in politics, presented as part of the reality of politics."[25] Milbank and VandeHei chronicle the deception used, much like Rutenberg, but go one step further and write, "But Bush has outdone Kerry in the number of untruths, in part because Bush has leveled so many specific charges (and Kerry has such a lengthy voting record), but also because Kerry has learned from the troubles caused by Al Gore's misstatements in 2000."[26] One article was the rule in campaign reporting, the other the exception.

For a 2005 survey we phrased a question about a hypothetical campaign in which journalists knew that one side was more deceptive than the other. That poll of journalists conducted for the Annenberg Public Policy Center and the Annenberg Foundation Trust at Sunnylands suggests that Rosen is correct: even when journalists conclude that one side is more deceptive they are reluctant to report it.[27] We asked, "In a political campaign, if one side is using deceptive tactics more often than the opponents, do most journalists usually report the greater use of deception by one side, just report that both sides are using deception, or avoid the matter completely?" A majority of those surveyed said they believe journalists usually report that both sides are using deception and that this creates the impression to the public that each side of the campaign is engaging in similar amounts of deception (see Table 6.8). The avoidance of comparative judgment, which is part of the he said/she said approach to campaigns in general, creates a sense of moral equivalence between the two campaigns.

We believe that five problems explain why so few news articles evaluate the relative truthfulness of each side in a major campaign. It is difficult for

Table 6.8 Survey of journalists on use of deceptive tactics in political campaigns

In a political campaign, if one side is using deceptive tactics more often than the opponents, do most journalists usually report the greater use of deception by one side, report that both sides are using deception, or avoid the matter completely?

	Journalists N = 673
Report the greater use of deception by one side	25%
Just report that both sides are using deception	58
Avoid the matter completely	11
Don't know	4
Refused	2

Under these circumstances, do you think that by failing to point out that one side is more deceptive, journalists are suggesting that both sides are engaged in a similar amount of deception or not?*

	Journalists N = 465
Suggesting similar amount	79%
Not suggesting similar amount	17
Don't know	2
Refused	2

*Based on those who believe that most journalists usually either report that both sides are using deception or avoid the matter completely.

reporters to determine: (1) What is deception? (2) What forms of advertising should be counted? (3) Whose ads should be counted? (4) How does one calculate amounts of deception—number of claims or claims weighted by advertisement buy? and (5) Are all deceptions are created equal?

First, defining deception is complicated in an arena in which most problematic statements in political advertisements are literally accurate, but invite false inference. In addition, as communication scholars are fond of noting, meaning exists at the intersection of text, context, and the predispositions of the receiving audience. Reporters are reluctant to assume that all viewers of a television advertisement have been misled. And it is indeed true, as the survey findings we reported suggest, that for whatever reason, many citizens are not misled by distorted claims.

Reporters are not comfortable with the words *deceptive* and *false.* In the language conventionalized in print and broadcast ad watches, the ads being treated in the two articles are usually cast as "misleading." Seldom will an ad watch use the term *false* to describe a campaign ad. Our search for the word *false* and the root *decept* in the ad watches in the "Ad Watch Database: Election

2004" by Media Literacy Clearinghouse for the month of October shows that only FactCheck.org used the word "falsely" in reference to a campaign claim.[28] How does a reporter tabulate "deception" when most fact-checking employs language that does not use the word?

Second, where should one look for deception? In speeches? Debates? Ads? When ads are the reporter's focus, tabulating deception requires a decision that limits the range of the claim. Should only televised content be counted? The importance of this question is increased by the fact that radio ads tend to be more deceptive than those on television. And direct mail ads and phone contact by campaigns are more deceptive than either radio or television ads.[29]

Third, whose advertisements should be counted? Should the Bush and Kerry campaigns be tagged with responsibility for the ads by their respective parties and Section 527 groups? The importance of this question is magnified by the fact that attacks have tended to migrate to noncandidate advertisements.

Fourth, how does one determine how much deception is contained in either an advertisement or a campaign globally? If one relies on a simple count of the number of misleading statements, the campaign that creates many ads with small amounts of air time behind each is disadvantaged. But weighting ads for exposure is time consuming and somewhat unreliable until "time buy" information for the entire nation becomes available. At the moment, the monitoring services ignore some markets.

Finally, once one has defined, located, and counted the deceptions, one needs to ask if all assertions are created equal. Is saying that someone did something he did not do more serious than exaggerating the effects of an actual action? Is saying that a person lied to take the country into war more or less serious or comparable to alleging that a candidate committed treason by giving aid and comfort to the enemy? Weighting deception is even more dangerous for the journalist than drawing conclusions about the amount of deception the campaigns use. If one could quantify the number of claims by employing some systematic methodology, the journalist could use the scientific method as a shield to fend off attacks of bias. Weighting misleading claims inherently involves personal judgment, however. What might seem serious to one citizen might seem comparatively innocuous to the next. At the same time, attaching weights to misleading campaign claims would put the reporter in the line of partisan fire that they try to avoid.

Apart from these difficulties, most reporters are not disposed to engage in the process of calculating deception at all. The "belief of reporters that their job is 'covering' news, not 'making the news' " leads them to avoid both fact checking and weighing in on the question: Is one side more deceptive than the other or engaged in more consequential or serious distortions?[30] When reporters duck these responsibilities, campaigns can deceive and mislead without the penalty such reporting could impose.[31]

When reporters do draw a comparative conclusion about the relative deception in a campaign, they often attribute it to supposedly neutral experts. This move sidesteps the problems we identified in defining and calculating amounts of deception. For example, Milbank and VandeHei did not conduct a systematic content analysis of all ads aired by each campaign. Instead the warrant for their conclusion is found in the subtitle of the article: "Scholars Say Campaign Is Making History with Often-Misleading Attacks." Citing experts frees journalists from drawing and voicing conclusions that might appear to advantage one side in the political contest. As journalism scholar Gaye Tuchman has argued, citing outside sources and using direct quotes allows journalists to distance themselves from the topic or event they cover and creates a "web of mutually self-validating facts."[32]

Drawing conclusions from individuals who are interviewed is problematic when the subject of the news report is the relative accuracy of campaigns. Asking partisans on each side to critique or calculate levels of deception in the ads of the other does not give readers access to dispassionate voices drawing conclusions. In campaigns each side routinely alleges that the other is engaging in far higher levels of distortion. And academically based research teams such as FactCheck.org are more likely to critique ads one at a time than to draw global conclusions for exactly the same reasons that constrain reporters. Scholars are no more eager than reporters to be tagged as partisans, a label that will be flung at them should they say that one side is engaging in more, or more consequential, deception. The result is evident in the exculpatory tone in the weak judgment offered by "scholars," Jamieson among them, in the *Post* article.

What is the impact of this journalistic (and scholarly) disposition and of the difficulties in assessing relative deception? Kathleen Hall Jamieson and Paul Waldman argue that when journalists fail to act as the custodian of facts, they tacitly reward campaign deception.[33] To that claim we here add the notion that when they expose deception but falsely imply that equivalent levels characterize the campaigns of the major contenders, they deny voters the capacity to punish those engaging in a higher level of problematic discourse and invite the cynical assumption that lying is endemic to politics.

Misleading Claims Lead to Misguided Voting

All of this matters because misconceptions based on deception can produce misguided voting. If campaigns did not believe they would benefit from it, they would not deceive. Meaningful participation in the most basic form of democratic life—including casting a vote—requires a degree of consistency between citizens' own issue stances and their votes. Believing falsehoods creates a false sense of such consistency, leading to misguided votes. Recent studies confirm the existence of the problem. During the 2000 and 2004 campaigns voters made mistakes in matching candidates' policy stances with their own policy stances.[34] These mistakes benefited incumbent George W. Bush with perceived agreement exceeding actual agreement and had the opposite effect for Democratic challenger John Kerry, with actual agreement exceeding perceived agreement.[35] The inconsistencies between candidates' positions and voters perceptions of them detailed in these studies are, in part, at least the outcome of the press's failure to deal well with deception in campaigns.

As we have outlined in this chapter, the press has the ability to provide the tools citizens need to discriminate truthful campaign claims from false claims. Our analysis suggests, however, that the press has a way to go to play the role it could in protecting citizens from campaign deception. Press critics and political theorists argue that more substantive news would produce a better informed and perhaps more engaged electorate.[36] Many scholars call for the media to devote less time to discussions of strategy and more to substance. To that call we add a plea for a notion of substance that unmasks deception.

Appendix

Exact Question Wording for Index of Campaign Claims

These questions were recoded into a dichotomous scale with those reporting 1 or 2 for true claims coded as 1 and 3 or 4 for true claims coded as 0 and vice versa for false claims. "Don't knows" were always recorded as zero. This may seem problematic because the "don't know" could refer to not knowing the truthfulness of the claim or a fact that the respondent never heard such a claim. The regression analyses reported in the chapter were also conducted with the "don't knows" coded as "missing values"; however, this did not affect the estimates of model.

1. John Kerry's health care plan would have taken medical decisions out of the hands of doctors and patients and put them under control of government bureaucrats. How truthful do you think that statement is? (FALSE)

1 very truthful

2 somewhat truthful

3 not too truthful

4 Or not truthful at all

8 Don't know

9 Refused

2. George W. Bush's Social Security plan would cut benefits 30 to 45 percent. (FALSE)

3. John Kerry's tax plan would increase taxes on 900,000 small business owners. (FALSE)

4. By limiting how much people could collect for pain and suffering in medical malpractice suits, Bush's health plan would significantly reduce the cost of medical care. (FALSE)

5. Saddam Hussein played a role in September 11. (FALSE)

6. Since George W. Bush became president, the economy has lost more jobs than at any time since the Great Depression. (TRUE)

7. George W. Bush's tax cuts reduced taxes for everyone who pays taxes. (FALSE)

8. George W. Bush increased federal funding for education. (TRUE)

9. Dick Cheney has profited from the contracts Halliburton has in Iraq. (FALSE)

10. George W. Bush's plan to cut Social Security would cut benefits for those currently receiving them. (FALSE)

11. The assault weapons ban outlawed automatic and semi-automatic weapons. (FALSE)

12. The new jobs created since George Bush became president pay, on average, $9,000 a year less than the jobs they replaced. (FALSE)

13. George W. Bush proposed creating a new Homeland Security Department right after September 11. (FALSE)

14. John Kerry's health plan would have provided health insurance for all Americans. (FALSE)

15. The AARP supported the Bush prescription drug plan. (TRUE)

16. The U.S. has found weapons of mass destruction in Iraq. (FALSE)

17. The unemployment rate is now about where it was in 1996 when Bill Clinton ran for a second term. (TRUE)

18. John Kerry said that every American soldier who served in Vietnam was a war criminal. (FALSE)

19. George W. Bush cut the number of students who receive Pell grants for college education. (FALSE)

20. The Bush administration permitted members of the bin Laden family to fly out of the United States while U.S. airspace was still closed after September 11. (FALSE)

21. Senator Kerry voted to ban pump action shotguns and deer hunting ammunition. (FALSE)

22. When George W. Bush took office as president there was a budget surplus, and now there is a deficit. (TRUE)

23. The Bush administration discovered that flu vaccines were contaminated and decided to stop their distribution. (FALSE)

24. George W. Bush was honorably discharged from the National Guard. (TRUE)

25. John Kerry said he would only use military force after the United States was attacked. (FALSE)

26. John Kerry wanted to repeal the use of wiretaps in the Patriot Act. (FALSE)

27. John Kerry wanted to pay for the $87 billion for Iraq by eliminating part of the Bush tax cut for those paying the highest income tax-rate. (TRUE)

28. The Bush administration sent some soldiers to Iraq without the latest body armor. (TRUE)

29. Tax breaks for corporations that outsource American jobs began under George W. Bush. (FALSE)

30. As a senator, John Kerry repeatedly supported an increase in the gasoline tax. (FALSE)

31. John Kerry voted for cuts in intelligence after September 11. (FALSE)

32. John Kerry voted against major weapons systems after September 11. (FALSE)

33. President Bush increased the tax burden on the middle class. (FALSE)

34. John Kerry promised to cut middle class taxes. (TRUE)

35. Ninety-five percent of the cargo containers coming into United States ports are not screened in any way. (FALSE)

36. Under the Bush administration, the United States has gained more jobs than it lost. (FALSE)

37. World opinion favored U.S. intervention in Iraq. (FALSE)

38. George W. Bush strongly supported having an independent commission to investigate the attacks of September 11. (FALSE)

39. When in Congress current Central Intelligence Agency head Porter Goss supported cuts in spending on intelligence. (TRUE)

40. In the videotape aired the weekend before the election, Osama bin Laden didn't endorse either Bush or Kerry. (TRUE)

41. George W. Bush has promised to nominate Supreme Court justices who will overturn *Roe v. Wade*. (FALSE)

Exact Question Wording for Table 6.3

Thinking about the 2004 presidential campaign, in general, how difficult did you think it was to figure out when the Democratic and Republican campaigns were telling the truth and when they were misleading? Was it:

1 Very difficult
2 Somewhat difficult
3 or, not at all difficult
8 Don't know (coded as missing value)
9 Refused (coded as missing value)

Exact Question Wording for Table 6.4

How often do you think John Kerry told the truth about George W. Bush's record? (None of the time, some of the time, or all of the time) (All of the time, some of the time, or none of the time)

1 None of the time
2 Some of the time
3 or, All of the time
8 Don't know (coded as missing)
9 Refused (coded as missing)

How often do you think George W. Bush told the truth about John Kerry's record? (None of the time, some of the time, or all of the time) (All of the time, some of the time, or none of the time)

1 None of the time
2 Some of the time
3 or, All of the time
8 Don't know (coded as missing)
9 Refused (coded as missing)

Notes

1. See James H. Kuklinski, Paul J. Quirk, Jennifer Jerit, David Schwieder, and Robert R. Rich, "Misinformation and the Currency of Democratic Citizenship," *Journal of Politics* 62 (2000): 790–816.

2. Arthur Lupia and Mathew D. McCubbins, *The Democratic Dilemma: Can Citizens Learn What They Need To Know?* (Cambridge, UK; New York: Cambridge University Press, 1998); Samuel L. Popkin, *The Reasoning Voter: Communication and Persuasion in Presidential Campaigns,* 2nd ed. (Chicago: University of Chicago Press, 1994).

3. Lupia and McCubbins, *The Democratic Dilemma.*

4. Kuklinski et al., "Misinformation."

5. FactCheck.org "is a nonpartisan, nonprofit, 'consumer advocate' for voters that aims to reduce the level of deception and confusion in U.S. politics. We monitor the factual accuracy of what is said by major U.S. political players in the form of TV ads, debates, speeches, interviews, and news releases. Our goal is to apply the best practices of both journalism and scholarship, and to increase public knowledge and understanding." From www.FactCheck.org.

6. Due to a split ballot design, each individual respondent was asked roughly half of the questions. Those who received form A were asked about twenty-one of the claims, and those who received form B were asked about twenty of the claims.

7. For those respondents who received survey form A, the descriptive statistics for this variable are as follows: Minimum = 0; Maximum = 18; Mean = 8.86; Standard deviation = 2.912. For form B: Minimum = 0; Maximum = 16; Mean = 8.38; Standard deviation = 2.573.

8. For example, see Markus Prior, "Any Good News in Soft News? The Impact of Soft News Preference on Political Knowledge," *Political Communication* 20 (2003): 149–171.

9. Paula M. Poindexter, Don Heider, and Maxwell McCombs, "Watchdog or Good Neighbor? The Public's Expectation of Local News," *Harvard International Journal of Press/Politics* 11 (2006): 77–88.

10. The relationship found in Table 6.2 holds for almost all campaign claims. Space limitations prevent us from detailing all fifty-two claims by party identification.

11. See Baruch Fischoff, Paul Slovic, and Sara Lichtenstein, "Knowing with Certainty: The Appropriateness of Extreme Confidence," *Journal of Experimental Psychology: Human Perception and Performances* 3 (1977): 552–564; Kuklinski et al., "Misinformation."

12. Roderick P. Hart, *Seducing America: How Television Charms the Modern Voter* (Thousand Oaks, Calif.: Sage, 1998).

13. "Would Kerry Throw Us to the Wolves? A Misleading Bush Ad Criticizes Kerry for Proposal to Cut Intelligence Spending—A Decade Ago, By 4% When Some Republicans also Proposed Cuts," Factcheck.org, October 23, 2004. Available at *www.factcheck.org/article291.html*.

14. Associated Press, "Bush Ad Uses Wolves to Suggest Kerry Weak on Terror; Democrats Counter with Eagle-Ostrich Spot," October 22, 2004.

15. According the U.S. State Department, the 2004 battleground states were Florida, Iowa, Missouri, New Hampshire, New Mexico, Ohio, Oregon, Pennsylvania, Wisconsin, and West Virginia. See U.S. State Department: *http://usinfo.state.gov/dhr/Archive/2004/Jul/12-250886.html* for information on why each state is considered a battleground state. Other news organizations, however, list as many as seventeen states in the battleground. See Time.com: *www.time.com/time/election2004/battleground*.

16. The exact question wording is "John Kerry voted for cuts in intelligence after September 11. How truthful do you think that statement is?" 1= very truthful, 2 = somewhat truthful, 3 = not too truthful, 4 = not truthful at all, 8 = don't know, 9 = refuse.

17. "Eleven Days to Go, 'Wolves' Ad released by RNC," *World News Tonight with Peter Jennings*, October 22, 2004, 06:30 PM ET.

18. Bennett Roth, "Bush, Kerry Spar over Approaches to Terror; The President's Ad Features Wolves, a Move His Rival Calls a Scare Tactic," *Houston Chronicle*, October 23, 2004, A1.

19. Associated Press, "Bush Ad Uses Wolves."

20. *St. Petersburg Times*, "Political Imagery Gets Wild in TV Ads," October 23, 2004, A9; Associated Press, "A Zoo Out There: Wolves, Ostriches and Eagles Populate Presidential

Ads," October 22, 2004; Associated Press, "Candidates Use Animals in Campaign Ads," October 22, 2004.

21. *Today Show,* "A Panel of Undecided Voters Weigh in on Political Ads and Their Effectiveness; Brooks Jackson of FactCheck.org Gives the Facts on the Issues Mentioned in the Ads," October 27, 2004, 07:00 AM ET.

22. Ibid.

23. Jim Rutenberg, "Campaign Ads Are under Fire for Inaccuracy," *New York Times,* May 25, 2004, A1; Dana Milbank and Jim VandeHei, "From Bush, Unprecedented Negativity: Scholars Say Campaign Is Making History with Often-Misleading Attacks," *Washington Post,* May 31, 2004, A1.

24. Jay Rosen, "He Said, She Said, We Said," *Press Think,* June 4, 2004. Available online: *http://journalism.nyu.edu/pubzone/weblogs/pressthink/2004/06/04/ruten_milbank.html.*

25. Ibid.

26. Milbank and VandeHei, "From Bush, Unprecedented Negativity."

27. The Annenberg Foundation Trust at Sunnylands and the Annenberg Public Policy Center commissioned Princeton Survey Research Associates International (PSRAI) to conduct a study of the media as a central democratic institution. This study involved 673 journalists—371 interviewed by telephone and 302 who completed an online version of the survey. The telephone interviews were conducted by Princeton Data Source, LLC, from March 14, 2005, to May 2. The online survey was administered by PSRAI from March 7, 2005, to April 26. The response rate was 49 percent. This study was designed to be representative of the national and local print and broadcast media. The sampling frame for the national print organizations included newspapers, national news magazines, and wire services. The sampling frame for national broadcast organizations included television, cable, and radio networks.

28. See *http://medialit.med.sc.edu/adwatchdatabase.htm.*

29. Kathleen Hall Jamieson, *Dirty Politics: Deception, Distraction, and Democracy* (New York: Oxford University Press, 1992).

30. Ibid., 29.

31. Kathleen Hall Jamieson and Paul Waldman, *The Press Effect: Politicians, Journalists, and the Stories That Shape the Political World* (New York: Oxford University Press, 2003).

32. Gaye Tuchman, *Making the News: A Study of the Construction of Reality* (New York: Praeger, 1978), 78.

33. Jamieson and Waldman, *The Press Effect,* chap. 7.

34. Kate Kenski and Kathleen Hall Jamieson, "Issue Knowledge and Perception of Agreement in the 2004 Presidential General Election," *Presidential Studies Quarterly* 36 (June 2006): 243–259; Paul Waldman and Kathleen Hall Jamieson, "Rhetorical Convergence and Issue Knowledge in the 2000 Presidential Election," *Presidential Studies Quarterly* 33 (2003): 145–163.

35. Kenski and Jamieson, "Issue Knowledge and Perception of Agreement"; Waldman and Jamieson, "Rhetorical Convergence and Issue Knowledge."

36. Michael X. Delli Carpini and Scott Keeter, *What Americans Know about Politics and Why It Matters* (New Haven: Yale University Press, 1996); Norman H. Nie, Jane Junn, and Kenneth Stehlik-Barry, *Education and Democratic Citizenship in America* (Chicago: University of Chicago Press, 1996).

Section III   The Public's Voice

7 Advertising and Citizen Voting Behavior

Darrell M. West

Since the mid-1990s American politics has suffered extensive polarization. The public saw a Democratic president impeached in 1998, a contested presidential election in 2000, a horrific terrorist attack in 2001, followed by a Republican chief executive presiding over an unpopular war in Iraq, which clearly contributed to a dramatic Democratic comeback in the 2006 congressional races. In this contentious atmosphere, it is not surprising that contemporary political campaigns feature sharp rhetoric, attack ads, and hotly contested campaigns. Republicans use images of firefighters carrying victims away from the World Trade Center, while Democrats say it is time for a new direction in national and international policy.

But how do we know which advertising appeals work? Commercials represent the largest single expenditure in most major contests. In some races, they total around 60 percent of the overall campaign budget. Politicians craft messages with great care and sometimes try them out on ordinary citizens before using them. Reporters dissect advertisements for accuracy, impact, and effectiveness. Yet in any particular race, both candidates run ads; and one wins, while the other loses.

Consultants judge the effectiveness of ads by the election outcome, leading to the belief that winners have great ads and losers do not. This type of test, however, is never possible to complete until after the election, and it unfairly equates victory with advertising effectiveness. Candidates win elections for many different reasons: public opinion trends may be in their favor; government performance may help or hurt specific candidates; or the money that buys the ads may also be associated with other features that sway voters, such as positive news coverage, strong organization, or effective appeals.

As an alternative, some analysts evaluate ads by asking voters to indicate whether commercials influenced them. When asked directly whether television commercials helped them decide how to vote, most voters say ads did not influence them. For example, in the 1996 election, the results of a Media Studies

Center survey placed ads at the bottom of the heap in terms of possible information sources. Forty-five percent of voters felt they learned a great deal from debates, 32 percent cited newspaper stories, and 30 percent pointed to television news stories, but just 5 percent believed they learned a lot from political ads. When asked directly about ads in a CBS News/*New York Times* survey, only 11 percent reported that any presidential candidate's ads had helped them decide how to vote.[1]

But direct questioning is not a meaningful way of looking at advertising. Such responses undoubtedly reflect an unwillingness to admit that external agents have any effect. Many people firmly believe that they make up their minds independently of the campaign. In much the same way teenagers do not like to concede parental influence, few voters are willing to admit they are influenced by television spots.

In this chapter, I look at three ways political ads affect voters: learning, agenda-setting, and priming. I use examples from several recent elections to illustrate how advertising influences voter choice. Campaign ads may affect voters directly or indirectly. It is not always the case that citizens see an ad and decide to vote for that individual. Political commercials may affect voters by providing information about candidate backgrounds and policy positions. Spots also may help set the agenda in ways that are relevant for the voters. Finally, ads may elevate certain criteria of evaluation that advantage particular candidates. In these ways, advertisements can be influential even if voters do not believe they are being affected by paid media.

Early Research

Early research downplayed the power of ads to mold the public images of candidates. The pioneering study was Thomas Patterson and Robert McClure's innovative effort, *The Unseeing Eye*.[2] Looking at ad content and effects, Patterson and McClure sought to dispel the concerns of the public and journalists regarding political commercials. They used a model of psychological reasoning based on voters' knowledge about candidates and examined whether television ads enabled voters to get more information about the policy views or personal qualities of campaigners. They found that voters learned more about the issues from the candidates' ads than from the news, because ads addressed issues, but the news was dominated by coverage of the "horse race"—who is ahead at a given time.[3]

The study's results fit with the general view among election experts of the 1960s and 1970s that short-term political strategies were not very decisive in determining election results. The era following the publication of the classic work on voting behavior, *The American Voter*, proclaimed long-term forces, such as party identification, as the most important. Although a few scholars disputed this interpretation, many argued that short-term factors related to media coverage, candidates' advertisements, and campaign spending were not crucial to vote choice. For example, Harold Mendelsohn and Irving Crespi claimed in 1970 that the "injection of high doses of political information during the frenetic periods of national campaigns does very little to alter the deeply rooted, tightly held political attitudes of most voters."[4] Even the later emergence of models based on pocketbook considerations did little to change this interpretation. Paid ads were thought to have a limited ability to shape citizens' impressions of economic performance.

Since that time, however, we have begun to see changes in these earlier points of view. Candidates have started to use commercials more aggressively; reporters have devoted more attention to paid advertising; and ad techniques have grown more sophisticated. It is now thought that voters' assessments can change based on short-term information and that candidates have the power to sway voters who are still undecided in the closing weeks of the campaign. Evidence from elections around the United States suggests that ads are successful in helping candidates develop the images they wish to project.[5]

This is particularly true when campaigners are unknown or running in multicandidate nominating contests. The more strategic options that are available with the larger number of candidates involved, the more potential there is for the campaign to affect citizen judgments. Lynn Vavreck, Constantine Spiliotes, and Linda Fowler's study of the 2000 New Hampshire primary, for example, found that a variety of campaign activities affected voters' recognition of and favorability toward specific candidates.[6]

Furthermore, candidates no longer hold the monopoly on advertising. Political parties, interest groups, and even private individuals run commercials, many of them negative. In fact, there are discernible differences in the percentage of attack ads run by different sources. The most negative messages were found in issue ads run by interest groups. Fifty-six percent of those ads were attack-oriented, compared with 20 percent of candidate-sponsored advertisements.[7]

Because paid ads are so important in contemporary campaigns, candidates take the development of advertising strategies quite seriously. Commercials often are pretested through focus groups or public opinion surveys.[8] Themes as well as styles of presentation are tried out before likely voters. What messages are most appealing? When and how often should particular ads be aired? Who should be targeted? How should ads best convey information?

The number of times an ad is broadcast is one of the most important strategic decisions of any political campaign. Professional ad buyers specialize in picking the time slots and television shows that are advantageous for particular candidates. A candidate interested in appealing to senior citizens may air ads repeatedly during television shows catering to the elderly; youth-oriented politicians may run spots on the Fox Network or MTV; and minority candidates may advertise on Black Entertainment Television. Candidates also place their ads on their own Web sites or run them on commercial links such as YouTube.com.

The content and timing of ads are crucial for candidates because of their link to overall success. Campaigns have become a blitz of competing ads, quick responses, and counterresponses. Ads have become serial in nature, with each ad building thematically on previous spots. Election campaigns feature strategic interactions that are as important as the individual ads themselves. Candidates often play off each other's ads in an effort to gain the advantage with voters.

Learning about the Candidates

Do the media provide information that increases voters' knowledge of where candidates stand on the issues and their personal backgrounds? Research studies have found that voters do not often cast ballots based on the issues. Citizens form many impressions during the course of election campaigns. These impressions range from views about candidates' issue positions and personal characteristics to feelings about the electoral prospects of specific candidates, and those views are decisive. As ads have become more gripping emotionally, affective models—which describe feelings—are crucial to evaluations of candidates' fortunes.[9]

Favorability is an example of an affective dimension that is important to vote choice. Citizens often support the candidates they like and oppose those they dislike. If all are disliked, they vote for candidates they dislike the least. Anything that raises a candidate's favorability also increases his or her likelihood of being chosen.[10] Candidates devote great attention to making themselves appear more likable. Values that are widely shared, such as patriotism and pride in national accomplishments, help candidates increase their favorability ratings among voters. Conversely, hard-hitting ads are used to pinpoint the opposition's flaws.

When public primaries replaced caucuses and smoke-filled rooms, that change brought new factors such as electability and familiarity to the forefront. Electability refers to citizens' perceptions of a candidate's chances for winning the November election. Because many citizens do not want to waste their vote on a hopeless choice, impressions of electability can increase voters' support of a candidate: people like to support the winner. Familiarity is important as a threshold requirement. Candidates must become known to do well on election day. The development of a campaign structure that encourages less widely known candidates to run makes citizens' assessments of a candidate's prospects a potentially important area of inquiry.

Examining elections since the late 1970s, we see that citizens' assessments of the candidates varied widely, depending on the electoral setting. Presidential general election candidates were the most well known, with a range of recognition levels from a low in 1992 for Bill Clinton (73 percent) and Ross Perot (67 percent) to a high for Gerald Ford (95 percent) in 1976. By the end of the 2004 campaign, 88 percent of respondents recognized John Kerry, and 90 percent recognized George W. Bush. But it took Kerry a long time to gain this recognition level. In March only 57 percent recognized him, and in mid-September 73 percent recognized him. Kerry's relative lack of recognition gave Republicans an opportunity to use advertising to create unfavorable portraits of the challenger.

Citizen perceptions of candidate likability and electability also have varied widely. For example, Ronald Reagan was the best liked (66 percent in 1984), and the least liked were George H. W. Bush (23 percent in 1992), Bob Dole (25 percent in 1996), and Perot (18 percent in 1996). In 2004 George W. Bush was liked by 48 percent, compared with 41 percent who liked Kerry, which put both of them around the midpoint of likability since 1984. With regard to electability, George McGovern in 1972 was the candidate seen as least electable (1 percent), and George H. W. Bush in 1988 was seen as the most electable (85 percent). In 1996, 83 percent of respondents believed Clinton was the most electable. In 2004, 49 percent of voters saw Bush as electable, compared to 33 percent for Kerry.

Voters also have a sense of the policy issues and personal traits associated with each candidate. In 2004 Bush was seen as having slightly stronger leadership skills (62 percent) than Kerry (52 percent) and saying what he believed (60 percent, compared with the 37 percent who felt that way about Kerry). Kerry was seen as slightly more caring (53 percent) than Bush (48 percent). In terms of the issues, Kerry held an advantage over Bush in improving health care, protecting Social Security, and improving schools, but Bush was seen as better at bringing fiscal discipline to the government.

How did political commercials influence citizens' perceptions of the candidates? In the 2000 presidential general election, there was a connection between individuals seeing news and candidate ads and thinking Al Gore and George Bush, respectively, were electable. The individuals who saw Gore's ads were more likely to report that he was electable. The same was true for Bush to an even greater extent.

There were interesting relationships between viewers seeing TV news and candidates' ads and how those viewers saw candidates' personal qualities and political views. Those who saw Gore's commercials were more likely to see him as providing fiscal discipline and less likely to believe that Bush would do so. Those who reported seeing national television news, however, concluded the opposite: Bush would be fiscally responsible and caring, and Gore would not likely be either.

In 2004 ads were linked to changing perceptions of the candidates. Voter impressions shifted during the course of the campaign. National surveys undertaken by CBS News/*New York Times* show that Kerry was far less known (57 percent recognition level in March 2004) than Bush (82 percent recognition), but Kerry became about as well known as the president by the end of October. Throughout most of the campaign, Bush held a higher favorability rating than Kerry.

From the beginning of the general election in spring 2004, Bush attacked Kerry as a wishy-washy politician who told voters what they wanted to hear. This perception stuck with voters. The polling data reveal that Bush consistently had a huge advantage over Kerry according to the criterion that he says what he believes. For example, in mid-October, 59 percent portrayed Bush as saying what he believed, compared to 37 percent who felt that way about Kerry. Bush also neutralized a traditional Democratic strength, that of being seen as caring and compassionate and understanding the needs of ordinary people. Ever since Herbert Hoover's inaction in the face of the Great Depression in the 1930s, voters have seen Democrats as caring more about ordinary folks than Republicans. On this major question, however, Bush was able to narrow the perception gap. In mid-October, 51 percent thought Kerry "understood the needs of people like you," and 44 percent felt that way about Bush. For a president whose tax cut policies had benefited wealthy Americans and who had passed billions in tax breaks for corporations, these numbers represented a major victory.

In addition, Bush tarred Kerry with the "liberal" codeword, as G. H. W. Bush had done to Michael Dukakis in 1988. At the beginning of the general election, 39 percent of registered voters saw Kerry as a liberal. By mid-October this number had risen to 56 percent.

Bush used attack ads during the campaign to portray Kerry in unfavorable terms. He characterized Kerry as a doctrinaire liberal who was also wishy-washy and unprincipled. These two critiques are noteworthy because in some respects they are inconsistent with one another. It is difficult to be wishy-washy and a doctrinaire liberal simultaneously. By repeating these messages over and over, Bush was able to reinforce negative perceptions about Kerry.

By the time of the 2006 congressional elections, the political context had changed dramatically. Rather than fearing an imminent terrorist attack, citizens were worried about a war in Iraq that was not going well. In national surveys, only 29 percent of Americans approved of the way Bush was managing the war, and 70 percent did not believe he had a plan to end it.[11] With more than $250 billion expended and nearly 3,000 dead American soldiers, Republicans were on the defensive, and Democrats framed the election as a referendum on President Bush. Overall spending on advertisements topped $2 billion, up from the $1.6 billion in 2004.[12]

Democratic candidates around the country ran advertising campaigns that played to voter discontent with Bush. One ad against Republican House member Dave Reichert of Washington criticized him by saying he "just sides with Bush on Iraq. Iraq is just a disaster. Iraq is a complete disaster. It's heartbreaking." Another spot targeting Republican representative Rob Simmons of Connecticut said, "Despite a war gone wrong and no plan for victory, politicians like Rob Simmons keep voting to stay the course again and again, following George Bush's failed leadership no matter what the cost."[13]

Republicans meanwhile centered their response on questioning the values and backgrounds of their Democratic opponents. In Tennessee, the Republican National Committee financed an independent ad against Democratic senatorial candidate Harold Ford Jr. The ad featured a scantily clad white woman claiming to have met Ford, an African American, at a Super Bowl party sponsored by *Playboy* magazine. The young woman leers into the camera and pleads, "Harold, call me."[14] After critics condemned the advertisement for playing on racial fears about a black man dating a white woman, the commercial was pulled off the air. But the damage was done: Ford lost his electoral bid to Republican Bob Corker, 51 percent to 48 percent. Corker aired more ads (12,007) than Ford (7,239) in the period from August 1 to October 15, which helped cement his victory.[15]

Republican senator Rick Santorum of Pennsylvania linked his opponent, Bob Casey Jr., to terrorist Osama bin Laden and North Korean dictator Kim Jong II. In an ad entitled "The Stakes," Casey was accused of being soft on terrorism and risking nuclear war.[16] But in an environment when nearly two-thirds of voters thought the country was headed in the wrong direction, Santorum lost his bid for reelection.

At the end of this hard-fought midterm election, the Democratic strategy of nationalizing the election and raising the negatives of Republican opponents on Bush and Iraq reaped tremendous dividends. Democrats picked up thirty-three seats in the House and six seats in the Senate, regaining majority control for the first time since 1994.

Setting the Agenda

Agenda-setting is the process by which issues evolve from specific grievances into prominent causes worthy of government consideration. In a political system in which citizens pay only limited attention to civic affairs, it is a mechanism through which the public can influence official deliberations by conveying its sense of which problems are important. It is well established that issues come and go and that at any given time only a few matters receive serious consideration by government officials.[17]

Television has long been thought to play a crucial role in setting the agenda.[18] Shanto Iyengar and Donald Kinder's experimental work strongly supports a model of media agenda-setting. The respondents in their study of network news regarded any problem covered by the media as "more important for the country, cared more about it, believed that government should do more about it, reported stronger feelings about it, and were more likely to identify it as one of the country's most important problems."[19]

Agenda-setting is an important part of political campaigns. Candidates use election contests to dramatize issues. They also try to deemphasize matters that may be problematic for themselves. In 1988 G. H. W. Bush's strategy was to steer the agenda away from certain aspects of Ronald Reagan's record and toward prisoners' furloughs and flag factories (Michael Dukakis's vulnerable areas) in an effort to make the campaign debate more advantageous for Republicans. The same thing happened in 2004 when George W. Bush sought to focus the agenda on terrorism and global security. Candidates' advertising therefore should be assessed to gauge its ability to change citizens' perceptions of what are the most important priorities.

Bush's "Revolving Door" ad in 1988 illustrates how a commercial can influence people's views about the country's most pressing policy problems.[20] The subject of the ad was Governor Dukakis's approval of prison furloughs for dangerous felons. Willie Horton, a convicted murderer had failed to return to his Massachusetts state prison after a brief furlough. While on the loose, Horton committed several brutal crimes, including a rape. The "Revolving Door" ad was aired frequently during the evening news, and news commentators discussed it extensively. Analysis of public opinion surveys demonstrates that the ad was linked to mentions of crime and of law and order as the most important problems facing the United States.[21] Among those who had not seen the ad, only 5 percent cited these problems, but 12 percent of those who had seen it named this area. These data fit with evidence cited by Marjorie Hershey, who found that "the proportion of respondents saying that George Bush was 'tough enough' on crime and criminals rose from 23 percent in July to a full 61 percent in late October, while the proportion saying Dukakis was not tough enough rose from 36 to 49 percent."[22]

Equally significant were the differences between men and women in regard to Bush's 1988 ads. For example, one of the strongest agenda-setting effects from the "Revolving Door" ad was among women on the crime issue.[23] After seeing this commercial, as well as the widely publicized Horton ad produced by an independent political action committee, women became much more likely than men to cite crime as the most important issue.

The fact that the ads mentioned rape clearly accentuated their impact on women. According to Dukakis's campaign manager, Susan Estrich: "The symbolism was very powerful . . . you can't find a stronger metaphor, intended or not, for racial hatred in this country than a black man raping a white woman. . . . I talked to people afterward. . . . Women said they couldn't help it, but it scared the living daylights out of them."[24]

The "Revolving Door" case demonstrates how the strategies of campaign elites and the overall cultural context are important factors in mediating the significance of advertisements. The way this commercial was put together—in terms of both subject area and timing—was a major contributor to its impact on viewers. If Horton had assaulted a fifty-year-old black man while he was at large, it is not likely that the "Revolving Door" ad would have affected voters' policy priorities as it did.[25]

In 2004 the campaign agenda featured a battle between terrorism and security concerns on the one hand and domestic economic issues on the other. American elections typically center more on domestic than on foreign policy considerations. But the September 11, 2001, terrorist attacks on New York City and the Pentagon and the subsequent wars in Afghanistan and Iraq placed foreign policy directly onto the political agenda. In terms of campaign-related topics, Bush attempted to portray Kerry as a flip-flopping liberal out of touch with the American mainstream.

In early advertising in spring 2004, Bush complained that Kerry would penalize drivers with a 50-cent-a-gallon gasoline tax, would "raise taxes by at least $900 billion," would "weaken the Patriot Act used to arrest terrorists," opposed "body armor for troops in combat," and "opposed weapons vital to winning the war on terror: Bradley Fighting Vehicles, Patriot missiles, B-2 stealth bombers, F-18 fighter jets."[26] A Bush spokesperson justified these attacks by saying, "Kerry sailed through the Democratic primary process with little or no scrutiny. In order to make an informed judgment about whether Kerry is a suitable choice for president, voters need to have this information." The Kerry campaign saw a more nefarious motive. Strategist Michael Donilon complained that Bush staffers "have decided that the only way to win this election is to destroy John Kerry."[27]

For his part, Kerry attempted to characterize Bush as "a corporate toady who wants to foul the air and water, outlaw abortion, and export U.S. jobs overseas." Ads from the Kerry camp argued, among other claims, that Bush "wants to roll back the Clean Air and Clean Water acts," name "anti-choice justices" to the U.S. Supreme Court, and supports "sending jobs overseas."[28]

In general, however, Kerry's early ads were more positive than Bush's. One study found that 52 percent of claims in Bush's spots were attack-oriented, compared to 19 percent for Kerry.[29] This strategy was in keeping with the general thrust of the Bush organization to paint Kerry in negative terms while he still was relatively unknown to the electorate as a whole.

When asked at the beginning of the campaign which one issue they most wanted to hear the presidential candidates discuss, voters named the war in Iraq (23 percent), economy and jobs (20 percent), health care and Medicare (13 percent), and education (5 percent).[30] By the fall, these priorities had shifted somewhat. Public interest in the economy and jobs was ranked the number one priority (20 percent), followed by the war in Iraq (18 percent), health care and Medicare (15 percent), and defense (4 percent).[31]

Throughout the fall, Bush attempted to maintain the focus on terrorism. One of his more provocative ads was called "Wolves." In it, a wolf runs through a forest, while a female announcer warns: "In an increasingly dangerous world, even after the first terrorist attack on America, John Kerry and the liberals in

Congress voted to slash America's intelligence budget by $6 billion. Cuts so deep they would have weakened America's defenses. [Image of a pack of wolves resting on a hill.] And weakness attract those who are waiting to do America harm."[32]

Not to be outdone by animal imagery, Kerry started broadcasting an ad featuring an eagle and an ostrich: "The eagle soars high above the earth. The ostrich buries its head in the sand. The eagle can see everything for miles around. The ostrich? Can't see at all. . . . Given the choice, in these challenging times, shouldn't we be the eagle again?"[33]

Within a day, individuals outside the campaign had put up a new Web site, WolfpacksforTruth.org, which advertised the "real story" on Bush's "Wolves" commercial. Taking on the voice of the wolves, the site explained that Bush had tricked them. "They told us we were shooting a Greenpeace commercial! When the camera crew showed up, we wondered why they were all driving Hummers. . . . Little did we know we were being tricked into this vicious campaign attack ad! We are not Terrorists! . . . We are a peaceful pack of wolves. All we want in life is: Live in tree-filled forests. Drink clean water from our rivers and streams. Breathe fresh and clean air."

By election day, it was clear how much Bush's effort at focusing the agenda on terrorism and moral values paid off for him. National exit polls revealed a clear tie between seeing particular issues as most important and voting for the president. Bush won 85 percent of the votes of those who cited terrorism as their most important issue, compared to 15 percent for Kerry. Seventy-eight percent of those naming moral values as the most important consideration in the election cast ballots for Bush, compared to 19 percent who did so for Kerry. In contrast, Kerry's top issues were the economy and jobs (he received 81 percent of the vote of individuals saying this was their most important issue), education (76 percent of their vote), and Iraq (75 percent).

These results suggest how potent a combination cultural values and security concerns have become for the general public. Bush successfully redefined the national agenda away from the economy, education, and health care to cultural and security issues. His unstated but clearly visible mantra during the campaign became, "It's terrorism, stupid." In so doing, he took advantage of voter anxiety in the post–September 11 world and repositioned his party as the one that would best defend America against threats both foreign and domestic.

Because voters are not able to focus on every important issue, campaigners seek to prioritize the contest by emphasizing a few items. If they can set the agenda in a way that is favorable to their own electoral interests, they help the campaign as a whole. Some issues such as national security are often thought to favor Republicans, while topics such as health care generally help Democrats. As seen in a number of different elections, setting the agenda through advertisements is one of the major strategic goals in any campaign.

Candidates cannot, however, make an issue important if it is not already salient with voters. It is impossible to raise relevance if none exists. If the campaign features a fixed agenda with one dominant agenda item, candidates have to address that topic. They have greater strategic flexibility when the agenda is fluid or varied. In that situation, their speeches and ads can increase or decrease the perceived saliency of a topic by giving it more attention. Raised issues can confer major electoral advantages if the candidate is seen as having greater competence or credibility on that particular topic.

In the 2006 congressional elections the national agenda centered on the war in Iraq, health care, stem cell research, the economy, and terrorism. According to a CBS News/New York Times survey undertaken right before the election, respondents were concerned about Iraq (26 percent), the economy (11 percent), terrorism and immigration (7 percent), health care (5 percent), foreign policy (4 percent), defense and military matters (3 percent), jobs and unemployment (3 percent), and education (2 percent).[34]

The indictments, convictions, and resignations of several Republicans gave Democrats the opportunity to campaign against Washington and call for a change in the national course. An ad for Democrat Francine Busby compared Republican Brian Bilbray to convicted representative Randy Cunningham and warned, "We don't need another congressman in jail."

Actor Michael J. Fox appeared in a commercial supporting federal funding for stem cell research and calling for the election of Democratic senatorial candidate Claire McCaskill.[35] Fox also called for the election of a new Democratic senator in Virginia by saying, "A vote for Jim Webb is a vote for hope and a better quality of life for Americans."[36] Republican George Allen responded by pointing out that Webb had written books that stereotyped women as sex objects. "His novels? Some are graphic, even deviant," the advertisement warned.[37]

Many of the ads across the country were unrelentingly negative. Indeed, of the spots broadcast by the national party committees, 91 percent of the National Republican Congressional Committee ads were judged negative, and 81 percent of those sponsored by the Democratic Congressional Campaign Committee fell into that category. Expert commentators, such as Kathleen Hall Jamieson, said that 80 percent of the ads in 2006 were negative, compared to 60 percent of commercials in 2004.[38]

With a wave of attack ads sweeping all the major House and Senate races, Democrat Ned Lamont of Connecticut produced a spoof ad mocking attacks on him. "Meet Ned Lamont," the ad stated. "He can't make a decent cup of coffee." As the candidate shuffled papers, flashy red text appeared on the screen warning "Messy Desk."[39] This commercial did not save Lamont's campaign. He lost to Joe Lieberman, running as an independent, in the Senate campaign.

Priming and Defusing

Priming is a perspective based on the notion that individuals review information sporadically in thinking about political matters. Developed in regard to the evening news, this approach proposes that people use readily available material to evaluate candidates and that in the media age one of the most accessible sources is television. By its patterns of coverage, television can influence voters' choices between candidates by elevating particular standards of evaluation. For example, television shows that devote extensive coverage to defense matters can increase the importance of defense policy in citizens' assessments. Likewise, news accounts that dwell on environmental concerns can raise the importance of those matters in voting choices.[40]

Priming has attracted attention in relation to television news, but little attention has been paid to its conceptual counterpart, defusing. This term refers to efforts on the part of candidates to decrease the importance of particular standards of evaluation. Candidates often have image problems, such as being seen as weak on defense or lacking a clear vision for the future. It obviously is in their interest to defuse their perceived shortcomings, which they can do either by lessening the overall importance of the issue to the public or by reducing the distance between themselves and their opponents to the point where the topic no longer affects the vote.

The concepts of priming and defusing are particularly applicable to the study of campaign advertising. In the same way that news can alter voter judgments, television commercials can prime (or defuse) the electorate by shifting the standards of evaluation. To understand priming, one must also understand the notion of information costs. Acquiring information costs people time and effort. Particularly during election campaigns, it is not easy for ordinary citizens to compile a full record of candidates' backgrounds, policy views, and personal attributes. Most citizens lack the inclination or ability to search for all relevant material, given the time and energy involved. Instead, people look for informational shortcuts, or what Daniel Kahneman, Paul Slovic, and Amos

Tversky call heuristics.[41] Rather than conducting a complete search that incorporates every nugget of material about candidates, voters use readily available cues. In the media era, television provides some of the most accessible material. By its patterns of coverage and emphasis on particular information, television plays a significant role in influencing the standards of evaluation used in voters' selection of candidates.

With no incumbent running in the 2000 presidential race, Al Gore sought to become the first sitting vice president since G. H. W. Bush in 1988 and Martin Van Buren in 1846 to win election in his own right. Gore secured the Democratic nomination over New Jersey senator Bill Bradley, and George W. Bush beat back a determined challenge from Arizona senator John McCain. Sensing that the race would be extremely close, both nominees campaigned in the middle. Bush sought to dispel the notion left over from Newt Gingrich's speakership that Republicans were dangerous extremists not to be trusted with America's future and that he was up to the job of the presidency. For his part, Gore attempted to continue Clinton's "New Democrat" leanings by emphasizing targeted tax cuts and prescription drug benefits for senior citizens and by promising that he would continue Clinton's capacity for strong leadership.

Several of these messages resonated with voters. The more ads people saw, the stronger was the connection between believing that Gore was a strong leader and expressing a willingness to vote for him. There also was a strong link between ad viewing and candidates' electability. Similar to the 1992 experience, academic models based on economic voting proved way off target. Scholars predicted that Gore would win comfortably, with something between 53 percent and 60 percent of the two-party vote. Peace and prosperity reigned in America, and these forecasters asserted that Gore would carry the day.[42]

These predictions, however, ignored the ability of campaigns to alter the terms of debate. Clinton in 1992 was able to make voters feel worse about the economy than warranted by objective evidence, but Gore was unable to reap the rewards of the strong economy of the Clinton years. Because of the Monica Lewinsky scandal, Gore distanced himself from Clinton and lost his chance to be the only beneficiary of economic voting. The inability of the party controlling the presidency to benefit from the economy was one of the most surprising results of the 2000 election.

In the 2004 election, national conditions did not look advantageous for the sitting president. Throughout the fall, Bush's job approval numbers remained below the 50 percent threshold assumed necessary for reelection. More than a thousand American soldiers had died in Iraq. Between 2001 and 2004, the economy had lost around 2.7 million jobs. It was not until 2004 that new jobs started to be created in large numbers.

In this situation, Bush's campaign primed the electorate to see Kerry in negative terms, while Bush's own poor governing record in several respects was deemphasized: Kerry was a wishy-washy flip-flopper and not to be trusted, while Bush cared about the downtrodden and was interested in helping middle income earners do better economically. Given that his administration's tax cuts went largely to the rich, the caring and compassion dimension represented clear points of vulnerability for his reelection bid.

Bush sought to prime trust and defuse caring through a series of ads attacking Kerry's trustworthiness and penchant for changing positions on the issues. On the Iraq war, the Patriot Act, and the education program known as "No Child Left Behind," Bush's advertisements said Kerry had voted for the policy but later switched his position. At the same time, the president surrounded himself with images of working class folks and made jokes about his poor speaking ability by saying English was not his first language.

Kerry responded by seeking to undermine Bush's credibility. Kerry's campaign ads said Bush had deceived the country by saying there were weapons of mass destruction in Iraq and had provided tax cuts for rich, corporate interests.

In this fight over problem definition, polling data on trust and caring demonstrated that Bush had made some gains. On the "saying what he thinks" dimension, voters were more likely to describe Bush (59 percent) than Kerry (37 percent) as sticking firm to his beliefs. On the caring and compassion dimension, Kerry held a small advantage over Bush (51 percent to 44 percent), but not as great a margin as Democratic presidential candidates typically hold over their Republican counterparts.

By the end of the campaign, both candidates were using highly emotional ads to scare voters to their side. A Bush spot showed a clock ticking while a father loaded his young children into a minivan. An announcer warned, "Weakness invites those who would do us harm." A Kerry ad had images of a soldier shooting a machine gun into the air and a car bursting into a gigantic fireball. The announcer proclaimed, "Now Americans are being kidnapped, held hostage—even beheaded."[43]

In addition to the commercials' highly emotional images were some highly questionable charges. Bush accused Kerry of wanting to create a huge new federal bureaucracy to oversee health care, while Kerry said Bush would restore a military draft. In the end, Bush was able to defeat Kerry by 3.6 million votes across the country.

During the 2006 midterm elections, candidate ads sought to elevate or undermine particular standards of evaluation, often related to candidate character. In Wisconsin, Republican challenger Paul Nelson attacked Democratic House member Ron Kind by saying his opponent supported federal grants for studies of human sexuality. "Ron Kind Pays for Sex!" shouted one ad, while visual text splashed "XXX" across his face. According to the commercial, Kind wanted "to pay teenage girls to watch pornographic movies with probes connected to their genitalia." Republican representative John Hostettler of Indiana aired radio spots saying if Nancy Pelosi of California became the new Democratic Speaker, she would "put in motion her radical plan to advance the homosexual agenda."[44] Another spot paid for by the National Republican Congressional Committee accused Democrat Michael Arcuri of calling a sex hotline and attempting to charge it to taxpayers. More detailed scrutiny of this ad claim found that the call was a wrong number by an associate of the Democratic candidate and that it lasted only a few seconds.[45]

Ads and the Vote

Advertisements may operate indirectly through learning, agenda-setting, or priming, or they may have direct impact on voting behavior. The most recent campaigns offer interesting opportunities to investigate how ads directly affect the vote.[46] In 2000 a national survey asked people which television ad run by a presidential campaign during the fall had made the biggest impression on them. Overall, 23 percent mentioned an ad, and 77 percent indicated that no ad had made an impression on them (about the same as in previous elections). The top individual ads mentioned were Gore's Social Security ad (twenty-one mentions), Gore's ad on Bush's Texas record (ten mentions), Bush's improving schools ad (nine mentions), Bush's ad on Gore exaggerations (eight mentions), a National Rifle Association ad supporting Bush (seven mentions), Bush's "RATS" ad in which that word flashed subliminally on the screen (six mentions), and Gore's health care ad (five mentions). In the eyes of voters, total ad mentions by candidate included Gore (seventy-six mentions), Bush (sixty-four mentions), Ralph Nader (five mentions), and Pat Buchanan (two mentions).[47]

An examination of the impact of ad exposure on the vote yielded interesting results. George W. Bush was the only candidate for whom ads produced a negative impact on the vote. The more people saw Gore's advertisements, the less likely they were to say they would vote for Bush. In addition, the more liberal, Democratic, and nonwhite respondents were, the less inclined they were to support Bush. These results are consistent with evidence about the memorability of particular commercials. More individuals were likely to cite Gore's ads than Bush's ads when asked which spot had made the biggest impression on them.

In September 2004 a poll of voters at the beginning of the general election gave President Bush an eight-point lead (46 percent to 38 percent). The president's advantage reflected several strengths. At that point, Kerry was not very well known. He had a 57 percent recognition level, compared to 82 percent for Bush. But the president was aided by voter perceptions that he was a strong leader serving in troubled times. His leadership ability and resoluteness created a strong reservoir of support for himself.

By the end of July, right after the Democratic convention, Kerry moved to his first lead in the race. According to the CBS News/*New York Times* national surveys, 48 percent of voters supported Kerry, compared to 43 percent for Bush. Kerry's rise reflected a convention acceptance speech that was well-received and positive press coverage that accompanied this presentation.

But August proved to be a difficult month for Kerry. His campaign was not able to go on the air with commercials during this month because he had exhausted his nomination funds and did not want to use his scarce general election dollars. At the same time, outside groups, such as the Swift Boat Veterans for Truth, were attacking Kerry's Vietnam record and alleging he was not trustworthy. Under these circumstances, he was not able to sustain his advantage. By September, Bush had regained the lead (50 percent to 41 percent).

Nevertheless, throughout the remainder of the campaign, the two candidates were locked in a tight race. Kerry's support rose a little when he gave strong performances in the three presidential debates. But Bush maintained his own support by attacking Kerry's liberal record and inconsistent stances on terrorism. The "Wolves" ad started airing October 22 and apparently proved effective. By the end of the campaign, Bush's postdebate margin had stood up. On a 51 percent to 48 percent popular vote, Bush beat Kerry and won reelection to the presidency.

Conclusion

Political advertising can be influential at several different levels. It can have direct consequences for voting behavior or it can operate indirectly by providing information voters use in their decision making, affecting people's sense of important problems, or raising or lowering certain standards voters use in their political assessments. The variety of ways that advertisements can affect voters makes their influence on elections very complex. Depending on voter predispositions, candidate strategies, media coverage, or electoral context, the same commercial can have very different consequences.

The only way to determine whether an ad is going to be effective is by understanding the broader political context in which it is viewed. Candidates who are relatively unknown are the most susceptible to ad effects, as are those in multicandidate races and those who find themselves in political contexts that are fluid in nature. The fewer fixed beliefs voters have about candidates or issues, the more likely that advertisements will sway their judgments. Quite apart from such factors and of the relative effectiveness of particular advertising campaigns, it can be argued that the simple fact of advertising or not and the scale on which it is engaged plays a major part in the outcome. In the campaign system as it now operates, not advertising is not an option.

Notes

1. The Media Studies Center poll is reported in the *Providence Journal*, "Hype Swells as First Presidential Debate Approaches," September 29, 1996, A7. The CBS News/*New York Times* numbers come from Richard Berke, "Should Dole Risk Tough Image? Poll Says He Already Has One," *New York Times*, October 16, 1996, A1.

2. Thomas Patterson and Robert McClure, *The Unseeing Eye* (New York: Putnam's, 1976). Also see Martin Wattenberg, *The Rise of Candidate-Centered Politics* (Cambridge: Harvard University Press, 1991); and Richard M. Perloff, *Political Communication: Press, Politics, and Policy in America* (Mahway, N.J.: Erlbaum, 1998).

3. Darrell M. West, *Air Wars: Television Advertising in Election Campaigns*, 4th ed. (Washington, D.C.: CQ Press, 2005).

4. Harold Mendelsohn and Irving Crespi, *Polls, Television, and the New Politics* (Scranton, Pa.: Chandler, 1970), 248.

5. Craig Leonard Brians and Martin Wattenberg, "Campaign Issue Knowledge and Salience: Comparing Reception from TV Commercials, TV News, and Newspapers," *American Journal of Political Science* 40 (February 1996): 172–193; and Xinshu Zhao and Steven Chaffee, "Campaign Advertisements Versus Television News as Sources of Political Issue Information," *Public Opinion Quarterly* 59 (Spring 1995): 41–65.

6. Lynn Vavreck, Constantine Spiliotes, and Linda Fowler, "The Effects of Retail Politics in the New Hampshire Primary," *American Journal of Political Science* 46 (July 2002): 595–610.

7. Alliance for Better Campaigns, "Spot Comparison," *The Political Standard*, June 2000, 1. Also see Jonathan Krasno and Daniel Seltz, "Buying Time: Television Advertising in the 1998 Congressional Elections," Brennan Center for Justice, undated.

8. Elizabeth Kolbert, "Test-Marketing a President: How Focus Groups Pervade Campaign Politics," *New York Times* magazine, August 30, 1992, 18–21, 60, 68, 72.

9. Larry Bartels, *Presidential Primaries and the Dynamics of Public Choice* (Princeton: Princeton University Press, 1988); and Edie Goldenberg and Michael Traugott, *Campaigning for Congress* (Washington, D.C.: CQ Press, 1984), 85–91.

10. See Stanley Kelley Jr. and Thad Mirer, "The Simple Act of Voting," *American Political Science Review* 68 (1974): 572–591.

11. Adam Nagourney and Megan Thee, "With Election Driven by Iraq, Voters Want New Approach," *New York Times*, November 2, 2006, A1.

12. Jonathan Weisman and Chris Cillizza, "Campaigns Set for TV Finale," *Washington Post*, November 3, 2006, A1.

13. David Espo, "Dems Counter Bush Attack With Iraq Ads," CBS News.com, October 31, 2006.

14. Rupert Cornwell, "Republican Advert Banned over Racial Slur," *The Independent*, October 27, 2006, 44.

15. Drew Jubera, "Corker Holds GOP Seat in Tenn.," *Atlanta Journal-Constitution*, November 8, 2006, A16.

16. "Out of Steam," *Los Angeles Times*, November 1, 2006, A18.

17. The classics in this area are E. E. Schattschneider, *The Semisovereign People* (Hinsdale, Ill.: Dryden Press, 1960); Roger Cobb and Charles Elder, *Participation in American Politics: The Dynamics of Agenda-Building*, 2nd ed. (Baltimore: Johns Hopkins University Press, 1983); and John Kingdon, *Agendas, Alternatives, and Public Policies* (Boston: Little, Brown, 1984).

18. See, for example, Maxwell McCombs and Donald Shaw, "The Agenda-Setting Function of Mass Media," *Public Opinion Quarterly* 36 (1972): 176–187; Ray Funkhouser, "The Issues of the Sixties: An Exploratory Study in the Dynamics of Public Opinion," *Public Opinion Quarterly* 37 (1973): 62–75; Jack McLeod, Lee Becker, and James Byrnes, "Another Look at the Agenda-Setting Function of the Press," *Communication Research* 1 (1974): 131–166; Lutz Erbring, Edie Goldenberg, and Arthur Miller, "Front-Page News and Real-World Cues: A New Look at Agenda-Setting by the Media," *American Journal of Political Science* 24 (1980): 16–49; and David Weaver, *Media Agenda-Setting in a Presidential Election* (New York: Praeger, 1981).

19. Shanto Iyengar and Donald Kinder, *News That Matters* (Chicago: University of Chicago Press, 1987), 112; and Samuel Kernell, *Going Public*, 2nd ed. (Washington, D.C.: CQ Press, 1993). Also see Benjamin Page, Robert Shapiro, and Glenn Dempsey, "What Moves Public Opinion?" *American Political Science Review* 81 (1987): 23–44.

20. The 1984 analysis of individual ads does not include a measure of media exposure; the October 1988 CBS News/*New York Times* survey regarding Bush's "Revolving Door" and Dukakis's "Family/Education" commercials incorporates media exposure as a control factor.

21. There often has been confusion between the Bush-produced "Revolving Door" ad, which did not mention Horton directly by name, and the ad aired by an independent political action committee, which used his name and picture. It is not clear whether viewers actually distinguished the two because both ads dealt with crime and Dukakis's lack of toughness.

22. Marjorie Hershey, "The Campaign and the Media," in *The Election of 1988*, ed. Gerald M. Pomper (Chatham, N.J.: Chatham House, 1989), 95–96.

23. I also confirmed this result through a logistic regression analysis that included an interaction term for gender and exposure to Bush's "Revolving Door" ad. The coefficient for the interaction term was 1.39 with a standard error of .62 (p > .05), indicating a strong relationship in the expected direction.

24. Quote taken from David Runkel, ed., *Campaign for President: The Managers Look at '88* (Dover, Mass.: Auburn House, 1989), 113–114.

25. For a related argument, see Darrell M. West, "Television and Presidential Popularity in America," *British Journal of Political Science* 21 (1991): 199–214.

26. Howard Kurtz, "Candidates' Ads Switch the Focus to Kerry," *Washington Post,* May 9, 2004, A4.

27. Ibid.

28. Ibid.

29. Ibid.

30. CBS News/*New York Times* poll, June 23–27, 2004.

31. Ibid., October 14–17, 2004.

32. Liz Sidoti, "New Bush Ad Uses Wolves to Suggest Terrorists Would Seize on Kerry Presidency," Associated Press, October 22, 2004.

33. Howard Kurtz, "In Ad Battle, GOP Unleashes Wolves, Democrats Use Ostrich," *Washington Post,* October 23, 2004, A6.

34. CBS News/*New York Times* national survey of 1,084 adults completed October 27–31, 2006.

35. Sylvester Brown, "Some Voters Will Buy into Misleading Political Ads," *St. Louis Post-Dispatch,* October 29, 2006, D1.

36. Michael Shear, "Vitriol Fills the Air and Airwaves," *Washington Post,* November 3, 2006, B2.

37. Ibid.

38. Ira Teinowitz, "No Shortage of Mudslinging in Midterm Run-Up," *Advertising Age,* October 31, 2006.

39. Alessandra Stanley, "Scary, Like Funny Scary," *New York Times,* October 29, 2006, D1.

40. A number of studies have investigated this relationship. See George Bishop, Robert Oldendick, and Alfred Tuchfarber, "Political Information Processing: Question Order and Context Effects," *Political Behavior* 4 (1982): 177–200; C. Turner and E. Krauss, "Fallible Indicators of the Subjective State of the Nation," *American Psychologist* 33 (1978): 456–470; and Amos Tversky and Daniel Kahneman, "The Framing of Decisions and the Psychology of Choice," *Science* January 1981, 453–458.

41. Daniel Kahneman, Paul Slovic, and Amos Tversky, eds., *Judgment Under Uncertainty: Heuristics and Biases* (New York: Cambridge University Press, 1982).

42. D. W. Miller, "Election Results Leave Political Scientists Defensive over Forecasting Models," *Chronicle of Higher Education,* November 17, 2000, A24.

43. Jim Rutenberg, "Scary Ads Take Campaign to a Grim New Level," *New York Times,* October 17, 2004, A1.

44. "Candidates Fight Dirty in Battle for Congress," *The Independent,* October 30, 2006, 2.

45. Jim Kuhnhenn, "Millions Spent on Negative Political Ads," *CBS News,* October 31, 2006.

46. Marion Just et al., *Crosstalk: Citizens, Candidates, and the Media in a Presidential Campaign* (Chicago: University of Chicago Press, 1996).

47. Brown University survey conducted October–November 2000.

8 Free Falls, High Dives, and the Future of Democratic Accountability

Scott L. Althaus

The health of a democracy rests on the vigilance of its citizens, and democracy works best when citizens pay attention to the governing process. Different models of democracy envision different roles for citizens to fulfill, but every theory of democracy agrees that the most basic role of the citizen is to hold leaders accountable for what they have done or intend to do.[1]

Yet we know little about the conditions under which citizens are most likely to exercise such vigilance by going out and seeking political information. Recent scholarship has demonstrated that threats of various sorts can motivate people to gather information.[2] It would seem that citizen interest in politics should be most acute when the political stakes are perceived as high, or when the risk of future harm is great. For example, citizen knowledge of politics over the latter half of the twentieth century hit an all-time high in the 1960s, presumably because of the social turmoil occurring during that decade.[3] Likewise, the American public receives higher scores on political knowledge tests given during presidential election campaigns than it does during midterm congressional elections, apparently because the highly visible presidential campaigns remind people how important it is to follow government affairs.[4] If citizen engagement in politics goes up when the political environment generates reasons to be attentive, then democratic accountability might occur most efficiently during periods of social unrest or economic hardship, as the history of "critical realignments" in American elections suggests.[5]

Editors' Note: Portions of the analysis of audience demand for network news broadcasts first appeared in Scott L. Althaus, "American News Consumption During Times of National Crisis," *PS: Political Science & Politics* 35, no. 3 (2002), and are used with permission from Cambridge University Press. Unless otherwise noted, all circulation and ratings data reported in this chapter were obtained from the 2004, 2005, and 2006 editions of the Project for Excellence in Journalism's "State of the News Media" reports, available at *www.journalism.org*.

If vigilance follows times of trouble, then complacence should emerge in the wake of peace and prosperity. Although this prediction implies that political accountability might be harder to achieve when things are generally going well, it also suggests a reassuring explanation for one of the most vexing trends confronting American political communication scholars: the long-term decline in the size of audiences for traditional news coverage in the United States.

At the height of the Vietnam War in 1969, fully half of U.S. households tuned in to one of the three nightly news broadcasts. By 2000 the combined audience for network nightly news had dropped to less than a quarter of U.S. households. The same historical decline has affected newspaper readership. Daily newspaper circulation in the United States was approximately one newspaper per household in 1970. By 2000 weekday newspaper penetration had fallen to slightly more than one newspaper for every two households, a drop of nearly 50 percent in just thirty years.[6]

What happened between the 1960s and the turn of the twenty-first century that could explain these declines in the size of news audiences? One factor might be the end of the Vietnam War. The post-Vietnam period was a time not only of peace for Americans but also of rapidly growing prosperity. Between 1970 and 2000 per capita disposable income in the United States grew by 188 percent after controlling for inflation and changes in the price of personal commodities.[7] If times of peace and prosperity are partly responsible for the apparent demobilization of news audiences, then the public's limited amount of attention to the news in 2000 compared to 1969 could be less ominous that it might seem. As long as Americans return to the news when times again become troubled, their waning interest during good times may be of no lasting consequence. Firefighters make for pleasant company, but showing up when the house is in flames is what really counts.

If popular vigilance is an essential ingredient to successful democratic governance, then we want to know whether diminishing levels of citizen attentiveness to politics is more like a free fall or a high dive. Leaving the safety of the airplane signals a point of no return for the parachutist. Pulling the rip cord can slow down but not reverse the jumper's fall. Once on the ground, the time and expense involved in reloading the chute and flying back to altitude makes the jumper unlikely to turn around and do it again. The same may be true of interest in the news. If people reach their "tipping point" and stop paying close attention to the daily doings of political leaders, then the declining size of newspaper and broadcast news audiences may signal a long-term demobilization that results in permanently smaller and more specialized sets of niche audiences for various types of political information.[8]

But news audiences may be more resilient than they appear. Plunging head-first from an aerial platform without a parachute sounds catastrophic, but not when the platform is a diving board suspended above a deep pool of water. The diver speeds downward but eventually bobs back up. Climbing out and scaling the ladder for another leap is easily done, and the cycle continues until the interest fades. The size of the news audience might fall when times are good, but rise again when bad times return. In such a situation, an apparent long-term decline in the health of the body politic may rapidly change for the better once a pressing need arises for renewed citizen vigilance.[9]

The difficulty in sorting out free falls from high dives comes from the challenge of identifying the unique impact of numerous factors that simultaneously influence the changing composition of news audiences over time. Comparing news habits during the Vietnam War to those at the start of the twenty-first century tells us little about the reasons for decline, as more than peace and prosperity transpired in the intervening years. The growth of cable news channels and the advent of the Internet contributed to the fragmentation of audiences for traditional news formats, just as the rise of radio and broadcast television ate away at newspaper audiences in the decades before the 1960s. Today's audiences are also lured away from news coverage by a wider range of non-news media choices than were available in 1970, from video games and personal computers to home theaters and MTV.[10] No simple comparison between the Vietnam era and today can control for the multiple influences of these other developments. To figure out not only whether the long-term contraction in the size of print and broadcast news audiences is temporary or permanent, but also how large the drop actually is, would require a census of audiences for all available news outlets. Given the complexity and scope of the contemporary media environment, such a survey may be impossible.

We have, however, a different way to approach the question that can help sort out the impact of these many competing influences. Sudden changes in the political environment following the onset of national crises provide opportunities to study the response of news audiences during times when technological advances and the state of the economy are more or less constant. This chapter considers patterns of surge and decline in news attention for three such cases: the Persian Gulf crisis of 1990–1991, the terrorist attacks of September 11, 2001, and the invasion of Iraq in March 2003. Two of the three cases have clear and sudden starting points: the 9/11 attacks were completely unanticipated, as was Iraq's invasion of neighboring Kuwait on August 2, 1990. Moreover, the Persian Gulf crisis occurred more than two years before the advent of the World Wide Web and during a time when CNN's tiny audience and lack of cable competitors made it a novel but relatively minor player on the media scene. The timing of these two crises allows for a comparison between the dynamics of audience response in the more concentrated television news system that existed in 1991, when the three network evening news broadcasts were the main source of news for American audiences, and the highly segmented multi-outlet system that was in place by 2001. The run-up to the 2003 invasion of Iraq was more gradual, but in all three cases it is possible to study the dynamics of news audience size long before and long after the start of each crisis. Comparing the percentage of adults attending to the news before and after each precipitating event should reveal how the crisis atmosphere stimulated changes in levels of popular attention to the news.

Free Fall or High Dive?

To understand whether the American public's appetite for political news is stimulated by the loss of peace or threats to prosperity, we must start by assessing the degree to which the public sees different sources of news as useful for keeping up with national and international events. National surveys conducted since 1991 by the Pew Research Center for the People and the Press provide detailed information about the media consumption habits of the U.S. public. Figure 8.1 shows that when people are asked where they were most likely to turn for news about national and international issues, television news has long been the most popular source of political information in the United States.[11] In 2006, three out of four respondents named television as one of their main sources of news about national and international issues. In contrast, only about four in ten respondents mentioned newspapers as a major source of such information in 2006; one in four named the Internet; and two in ten relied on radio.

Because Pew allows respondents to mention up to two main sources of news about national and international issues, the numbers for each year can add up to far more than 100 percent. The best way to interpret these survey results is to note the trends over time and whether use of different media for surveillance changes in response to the onset of wars, major political events, or national crises. The relative importance of television, newspapers, and radio for keeping up with national and international issues has been relatively stable since 1990. Television's overwhelming popularity waned somewhat during the late 1990s, but revived after 9/11. Newspapers are the second-most popular source for following news of global and domestic importance, but reliance on newspapers for this purpose peaked in the mid-1990s and has been waning ever

Figure 8.1 Where Americans get most of their news about national and international issues, 1990–2006

Percentage of adults

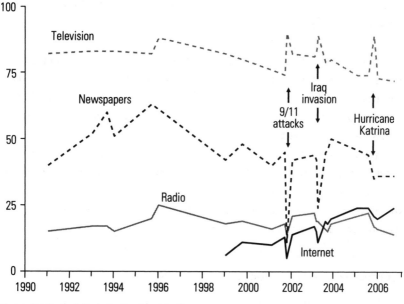

Source: Pew Research Center for People and the Press.

since. Radio used to be the third-most mentioned source of political news, and its use for this purpose has remained relatively steady since 1990. Of the four media considered here, the Internet was the least-turned-to news medium for national and international issues until after the invasion of Iraq. But popular interest in using the Internet to follow news of the world has been building steadily since the late 1990s. Starting in July 2003 the Internet has been consistently mentioned by more people than radio as an important source of news about major events.

Yet when national crises erupt, these conventional patterns of self-reported media reliance can change quite dramatically. Figure 8.1 shows how reliance on television news spiked after the September 2001 attacks, the March 2003 invasion of Iraq, and Hurricane Katrina in September 2005. Short-term increases in reliance on television for news of national and international issues were accompanied by short-term declines in the use of radio and the Internet, as well as the dramatic abandonment of newspapers as a main source for political surveillance in the case of the two threats to national peace. Americans, however, did not stop reading newspapers or listening to radio news during these national crises. Instead, these data tell us merely that the perceived usefulness of the four media changed abruptly when circumstances became dire, and that television is seen as the most important news source for national and international information during times of national crisis.

Claiming to rely on a medium for keeping up with a particular kind of news does not imply doing it often. It is important to place the trends in Figure 8.1 into perspective. Interest in national and international news topics is not widespread in the American public. For example, Pew data show that during most of 2005 and 2006 only four in ten Americans said they paid very close attention to news about the war in Iraq.[12] For this reason, we need to examine what Americans do, not just what they say. Do sudden changes in national fortunes precipitate rapid growth in the size of news audiences for television, radio, newspapers, and the Internet? Addressing this question requires examining trends in ratings and circulation data for each medium in turn, beginning with national television news programming.

Audience Demand for Broadcast Television News

Nightly network news broadcasts hold the attention of a larger portion of Americans than any other single news product in the United States, including cable news. For example, *CBS Evening News with Katie Couric* was the lowest-rated network evening news program at the end of 2006. During the week of December 18, the average nightly audience for Couric's broadcast was 7.4 million viewers, compared to 8.5 million for ABC's *World News Tonight* and 9.5 million for NBC's *Nightly News*. Yet Couric's average nightly audience was more than two and a half times as large as the total audience for the top-rated programs on Fox, CNN, and MSNBC combined. For the week of December 18, the combined audience for Fox's *O'Reilly Factor*, CNN's *Paula Zahn Now*, and MSNBC's *Countdown with Keith Olbermann* averaged just 2.8 million viewers per night.[13] In contrast, the combined nightly audience for the three network news programs during the week of December 18 was nine times as large. Although network news audiences have been in decline for many decades, they still dwarf the nearest competitor on cable television.

To track short-term changes in the size of network news audiences over time, I combined weekly television ratings data collected by Nielsen Media Research for ABC's *World News Tonight*, CBS's *Evening News*, and NBC's *Nightly News*.[14] Translating these ratings data into the percentage of American

Figure 8.2 Average combined audience for evening network news broadcasts around the time of the Persian Gulf Crisis and the 9/11 attacks

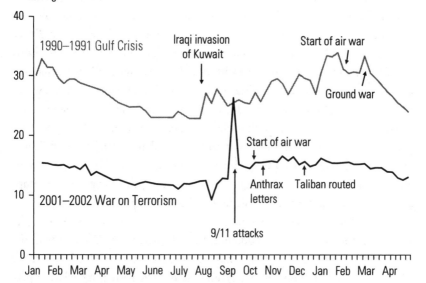

Percentage of adults

Source: Nielsen Media Research, compiled from various sources.

adults tuning in to the nightly news corrects for population growth in the United States that occurred between 1990 and 2001.[15]

One striking feature of these trends (see Figure 8.2) is that the evening news audience was only about half as large in 2001 as it was a decade before. During the 1990–1991 period, between 23 percent and 33 percent of American adults watched nightly network news broadcasts, depending on the time of year. Since January 2001 Nielsen data put the total size of nightly news audiences at between 11 percent and 16 percent of American adults (not counting the week of 9/11). Today's total audience for all forms of public affairs content is probably smaller than it was a decade before, but the main reason for today's smaller network television news audience is that the once-larger broadcast news audience of 1990–1991 is spread across a wider range of news products, with cable, the Internet, and local television news now attracting sizable portions of a national news audience that in 1990 was shared mainly by the three evening news programs.

Because news audiences have become fragmented, absolute differences in the percentage of adults watching network news during each crisis period are less telling than the relative changes in audience size within each trend. If we begin our analysis immediately before the onset of each crisis and follow the trends over the next several months, the two cases appear to reveal different patterns of audience response. The Iraqi invasion of Kuwait produced an immediate four percentage point spike in the U.S. news audience. The nightly news audience then grew steadily during the fall as the U.S. military buildup in Saudi Arabia signaled a looming confrontation with Iraq. Nearly a third of U.S. adults were directly exposed to one of the three nightly news broadcasts during the weeks leading up to and immediately following the start of the air war on January 16, 1991. The news audience shrank somewhat in early February but jumped three percentage points during the week of ground combat, which began on February 23. A rapid victory over Iraqi ground forces was followed by an abrupt turn away from the news, and the nightly audience dropped nearly ten percentage points over the eight weeks following the close of the ground campaign.

A decade later, the tragedies of 9/11 had the immediate effect of doubling the size of the evening news audience, from 13 percent of U.S. adults in the week of September 3–9 to more than 26 percent in the week of September 10–16. Just as swiftly, however, the evening news audience contracted to 15 percent of adults in the week of September 17–23 and never rose more than 1.5 percentage points above that level in the following seven months. In contrast to frequent event-driven surges in news attention throughout the Persian Gulf crisis, network news attention in the post-9/11 United States held quite stable at about four percentage points above pre-9/11 levels for several months before declining steadily after the start of the new year in 2002. By the middle of April 2002, the size of the evening news audience had returned to the previous July's level of just 13 percent of adults.

When interpreting these postcrisis trends using the immediate precrisis period as a benchmark, it appears that the Persian Gulf crisis produced a gradual mobilization of Americans into the television news audience, but that the onset of the war on terrorism generated a smaller shock to the size of news audiences that started decaying soon after it began. During the Persian Gulf crisis, the average size of the evening news audience grew by 13.8 million persons between the last week of July 1990 and the first week of January 1991. During the onset of the war on terrorism, the growth in the evening news audience between these same two weeks was only half as large, amounting to 7.4 million more audience members in January 2002 compared to the previous July.

This interpretation of postcrisis growth in the news audience, however, requires us to ignore the left-hand side of Figure 8.2. The longer-term trends leading up to each precipitating event call into question whether either of these national crises fundamentally increased the size of the broadcast news audience. Network television news audiences swell during the winter months, when people spend more time indoors, and shrink in the summer months. Once we take into account these cyclical shifts in the size of television news audiences, the apparent changes prompted by each crisis become harder to distinguish from normal seasonal movement. It seems impressive at first glance that 32.7 percent of adults were following the evening news in a typical week during the critical month of January 1991, up from 23.2 percent for July 1990. But this number loses some of its luster when we recognize that the evening news audience was nearly as large—31.4 percent of adults—in the previous January. Because of the seasonal variation, a more appropriate way of measuring the impact of national crises is to calculate the size of the news audience after the precipitating event compared to its size from the same period in the previous year. This comparison paints a very different picture. During the Persian Gulf crisis an average of approximately 2.4 million more adults per day were watching evening news broadcasts in the first four months of 1991 compared to the first four months of 1990. The same comparison for the onset of the war on terrorism produces a mean difference of just less than 900,000 more audience members per day in 2002 than in 2001. Seasonal-adjusted growth in the news audience was nearly three times as large during the Persian Gulf crisis as during the current war on terrorism, but in both cases the magnitude of growth was rather small, amounting to 0.4 percent of adults in 2001–2002 and 1.3 percent in 1990–1991.[16] Seen from this perspective, the clearest impact of the Iraqi invasion of Kuwait was the increase in the amount of weekly variance around the seasonal mean rather than a shift in the mean itself. Similarly, 9/11 appears to have accelerated the seasonal growth curve for the evening news audience during the fall of 2001 without producing a substantive shift in its average size.

This seasonal variation becomes easier to see when the points of comparison are closer together in time. Figure 8.3 shows twenty-four months of weekly ratings data for January 2001 through January 2003 and January 2002 through January 2004. Staggering these ratings trends by a year helps to distinguish event-induced spikes in the size of news audiences from normal seasonal movement. Because the 9/11 attacks occurred during the first period and the 2003 invasion of Iraq during the second, this comparison also helps to clarify how these events influenced the size of news audiences in the months that followed. Looking first at the impact of the 9/11 attacks compared to audience trends in the following year, we see that network news audiences grew by

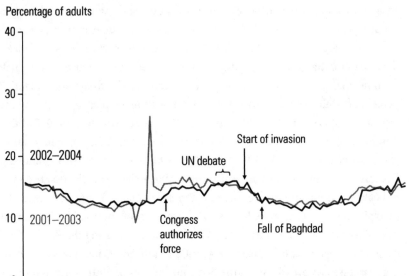

Figure 8.3 Average combined audience for evening network news broadcasts around the time of the 9/11 attacks and the invasion of Iraq

Percentage of adults

40

30

20 — 2002–2004

Start of invasion

UN debate

10 — 2001–2003

Congress
authorizes
force

Fall of Baghdad

0

Jan Feb Mar Apr May Jun Jul Aug Sep Oct Nov Dec Jan Feb Mar Apr May Jun Jul Aug Sep Oct Nov Dec Jan

Source: Nielsen Media Research, compiled from various sources.

approximately 2 percent of the adult population beginning in the week following the terror attacks until roughly a month later. From mid-October 2001 until mid-January 2002, the network news audience was about 1 percent of the adult population larger than it would be a year later. After mid-January 2002 the size of the network news audience appears almost indistinguishable from the audience trend of the following year.

If the 9/11 attacks produced a small but temporary increase in the size of network news audiences, the March 2003 invasion of Iraq registered hardly at all. Figure 8.3 shows that the initial run-up to war produced little noticeable growth in the network news audience, beginning with the congressional vote on October 11, 2002, to authorize the use of military force against Iraq and continuing with the debate before the United Nations from late January through mid-February 2003. After the testimony of UN chief weapons inspector Hans Blix and Secretary of State Colin Powell on whether Iraq possessed weapons of mass destruction, the size of the broadcast news audience dropped slightly until the beginning of the war against Iraq. The week including the start of the Iraqi invasion saw a temporary 1 percent jump in audience levels over the previous week, but the size of the network news audience dropped precipitously over the following month as the invasion forces ground on toward Baghdad. The data in Figure 8.3 show that this decline in news attention followed the normal seasonal trend for March and April and did not seem to be influenced in any significant way by the progress of the war.

In short, the daily news audience for network news broadcasts is much larger than any other daily broadcast or cable news audience in the United States. But short-term changes in the size of the network news audience are typically influenced less by the current state of national security than by the current state of the weather.

Audience Demand for Cable Television News

The size of audiences for cable news channels is hard to pin down because of the format differences between traditional network broadcasts and cable channels. Audiences for nightly news broadcasts are concentrated into a single thirty-minute time period per day, but audiences for cable news channels come and go around the clock. Cable viewership can therefore be very small for any given program but fairly large when the number of unique viewers is considered over longer periods of time. Researchers use two methods to measure audience size for cable news channels: the average number of viewers in a typical minute of a day, and the cumulative number of unique viewers that have watched the channel at some point during an entire month.

The average number of people watching cable news channels at any given minute of the day is usually quite modest by network news standards. Figure 8.4 shows the combined average audience per minute for the top three cable news channels: CNN, Fox, and MSNBC. The impact of the 9/11 attacks on long-term trends in cable news viewership is unmistakable. From January 1998 to August 2001, the combined daytime audience for the three cable channels averaged just less than 0.4 percent of adults, or about 770,000 persons, while the combined primetime audience per minute averaged nearly 0.7 percent of adults, or about 1.4 million persons. From September 2001 to December 2005, the average daytime cable audience grew to nearly 0.9 percent of adults, or approximately 1.8 million people, while the average primetime audience expanded to 1.4 percent of adults per minute, or 2.9 million viewers. The increased national security threat following 9/11 effectively doubled the audience for cable news channels.

Figure 8.4 Average combined audience for CNN, Fox, and MSNBC cable news channels during daytime and primtetime hours, 1998–2005

Percentage of adults

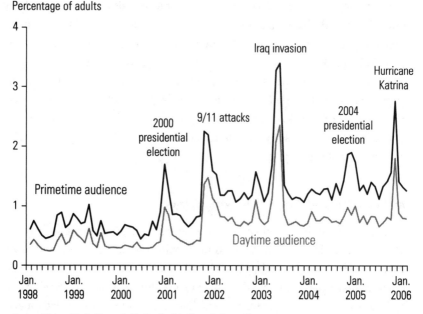

Source: Nielsen Media Research, Project for Excellence in Journalism.

In addition to expanding the regular audience for cable news, national crises and high-visibility political events can have even stronger short-term effects on public attention to cable news programming. Figure 8.4 shows that as recounts were ordered in several states after the 2000 presidential election, the average cable news audience in November 2000 was three times the size of the average cable news audience when the campaign began in September. Likewise, comparing cable news attention in August and September 2004 shows that the start of the presidential campaign increased the size of the primetime viewing audience by nearly a third for all three cable channels combined. Dramatic crises had a similar effect on the size of cable news audiences. The 9/11 attacks produced a fourfold increase in the size of the average cable news audience, from 1.6 million primetime viewers in August 2001 to 4.6 million primetime viewers in September. But the average cable news audience contracted swiftly in the months following the attacks. By January 2002 the combined per-minute audience for the three cable channels averaged 2.4 million primetime viewers, just half the size of the peak audience in September 2001. More dramatic changes in the size of the average cable news audience followed the invasion of Iraq in March 2003 and the aftermath of Hurricane Katrina in September 2005. The average minute of primetime cable news programming during the intense ground combat in April 2003 drew 3.5 million more viewers than in February 2003, a month before the invasion. The flooding of the Gulf Coast after the hurricane temporarily expanded the average audience for primetime cable news from 1.5 percent of adults in August 2005 to 2.7 percent in September, before just as swiftly snapping back to 1.4 percent in October.

Although Figure 8.4 shows that the average cable audience remains far smaller than the average broadcast news audience, the cumulative cable news audience—that is, the total number of unique viewers over a period of time—can include a fairly large proportion of American adults. For example, Hurricane Katrina drew an average primetime cable news audience of 2.0 million per minute for CNN and 2.8 million per minute for Fox during September 2005. But the number of different people who watched at least six minutes of programming at some point during that same month was 101.1 million for CNN (or about 49 percent of American adults) and 87.2 million for Fox (or about 34 percent of American adults). Even if there is a large overlap in the individuals making up these two audiences, we can safely conclude that a majority of the American public sought out at least a few minutes of cable news programming as this natural disaster unfolded. Hurricane Katrina caused the cumulative cable news audience to increase by between 25 million and 37 million unique viewers per channel—representing between 12 percent and 18 percent of American adults each—during September 2005 relative to cumulative audiences for the previous month. But by November 2005 the size of cumulative cable news audiences had fallen back to pre-Katrina levels. At the time of this writing, trend data for cumulative ratings suggest that in any given month around a third of the U.S. adult population tunes in to six or more minutes of cable news programming.[17]

The cumulative number of unique cable news viewers per month may be more than twice as large as the average nightly audience for the three network newscasts, but comparable data for cumulative network news audiences are not publicly available. It is difficult therefore to tell whether cable news attracts more or fewer unique viewers per month than broadcast news. It is also important to consider that this measure of the cable audience includes persons who tune in for just six minutes per month, whereas network news viewers tend to be habitually attentive. Of the two available measures, the size of the regular audience for cable news is therefore better estimated by the smaller average audience per minute ratings, even though these understate the size of the daily audience for cable news programming. Moreover, it is unclear whether even regular cable viewers are getting a mix of news comparable to that received by network audiences. A content analysis of primetime news programming on CNN, Fox, and MSNBC during late January 2002 found that cable news shows focused on a small number of "headline" stories and that much of the primetime programming took the form of personal interviews or panel discussions rather than traditional news reporting.[18] The cumulative cable news audience can include a large cross-section of the public, but this cross-section constitutes an irregular audience for news programming, tuning in to catch up with developing stories or breaking events but probably relying on noncable sources for whatever regular news diet they might choose to consume.

Audience Demand for Newspapers

Reading newspapers is relatively more habit-driven than watching television news. Eight out of ten regular newspapers readers are subscribers who have made a long-term financial commitment to a paper.[19] For this reason, levels of newspaper reading tend to remain stable even during times of national crisis.

The 1930s marked the beginning of a steady, long-term decline in American newspaper readership that has continued undisturbed by wars and other catalyzing events. Figure 8.5 shows a steady pattern starting with 1964, the year that the Gulf of Tonkin incident propelled the United States into a large-scale military involvement in Vietnam, and continuing through 2006.[20] The straight line in Figure 8.5 illustrates the predicted erosion of the newspaper audience over time, and, compared to the actual decline, shows how little impact wars and other dramatic events have had on newspaper readership over time. Daily newspaper readership during the Vietnam War started at 81 percent in 1964 but fell to 78 percent by 1970. The declining interest in newspapers continued through the 9/11 attacks[21] and the war in Iraq.

By 2006 only 50 percent of U.S. adults were estimated to read a daily newspaper. Although this sounds like a sizable news audience, research shows that only half of those readers pay regular attention to national or international news items, about the same proportion that reads the sports pages. Instead, newspaper readers disproportionately specialize in local news.[22] But because nearly nine in ten newspaper readers report paying attention to stories on the front page, it is likely that a fairly large proportion of Americans read prominent newspaper coverage of national or international news.

Figure 8.5 Combined national weekday readership for daily newspapers, 1964–2006

Percentage of adults

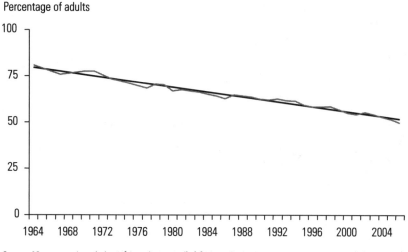

Source: Newspaper Association of America, compiled from various sources.

Audience Demand for Radio News

Like newspaper readers, the radio news audience consists mainly of habitual rather than occasional listeners. The highest levels of weekday radio news exposure occur during the morning and evening rush hours, mainly among motorists commuting between work and home.[23] Because commutes occur without regard to the weather or major events of the day, radio listeners constitute one of the most loyal and stable of news audiences.

It is important to distinguish between commercial and public radio news audiences, because commercial news-talk formats combine shorter headline-style reports with call-in discussion and interview programs, while public radio news formats tend to combine longer stories on events of the day with in-depth analysis. Figure 8.6 reports quarterly estimates of the average quarter-hour radio audience for all commercial news and talk radio formats combined, excluding sports-only stations. Quarter-hour ratings provide the average number of different persons who are listening to a format for at least five minutes in any given fifteen-minute block of time. They are therefore directly comparable in magnitude to the average audience estimates for network television and cable news. The largest audience for news formats on commercial radio listens during the morning and afternoon weekday drive times, averaging around 2 percent of American adults. The second measure in Figure 8.6 includes weekends and the

Figure 8.6 Combined average quarter-hour audience for news stations on commercial radio, 1998–2006

Percentage of adults

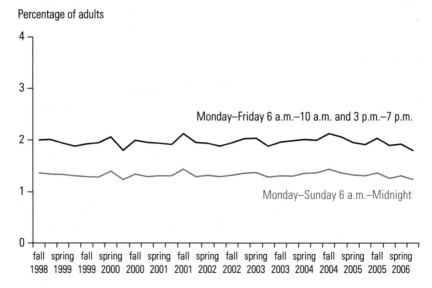

Source: Arbitron National Radio Services.

full span of daytime listening hours when calculating the size of the average quarter-hour audience for commercial news formats.

A comparison of the radio trends in Figure 8.6 with the cable news trends in Figure 8.4 shows just how much larger and more stable the radio news audience is relative to the cable news audience. Between 1998 and 2006, roughly 2 percent of American adults were listening to radio news during the peak weekday commute hours, compared to an average primetime cable news audience of about 1 percent during the same period. Slightly more than 1 percent were listening on average to commercial radio news stations in any given fifteen-minute block of time between 6 a.m. and midnight, compared to an average of just more than half a percent for daytime cable news programming.

Like cable, the size of the radio news audience at any given time of day is proportionally quite small, but unlike cable, it is largely unaffected by the onset of national crises. Short-lived surges in the size of the commercial radio news audience are visible for the quarterly periods including the 9/11 attacks and the 2003 invasion of Iraq, as well as the presidential elections of 2000 and 2004, but these changes are so small as to be hardly distinguishable from normal quarterly movement in the audience trends. As unresponsive as commercial news radio audiences can be, the radio audience as a whole can sometimes surge in impressive ways. An Arbitron study of radio audiences before, during, and after the 9/11 attacks found that the combined national audience for all forms of radio programming on the day of the attacks was 5 million persons above normal listening levels, a surge of roughly 2 percent of American adults within a single day.[24]

It is harder to gauge the response of public radio news audiences to national crises, because public radio's lack of commercial advertising means that traditional ratings data were not collected for these audiences until recently. According to Arbitron ratings data for 2006, combining the listeners for National Public Radio, Public Radio International, Pacifica Radio, and American Public Media yields an average quarter-hour audience for news-based public radio formats of roughly 0.8 percent of adults during the morning drive time hours and 0.5 percent during the afternoon drive time.[25] Averaging these estimates together and comparing that average to the drive-time audience for commercial news stations suggests that the news audience for public radio is less than half the size of the audience for commercial news radio. But as with cable news, the cumulative audience for radio news can be much larger than the average audience. In 2006 the weekly cumulative audience for news-based program formats on public radio stations averaged 22.2 million unique listeners for the four public radio networks combined, which translates to 10.8 percent of the adult population.[26]

It is less clear how much the size of this audience for public radio news has changed over time. Data provided by NPR suggest that its 2005 combined audience for news and music formats is 50 percent larger than in 2001 and 315 percent larger than its combined audience in 1985. Survey data from the Pew Center for the People and the Press, however, suggest a different trend. According to the Pew data, the percentage of adults saying they regularly listen to NPR nearly doubled between 1994 and 1995, from 9 percent to 15 percent, but grew more slowly from that point until 2006, when 17 percent called themselves regular NPR listeners.[27] On this measure, most of the audience growth for public radio programming occurred well before the 9/11 attacks and the Iraq war, suggesting again that the size of the radio news audience is relatively unaffected by current events.

Audience Demand for Online News

The online news audience is the hardest to measure, because we have no widely accepted methods for estimating the size of Internet audiences that can

Figure 8.7 Self-reported intentional, accidental, and back-channel exposure to news on the Internet, 1995–2006

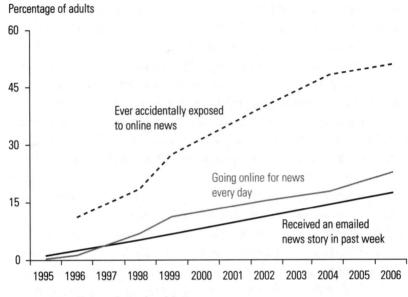

Percentage of adults

Ever accidentally exposed to online news

Going online for news every day

Received an emailed news story in past week

Source: Pew Research Center for People and the Press.

compare to television and radio ratings or newspaper circulation figures. Estimates of audience size based on the observed behavior of a random sample of the population are the best gauges of audience demand, because the estimates are based on what individuals actually do. Ratings and circulation trends are behavioral data, and for that reason are highly regarded within the media industry. Estimates of the total size of online news audiences, however, are often based on what individuals say they do. Self-reported media exposure measures are notorious for overstating the degree to which people follow news coverage of public affairs.[28] These self-reported survey estimates, however, remain the best gauge available for tracking changes in national online news audiences over time.

Popular access to the World Wide Web began with the advent of the Mosaic browser in 1993. National media use surveys conducted by the Pew Center show that online news audiences grew rapidly thereafter. Figure 8.7 shows that less than a quarter of a percent of adults reported visiting Internet news sites every day in 1994. That number grew to 11 percent by 1999 and 23 percent by 2006. Not only have online news sites become more popular during a period of declining interest in traditional news outlets, but decisions to seek out online news seem to be driven less by habit than by the occurrence of newsworthy developments. Figure 8.1 showed that Americans report slightly less dependence on the Internet for news during periods of national crisis than during normal times, but other research suggests that breaking news events are associated with temporary surges in the size of audiences for Internet news sites. This research suggests that event-driven interest in Internet news sites surges and declines in a way similar to that of cable news audiences, in contrast to the more stable viewership for broadcast television news, radio news, and newspapers during periods of national crisis.[29]

Although online news sites are growing in popularity, less is known about which news sites are attracting audiences and what kinds of news stories those audiences are seeking online. Research on the Internet use habits of a random sample of the population found that the most popular online news sites corresponded closely to the most popular off-line news outlets: the top six national news sites, in descending order of page-hit popularity, belonged to CNN, CBS News, *USA Today,* the *New York Times,* the *Washington Post,* and ABC News. This pattern suggests that the news stories people read online are likely to be quite similar to the stories they follow in traditional mainstream news outlets. This conclusion is underscored by the finding that visitors to online news sites, like the readers of printed newspapers, tended to pay slightly more attention to sports news than to news of national and world events.[30]

The proliferation of news outlets on the Internet has, however, produced new modes of exposure that have the potential to disseminate public affairs information far beyond the ranks of those who seek it out intentionally. The widespread use of Web portals combined with imprecise methods for locating Web-based information has caused ever more people to accidentally expose themselves to news stories online. Figure 8.7 shows that the percentage of Americans who have come across news stories when going online for a purpose other than to search for news rose from 11 percent in 1996 to 51 percent in 2006.[31] This number is especially impressive when we consider that only 67 percent of Americans reported ever going online at all as of 2006, which means that 76 percent of Internet users report being accidentally exposed to news stories. However, an early study on the types of people who report being accidentally exposed concluded that "those who tend to look for news online are the ones who tend to come across it by accident as well," suggesting that incidental exposure may not substantially broaden the flow of public affairs information reaching the politically disinterested.[32]

How frequently these accidental exposures occur remains unclear, but Pew Center surveys shed light on the percentage of adults that receive unsolicited news stories by e-mail. In 1995 only 1 percent of Americans reported receiving a news story by e-mail from a friend or acquaintance within the past week, but by 2006 fully 17 percent of Americans said they had been e-mailed a news story within the past week. This finding suggests a sizable back-channel audience at the receiving end of e-mailed news stories. But little is yet known about the types of news stories that are passed around the Internet in this fashion.

The Future of Democratic Accountability

The short-term dynamics of news attention following sudden threats to national peace and prosperity offer a mix of sobering and encouraging trends. The proportion of Americans following network newscasts, newspapers, and radio news stations tended to be relatively stable before, during, and after times of national crisis. The main exception proves the rule when it comes to popular use of traditional news media: the network news audience doubled in size following the 9/11 attacks, but this surge lasted no longer than a week; radio saw a small but temporary bump in listeners for the fall 2001 quarter; and the steady slide of newspaper audiences continued uninterrupted. Although the audiences for traditional news products were largely unperturbed by sudden changes in national fortune, the average size of the cable news audience doubled after 9/11 and has held steady at the new level ever since. Moreover, the cable news audience surges when threats are imminent and recedes when the immediate outlook improves. Internet news audiences seem to follow a similar pattern.

Demand for news therefore seems sensitive to current events when it comes to cable and Internet audiences, but relatively inelastic when it comes to newspapers, radio, and broadcast television. Countering the long-term demobilization that might be occurring in the U.S. news audience is a short-term responsiveness when peace and prosperity are threatened that is heartening but difficult to evaluate. The proportion of Americans tuning in to Fox and CNN for anything more than a brief glimpse at the latest headlines remains unclear, but the growing popularity of Internet news outlets is another positive sign for the health of American democracy.

As encouraging as these findings may be, the long-term trends in news attentiveness give pause. Newspaper and network television news audiences keep draining steadily away, as they have for decades, while radio audiences remain stable but small. That the normally small cable news audience doubled in size after 9/11 and that the online news audience is growing over time suggests that the long-term loss of audience shares for traditional news products may partly represent changing preferences for newer news products. If so, then the shrinking audience for network broadcasts and newspapers might be driven more by changes in the technology of news delivery than by any long-term popular demobilization from the world of public affairs. If a direct transfer of audience shares from old media to new media is under way, then it is possible that today's news audience could be numerically as large in the aggregate as it was in the 1970s. But even if the number of attentive Americans has held steady over time, the size of the adult population in the United States nearly doubled over the second half of the twentieth century. This ensures that even numerical stability in the size of news audiences would translate into a proportional decline in news attentiveness as the number of American adults increases over time. This is the optimistic view.

The pessimistic view is that overall news consumption levels may be substantially lower today than they were in the 1970s. The steady loss of newspaper readers and network news viewers predates the advent of CNN and the World Wide Web. And given the flourishing array of entertainment media alternatives that have sprung up since the late 1960s to occupy the attention of ordinary citizens, it is unlikely that a direct transfer of audiences from old news to new news has been taking place. Instead, the new era of multimedia entertainment has almost certainly eroded the audience base for news products in the United States.[33] The question is by how much. We know that news audiences today are spread out among a broader range of information sources, but our ability to accurately measure the size of audiences for cable and Internet news remains tentative and imprecise. We do not yet have a gauge that can tell us how much less attention the American public pays to political news today compared to the 1970s. A long-term free fall in news interest could therefore be under way, albeit more gradually than some might have expected given the rapid drop-off in attention to network news since the 1980s.

Although the seriousness of the free fall remains unclear, there is no question that audiences for broadcast television news and newspapers—the two most popular news media in the United States—are suffering a long-term and probably irreversible bleed-out. When it will stop and whether less traditional news products will inherit these audiences are questions of some importance to the future of popular governance in the United States. Regardless of what the future holds, one consequence of these long-term trends is already upon us. The loss of audience for any particular news medium undermines that medium's ability to supply the information needs of the audience it manages to hold on to, an unfortunate dynamic that has already taken hold in the newspaper and broadcast news industries.

For example, in March 2003 around six hundred reporters were embedded with American troops to cover the invasion of Iraq. Six months later only about one hundred remained, and by late 2006 the number may have declined to fewer than ten.[34] Security concerns and the logistical difficulties of reporting from Iraq explain part of the decline, but the main reason undoubtedly stems from the lack of widespread audience demand for in-depth news coverage from Iraq. Although popular news interest in the invasion itself was high, no long-term expansion of the network or cable news audiences survived the fall of Baghdad, despite the quickening pace of an organized insurgency that was already apparent by late summer of 2003. Without a sizable audience for Iraq news to attract advertising money, none of the major U.S. news organizations could long afford to keep a large number of reporters stationed there.

Gone are the early days of broadcasting when the evening news was a loss-leader. Back then, the networks chose to burnish their reputations on the quality of their news programs but make their money on entertainment shows. In the United States, mainstream journalism has always been a commercial enterprise that needed to cover its own expenses like any other business, but today the fiscal discipline of the bottom line is more rigidly enforced than in the past. As much as journalists might like to provide in-depth reporting on national and international affairs, the costs involved must ultimately be passed on to their readers and viewers. And if quality reporting on important stories is unable to sustain the attention of a news outlet's target audience, that outlet must find other ways to deliver its target audience to advertisers.

This is why the May 18, 1998, covers of *Time* and *Newsweek* featured the death of singer Frank Sinatra instead of the other big event of that week: India's unanticipated and ominous detonation of five atomic weapons—the first nuclear tests that had been conducted anywhere in the world in nearly a quarter century—an event that immediately precipitated a nuclear arms race in South Asia. It had not escaped the attention of news magazine editors that newsstand sales dropped by as much as 25 percent whenever a foreign news subject was on the cover.[35] The result was a form of journalism that gave profitable audiences the news they wanted. Their way.

In 1969, when nightly news broadcasts were watched by half of all the adults in America, six of ten nightly news stories dealt with national and international issues. Almost thirty years later, the nightly news devoted nearly two-thirds of its stories to topics other than government and foreign affairs.[36] It is no coincidence that recent nightly newscasts have half the ratings as well as half the amount of political coverage compared to newscasts from the Vietnam era. In the 1980s and 1990s news executives began responding to a decades-long erosion of print and broadcast audiences by aggressively retooling news content to feature less-sophisticated and less-demanding political coverage. The emergence of *USA Today* in the early 1980s and the "You News" concept for NBC's *Nightly News* in the mid-1990s were important developments signaling change in the mainstream U.S. news industry. Compared to their respective national competitors, both outlets reduced the number of stories they reported, provided less coverage of politics and current events, and featured more coverage of "news you can use" about personal finances, health, and lifestyle issues.[37] The growing popularity of *USA Today* during the 1980s and the rapid success of the more audience-friendly NBC *Nightly News* in the 1990s began silencing scoffers who had initially dismissed the formats as "McNews" and "News Lite," respectively. The die was cast for a new style of market-driven news reporting for national audiences, and to this day they remain the most popular newspaper and network newscast in the United States.

Audience attrition has led many media outlets to undersupply in-depth reporting of domestic and foreign political news for at least three reasons. First, to the extent that dwindling ratings or circulation numbers are taken as a sign of dissatisfaction with the existing news product, news outlets will attempt to repackage their content to be more attractive to their target audiences. Newspapers and television news traditionally served a steady diet of current events coverage to readers and viewers. If audiences were turning away from the traditional formulas, the losses could perhaps be reversed or at least softened with a less-demanding mix of feature stories and dramatic coverage of crime, disaster, and scandal. When interest is high, news outlets supply. When interest is low, frivolity grows.

Second, although a large segment of the departing news audience leaves because the news is too political, another portion deserts traditional news outlets because they are not covering politics enough.[38] Cable news channels and specialty Internet news outlets have emerged to cater to the tastes of political sophisticates. Because these specialty outlets are able to meet the information preferences of news junkies better than traditional mass-audience outlets, a gradual exodus from network newscasts and daily papers of people who prefer a timely diet of hard news leaves the audiences for traditional outlets relatively less interested in politics and public affairs. Separating the sheep from the goats in this way makes both groups happier, because the distinctive news preferences of each can be served by different types of news products. But an unintended consequence of increasing the diversity of news offerings is to concentrate ever more public affairs reporting into smaller and more specialized news outlets, thereby relieving traditional mass-market television news and newspaper products from the financial burden of having to provide more than a modicum of headline news about the nation and world.

Third, most of the news media's revenue comes from advertising, and the amount of revenue depends largely on audience size. Regardless of whether a share of its old audience is being divided among new competitors or exiting the news market altogether, the result to any given outlet is the same: less money that can be spent on gathering and reporting the news.[39] What typically follows are reductions in the number of newsroom staff; cuts in the number of news bureaus, particularly expensive foreign bureaus; a greater reliance on wire service coverage, which is usually less costly to acquire than sending an outlet's own reporters to cover the same story; and, because airtime can be filled more cheaply with talk than with action, an increased use of talking head and interview formats instead of traditional enterprise and investigative reporting. The inevitable result is greater homogeneity in the content and appearance of news stories reported by competing outlets, and reduced investment in the most essential functions performed by political journalism in democratic societies: gathering facts about important developments affecting the common welfare, reporting those facts in ways that help citizens make sense of the world beyond, and helping citizens hold the government accountable for the choices their leaders make.

Conclusion

In May 2006 a previously unknown singer named Taylor Hicks was propelled to national prominence when he won the hit television show *American Idol*. Two months later, a Zogby poll found that nearly a quarter of Americans could spontaneously name Hicks as the show's most recent winner, but the same poll found that only half as many could identify Samuel Alito as the newest justice on the Supreme Court.[40] On the night of the 9/11 attacks, Nielsen Media Research found that 79.5 million viewers—nearly four in ten American adults—were tuning into any of the eleven broadcast or cable networks that were showing news coverage of the attacks. As impressive as this level of attention seems, about the same number of viewers watched the January 2001 Super Bowl.[41] Indeed, an audience of this size assembles just about every year to watch the Super Bowl.

The lesson to draw from these examples is not that the American public is stupid or intellectually lazy. Instead, these comparisons underscore how politically alert and responsive the American public could be if its interest in national and international news was as great as its interest in popular culture. It is unlikely that most Americans had even heard of the disease anthrax before late September 2001, when several letters containing anthrax spores were mailed to U.S. news organizations and government offices. Yet by early 2002 a national survey found that nine of ten adults not only knew something about the disease, but also could state correctly that the inhaled form was more deadly than the kind found on the skin.[42] It is remarkable that this level of insight occurred at a time when only half of the U.S. public understood that antibiotics do not kill viruses.[43] When the slumbering Leviathan awakes, its capacity for watchfulness can be astonishing.

Different theories of democracy envision different roles for citizens to play, with some limiting citizen involvement to participating in occasional elections and others expecting citizens to deliberate actively and frequently about important matters of public policy.[44] Contrary to popular myth, few theories of democracy require anything like a highly informed citizenry as a precondition for popular rule.[45] But the efficiency and quality of representation is likely to be enhanced under all theories of democracy as citizens become better informed about the actions of their elected representatives and the important public issues confronting the nation.[46]

The more we learn about politics, the closer our political preferences should come to resemble our political interests, and the greater the chance that our votes and voices will properly reward our political leaders for what they have done well and punish them for what they did poorly or left undone. It is the quality of popular judgment underlying the system of rewards and punishments that is threatened by waning levels of interest in public affairs and the resulting undersupply of politically informative news coverage to the attentive audience that remains. The less attention the public routinely pays to the news, the greater the chance that voters will get it wrong on election day by rewarding irresponsible leadership and bestowing punishments on those whose sober and judicious views should have rightly carried the day.

Notes

1. David Held, *Models of Democracy,* 2nd ed. (Stanford: Stanford University Press, 1996); Bernard Manin, *The Principles of Representative Government* (New York: Cambridge University Press, 1997).

2. Ted Brader, *Campaigning for Hearts and Minds: How Emotional Appeals in Political Ads Work* (Chicago: University of Chicago Press, 2006); George E. Marcus, W. Russell Neuman, and Michael MacKuen, *Affective Intelligence and Political Judgment* (Chicago: University of Chicago Press, 2000).

3. Michael X. Delli Carpini and Scott Keeter, *What Americans Know about Politics and Why It Matters* (New Haven: Yale University Press, 1996), 120–122.

4. Scott L. Althaus, *Collective Preferences in Democratic Politics: Opinion Surveys and the Will of the People* (New York: Cambridge University Press, 2003), 207–217.

5. Walter Dean Burnham, *Critical Elections and the Mainsprings of American Politics* (New York: Norton, 1970); Peter F. Nardulli, *Popular Efficacy in the Democratic Era: A Reexamination of Electoral Accountability in the United States, 1828–2000* (Princeton: Princeton University Press, 2005).

6. Project for Excellence in Journalism, "The State of the News Media 2006," available at *www.journalism.org.*

7. Personal income statistics are from the U.S. Department of Commerce's Bureau of Economic Analysis, available at *www.bea.gov/bea/dn/nipaweb/index.asp.* The 188 percent figure is in "chained" 2000 dollars. The growth of per capita disposable income in constant 2000 dollars, which adjusts for inflation but not for the changing price of consumer goods, is 710 percent over the 1970–2000 period.

8. Markus Prior, *Post-Broadcast Democracy: How Media Choice Increases Inequality in Political Involvement and Polarizes Elections* (New York: Cambridge University Press, 2007).

9. Michael Schudson, *The Good Citizen: A History of American Civic Life* (New York: Free Press, 1998); John Zaller, "A New Standard of News Quality: Burglar Alarms for the Monitorial Citizen," *Political Communication* 20, no. 2 (2003).

10. Prior, *Post-Broadcast Democracy.*

11. Pew's question is "How have you been getting most of your news about national and international issues? From television, from newspapers, from radio, from magazines, or from the Internet?" Up to two answers are accepted, and respondents who provide only one are prompted for (but not required to give) a second answer. Pew asks about magazines as a source of national and international news, but because the proportion relying mainly on magazines has never been higher than 10 percent since the question was first asked in 1991, this chapter focuses instead on the more popular sources of public affairs news.

12. These data are from the 2006 Pew Biennial Media Consumption Survey questionnaire reported in Pew Research Center for the People and the Press, "Online Papers Modestly Boost Newspaper Readership: Maturing Internet News Audience Broader than Deep," issued July 30, 2006. Available at *http://people-press.org/reports/display.php3?ReportID=282.*

13. Ratings data for the week of December 18, 2006, are from *http://mediabistro.com.*

14. The author compiled these data from various media sources available from the LEXIS-NEXIS database. Nielsen uses representative national samples of five thousand television households to estimate television viewing trends for all households in the United States. Electronic "people meters" continuously monitor all broadcast television, satellite, cable, and VCR viewing activity for each individual in a household.

15. Nielsen currently publishes ratings in terms of millions of audience members viewing a particular program. According to the 2000 Census, there are 205.05 million persons aged nineteen or older in the United States. Because household television penetration has been nearly universal since before 1980, simply dividing the former by the latter produces a reasonable estimate of the percentage of American adults watching nightly news programs. During the 1990–1991 period, Nielsen reported ratings information using its measure of rating points, in which each point represents 1 percent of American television households viewing a particular program. To create comparable trends for the Persian Gulf crisis, the combined rating points for all three network news broadcasts were multiplied by the mean number of persons aged nineteen or older per U.S. household (1.87, according to the 1990 Census) and then by the number of U.S. households (91.99 million in 1990). This joint product was then divided by the total number of persons aged nineteen or older (181.50 million) to estimate the percentage of adults watching nightly network news programs.

16. These percentages come from comparing the January through April averages for each case.

17. Project for Excellence in Journalism, "The State of the News Media 2006."

18. "Cable News Wars: Behind the Battle for Cable News Viewers—March 2002," *Online NewsHour,* available at *www.pbs.org/newshour/media/cablenews/index.html.*

19. Newspaper Association of America, "Leveraging Newspaper Assets: A Study of Changing American Media Usage Habits, 2000 Research Report," 36. Available at *www .naa.org/marketscope/MediaUsage_2000.pdf.*

20. Daily newspaper readership data for the total U.S. population that are used in this section were compiled from various sources by the Newspaper Association of America and are available at *www.naa.org/ReadershipPages/Research-and-Readership/readership statistics.aspx.*

21. Audit bureau data released by the Newspaper Association of America showed that U.S. daily newspaper circulation in the period from September 31, 2001, through March 31, 2002, was 0.6 percent lower than in the prior six-month period that ended in September 2001. Felicity Barringer, "Some Big Papers Buck Trend of Circulation Drops," *New York Times,* May 7, 2002, C9.

22. Business Analysis and Research Department of the Newspaper Association of America, "Daily Newspaper Section Readership 2006." Available at *www.naa.org/market scope/readership2006/2006_newspaper_section_readership_daily.pdf.*

23. Arbitron National Radio Services, "Radio Today: How America Listens to Radio," 2006 ed. Available at *www.arbitron.com/downloads/NRT_2006.pdf.* Unless otherwise noted, all radio audience data in this section are from Arbitron National Radio Services and available at *www.arbitron.com/national_radio/home.htm.*

24. Arbitron, "Radio's Role During a National Crisis," 2002. Available at *www.arbitron .com/downloads/radio_911.pdf.*

25. Arbitron, "Public Radio Today." Available at *www.arbitron.com/downloads/Public RadioToday06.pdf.* These estimates come from multiplying the drive time average quarterly hour ratings for all public radio programming reported on page 8 of the report (approximately 1.0 percent of persons twelve and older during the morning drive time, and approximately 0.6 percent of persons twelve and older during the afternoon drive time) by the combined 6 a.m. to 10 a.m. shares reported for news/talk, news-classical, news-music, and news-jazz formats (summing to 81.7 percent, found on pages 20, 22, 31, and 37).

26. The 22.2 million figure comes from adding the weekly listener estimates reported by Arbitron for public radio stations broadcasting in news-talk, news-classical, news-music, and news-jazz formats. Source: Arbitron, "Public Radio Today," 2006.

27. National Public Radio audience data were reported in Project for Excellence in Journalism, "The State of the News Media 2006." The Pew survey estimates of NPR's audience were reported in the 2006 Pew Biennial Media Consumption survey, ibid.

28. Vincent Price and John Zaller, "Who Gets the News? Alternative Measures of News Reception and Their Implications for Research," *Public Opinion Quarterly* 57 (1993): 133–164.

29. David Tewksbury, "Exposure to the Newer Media in a Presidential Primary Campaign," *Political Communication* 23, no. 3 (2006): 313–332.

30. David Tewksbury, "The Seeds of Audience Fragmentation: Specialization in the Use of Online News Sites," *Journal of Broadcasting & Electronic Media* 49, no. 3 (2005): 332–348; David Tewksbury, "What Do Americans Really Want to Know? Tracking the Behavior of News Readers on the Internet," *Journal of Communication* 53, no. 4 (2003): 694–710.

31. These percentages were obtained by multiplying the proportion of respondents saying yes to the question, "When you go online do you ever come across news when you may have been going online for a purpose other than to get the news?" with the proportion saying yes to the question: "Do you ever go online to access the Internet or to send and receive email?"

32. David Tewksbury, Andrew J. Weaver, and Brett D. Maddex, "Accidentally Informed: Incidental News Exposure on the World Wide Web," *Journalism & Mass Communication Quarterly* 78, no. 3 (2001): 542.

33. Prior, *Post-Broadcast Democracy*.

34. David Vaina, "The Vanishing Embedded Reporter in Iraq," Project for Excellence in Journalism, 2006. Available at *www.journalism.org/node/2596*.

35. J. F. Hoge Jr., "Foreign News: Who Gives a Damn?" *Columbia Journalism Review* 36 (4) (1997): 48–52; Neil Hickey "Money Lust: How Pressure for Profit Is Perverting Journalism," *Columbia Journalism Review* 37 (4) (1998): 28–36.

36. John Zaller, "A Theory of Media Politics: How the Interests of Citizens, Journalists, and Citizens Shape the News," University of California, Los Angeles, 1999, 47. Available at *www.polisci.ucla.edu/faculty/zaller/media%20politics%20book%20.pdf*.

37. The "You News" concept is explained in Andie Tucher, " 'You News': It's Not Your Father's Newscast Anymore," *Columbia Journalism Review* 97, no. 3 (1997). See also James McCartney, "USA Today Grows Up," *American Journalism Review* 19 (September 1997); and James McCartney, "News Lite, " *American Journalism Review* 19 (June 1997).

38. Thomas Patterson, "Doing Well and Doing Good: How Soft News and Critical Journalism Are Shrinking the News Audience and Weakening Democracy—And What News Outlets Can Do About It," Working paper, Cambridge, Harvard University, 2000.

39. James T. Hamilton, *All the News That's Fit to Sell: How the Market Transforms Information into News* (Princeton: Princeton University Press, 2004); Philip M. Napoli, *Audience Economics: Media Institutions and the Audience Marketplace* (New York: Columbia University Press, 2003); Robert G. Picard, *Media Economics: Concepts and Issues* (Thousand Oaks, Calif.: Sage Publications, 1989).

40. Complete results from the July 2006 Zogby Poll for AOL.com are available at *www.zogby.com/wfAOL%20National.pdf*.

41. Lisa de Moraes, "For an Extraordinary Week, Nielsen Puts the Ratings Aside," *Washington Post*, September 20, 2001, sec. C.

42. Markus Prior, "Political Knowledge after September 11," *PS: Political Science & Politics* 35, no. 3 (2002): 523–529.

43. National Science Foundation, *Science and Engineering Indicators 2002*, Vol. 1 (Washington, D.C.: National Science Board, 2002), chap. 7.

44. C. Edwin Baker, *Media, Markets, and Democracy* (New York: Cambridge University Press, 2002); Jürgen Habermas, "Three Normative Models of Democracy," in *Democracy and Difference: Contesting the Boundaries of the Political*, ed. Seyla Benhabib (Princeton: Princeton University Press, 1996); and Held, *Models of Democracy*.

45. Scott L. Althaus, "False Starts, Dead Ends, and New Opportunities in Public Opinion Research," *Critical Review* 18, no. 1–3 (2006): 75–104.

46. Althaus, *Collective Preferences in Democratic Politics;* Delli Carpini and Keeter, *What Americans Know.*

9 But What Do the Polls Show?

Andrew Kohut

In 1993 the Times Mirror Center, the forerunner of the Pew Research Center, began a series of comprehensive opinion surveys about foreign policy. Called "America's Place in the World," the surveys were conducted every four years. They were aimed at providing policymakers, the press, and the public with an exposition of public opinion on the international issues of the day in the first year of a president's term. Over the years, the surveys have traced the currents in public opinion through the seemingly carefree days of the 1990s when "the United States had no enemies," to the time when public concerns soared following the September 11, 2001, attacks and Americans began a contentious debate about how best to deal with the terrorist threat.

The results of these surveys have been closely followed by the foreign policy community and well covered by the news media. Still, of all the briefings, press conferences, and events associated with the "America's Place in the World" surveys, one meeting in the mid-1990s stands out in my mind. I was introduced to my audience by Theodore Sorenson, once a principal adviser to and speechwriter for President John F. Kennedy. Sorenson remarked in his opening comments, "*Now that we have to consider public opinion* in the conduct of foreign policy, it's worth listening to what Kohut has to say about what his polls show."

I was unsure how to react to such an introduction, but coming from a senior policymaker of another era, it drove home to me quite clearly how much the role of public opinion had changed over the years. Indeed, in my tenures at Gallup, Times Mirror, and Pew, I have observed the growing impact that public opinion has on the course of the nation.

Public opinion has granted presidents permission to go to war, denied them permission, and even given them limited permission. Public opinion has rescued embattled presidents and condemned others. It has welcomed, if not solicited, some major policy changes and rejected others. The views of ordinary Americans have never had a greater say in public policy than in the closing decades of the twentieth century and in the new twenty-first century. Public opinion polls have become a megaphone for the voice of the people, fulfilling George Gallup's dream in the 1930s:

There is a growing conviction that public opinion must be measured. . . . In the democratic community, the attitudes of the mass of the people determine policy. "With public opinion on its side," said Abraham Lincoln in the course of his famous contest with Douglas, "everything succeeds."[1]

Nevertheless, from the start, opinion polls have had many detractors. Today, with polls being both part of the news and the news itself, as Kathleen Frankovic has noted,[2] those criticisms have certainly deepened. But more on that later. First, this chapter describes how opinion polls have come to speak with such a loud voice in American society. Next, it presents a number of case studies that illustrate the role of public opinion in shaping U.S. public policy. Finally, the chapter considers the limits and liabilities of the voice given to the public through polling conducted by and on behalf of the news media.

The Emergence of Modern Polling

As is the case with so many big changes in modern society, many either credit or blame technology for the emergence of public opinion polling. The advent of inexpensive computing and low-cost communications was central to the rise in prominence of polls. As late as the 1960s most public opinion surveys were conducted by personal interviews. Telephone ownership did not become nearly universal until about the mid-1960s, and even at that point "long distance" telephone calls were expensive.

Personal interviewing required that polling organizations maintain national networks of interviewers across the country that carried out their surveys in randomly selected neighborhoods. Questionnaires were mailed to interviewers who would complete their assignments, and then mail them back to the research organizations. The entire procedure took about a month. It included printing the questionnaire, drawing maps for interviewers, mailing out, mailing back, and finally data processing on punch cards and on the slow computers of that era. This was not a quick process in which polls could be carried out and reported in just a few days, as they are now.

In the personal interview era, just a few organizations, notably Gallup and Harris, had the facilities and national field staffs to conduct public opinion polls on politics and other issues for news organizations. In *The Powers That Be*, David Halberstam reports a conversation that outgoing president Lyndon B. Johnson had with incoming vice president Spiro T. Agnew:

"Young man," Johnson said, "we have in this country two television networks, NBC and CBS. We have two newsmagazines, *Newsweek* and *Time*. We have two wire services, AP and UPI. We have two pollsters, Gallup and Harris. We have two big newspapers: the *Washington Post* and the *New York Times*. They are all so damned big they think they own the country."[3]

LBJ was correct for 1968, but things would soon change for the media and the pollsters. National public opinion polls would not long be the sole provenance of two firms. In the early 1970s AT&T began to offer discounted costs for nationwide telephoning on its WATS lines. At the same time, computing became less expensive, faster, and more efficient. These changes ushered in widespread use of nationwide telephone surveys, which were far less expensive than field interviewing and did not require an elaborate infrastructure.

National opinion surveys could now be conducted by any organization that could afford a bank of telephones and had a technique for drawing a random sample of telephone numbers. Survey research blossomed. Political pollsters emerged to conduct surveys for candidates at all levels of government—not just the presidency. And the media, which had relied on Gallup and Harris, could now embrace opinion surveys more fully. Opinion surveys became the work product of news organizations.

The ascendancy of the telephone surveys made it *possible* for the news media and others to conduct polls, but it is fair to say that the turbulence of the late 1960s and early 1970s made it *imperative* that news organizations better understand a nation that was experiencing extraordinary social and political change. The civil rights movement, race riots, the Vietnam War, the antiwar movement, the rise of the counterculture, and the women's movement had changed the country and made its people far harder to understand than the American public of the 1950s.

The public was the story. No one understood that better than Phil Meyer. His pathbreaking book, *Precision Journalism: A Reporter's Introduction to Social Science Methods,* spelled out this idea to news media willing to consider ways to improve their reporting on social changes they found difficult to understand. Meyer starts the book by detailing the major stories that the media got wrong in coverage of the public's reaction to the national turmoil of that era. His examples include the role of antiwar sentiment in the 1968 presidential election, opinions about race following Martin Luther King's assassination and the Watts riots, and views of other major domestic policy reforms.[4]

In each of these cases, Meyer underscored the differences between what reporters were writing and what carefully conducted surveys were showing.

Figure 9.1 Opinion poll mentions in U.S. news and wires

Mentions

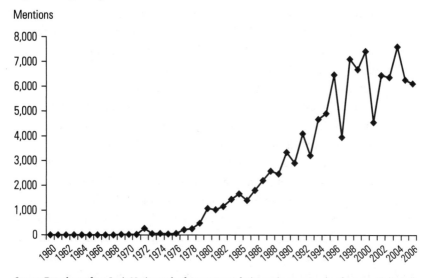

Source: Data drawn from Lexis-Nexis search of newspaper and wire service reports using the term *opinion poll.* We searched newspapers published in the United States and wire services where more than 60 percent of the stories originate in the United States for a total of 463 news sources.

Coverage of the Watts riots emphasized that the upheaval came at a time when relations between whites and blacks were worsening; polling showed just the opposite. Eugene McCarthy's strong showing in the 1968 New Hampshire primary was interpreted as a manifestation of antiwar sentiment.[5] Meyer noted that University of Michigan surveys at the time found that hawks outnumbered doves among McCarthy's supporters. And, although the headlines following the King assassination proclaimed the end of nonmilitancy among blacks, the polling showed more support for King's philosophy, not less.

So conditions were right for the news media to embrace polling: the costs of polling were now bearable, looming social and political changes challenged traditional reporting methods, and a new generation of journalists spurred on by Meyer and others urged the adoption of the methods of social science. And they did (see Figure 9.1). The CBS/*New York Times* poll started regular news surveys in 1975. NBC's first partner was the Associated Press, and it began polling in 1978. The ABC/*Washington Post* poll was launched in 1981. The impact of this on reporting of the findings of opinion polls is quite clear.

It is not an overstatement to say that regular reporting of public opinion polls by the national media put public opinion front and center in politics and policy in a way that had never before been the case. This development is relatively recent. Gallup has been part of the public scene since the 1930s, and Roper and Harris followed in the 1940s and 1960s, respectively, but the intensive and routine coverage of public reactions to major national stories, political or otherwise, is a relatively new phenomenon.

The pioneering independent pollsters did ask a few questions of their national samples about Sen. Joe McCarthy in the 1950s and the Cuban Missile Crisis and civil rights movement in the 1960s. But they were, indeed, just a few questions. Coverage was neither routine nor comprehensive.

President Jimmy Carter's administration was the first to experience full bore the thorough polling scrutiny that has been the rule since. Presidential approval is continuously rated, and measures of opinion are tallied about every major policy initiative and event. Polling covers not only the White House but also Congress and most other national institutions. Whether it is the economy, the budget deficit, health care, the environment, or any number of domestic issues, polls explore and chart public reactions. National security and foreign policy, once the purview of the elites, are now subject to the scrutiny of the American public.

Since the late 1970s, surveys have also set the stage for reporting about new proposals or changes of national course: *The public is ready, restless, or likely resistant to what is coming.* Polls provide tracking of popular reactions: *Public support is holding steady, increasing, or faltering.* And then in the final stages, the surveys provide material for epitaphs: *Popular backing propelled, rescued, or doomed the venture.*

Most important, at all stages, a sense of what the polls are showing affects the perspective of policy makers, political leaders, and the press itself. Polls provide leaders with capital or impoverish them in their efforts to promote policies. Claims of having the public on one's side are the common refrain of all promoters of public policy. Those who can back up their assertions by pointing to poll results find the going easier than leaders who cannot. In turn, news organizations cover policy initiatives differently when programs appear to have popular support compared with when they do not.

Regular public opinion reporting by the national news media has made the voice of the public inescapable. As a result, the public has become a more important player in national affairs over the past three decades. It is not possible to find a major national policy initiative for which polling has not played a significant, even critical, role. When the only public polls were Gallup and Harris, poll results were not nearly as ubiquitous and did not go hand in glove with traditional reporting as they do now. In 1998 Frankovic wrote:

In the past twenty-five years, something fundamental has changed. Polls have become even more important and necessary to news writing and presentation, to the point where their significance sometimes overwhelms the phenomena they are supposed to be measuring or supplementing.[6]

What follows are some well-known cases illustrating the interplay among public opinion—as reported in national opinion surveys—public policy, and politics. Along with other examples, the cases provide a basis for considering how polling has changed relations between the people and the press and the people and their leaders.

The Public Restrains Reagan in Central America

In 1985 Ronald Reagan was riding high. It was indeed "morning in America," and Reagan had been reelected in a landslide. The U.S. economy was on the mend as the misery index receded. But the president, whose policies would later be credited with helping speed the collapse of the Soviet Union, faced a challenge in his own hemisphere from leftist insurgents in Central America. In particular, the rise to power of the Sandinistas in Nicaragua represented an unacceptable threat to regional stability and, according to the administration, U.S. national security.

But the popular president's options in dealing with the problem were severely limited by U.S. public opinion. With the debacle of Vietnam still fresh in their memory, Americans were wary of the president's hard-line approach to the region fearing that it might lead to the engagement of American forces battling insurgents in the jungles of another war-torn country. The public's concerns were apparent in the disparities between Reagan's overall approval rating and his ratings in particular policy areas. In summer 1986 his overall approval rating was 63 percent; by comparison, just 34 percent approved of his handling of Nicaragua.[7] White House polling, conducted by Richard Wirthlin, confirmed the findings of the public polls. Robert Merry, writing for the *Wall Street Journal,* observed:

To Mr. Reagan, the existence of the pro-Soviet Sandinista regime in the Americas is a dangerous threat to regional stability and, eventually, to the U.S. itself.... But the voters and Congress are skittish about U.S. involvement in the jungles of

Central America, largely, it seems, because of their vivid memories of the country's ill-fated involvement in Vietnam.[8]

Turning to the poll conducted by Wirthlin, a longtime supporter of the president, Merry went on to note, "Americans are aware of the Central American problem, don't much like the Sandinistas and consider political instability in the region a serious threat to the U.S. But they don't want to do anything about it."[9]

The Reagan administration's acknowledgment of public opposition to intervention in Nicaragua raised, at least for some, an enduring criticism of the role of public opinion polls: they subvert leadership. Mike Getler and David Ignatius, writing for the *Washington Post*, expressed this opinion: "The soul of Reagan's foreign policy, in this view, is politics rather than ideology. It is a foreign policy of adjustment, a statecraft driven by public-opinion polls as much as by a coherent strategy."[10]

Getler and Ignatius were not alone in charging that the Reagan administration was poll-driven in its conduct of foreign policy. But, unlike most other critics, they pointed to an adverse consequence of the way the White House was coping with its lack of public support. Writing at the time of revelations about the secret mining of Nicaraguan ports, they noted:

These two traits—secrecy and the stress on public relations—have combined to produce the worst aspects of the Reagan approach to foreign policy: its reactive, ill-planned, ad-hoc quality. The administration, fearing a public backlash, has tended to plan its most important policies in secret, without adequate interagency discussion or expert advice.[11]

This was, as we know, a prelude to the exposure of more serious Iran-contra dealings, which cast a shadow over the last three years of Reagan's presidency.

The Public Is Persuaded to Go to War in the Gulf

When Saddam Hussein invaded Kuwait in August 1990, President George H. W. Bush and his administration had forgotten neither the lessons of Vietnam nor of the Iran-contra scandal. Polls showed the public ambivalent about the prospect of using military force to drive the Iraqis out of Kuwait. The news media polls found broad backing for sending troops to Saudi Arabia to protect the oil fields, but public reaction to a deeper involvement was decidedly mixed. In early August 1990 an ABC poll found the public opposed to bombing Iraqi military targets.[12] During that same period, a Gallup poll showed the public divided about whether the Gulf was worth fighting for.[13] Bush, however, masterfully took public opinion head on and built support for going to war.

Over the course of the subsequent six months a huge political debate raged, punctuated by regular reports on the shifting sentiments of the American public in news media polling reports. In particular, the polls monitored the president's success in communicating what was at stake in the Gulf region. A report Robert Toth and I wrote for the Aspen Institute in 1994 recapitulated the mounting public support for military action recorded by various polls:

[I]n the first week of August, a CBS/*New York Times* poll found the public divided by a margin of 50 percent yes, to 41 percent no, about whether George Bush had "explained clearly what's at stake and why he is sending troops to Saudi Arabia." However, by as early as the first week in September, no fewer than 77 percent in an ABC/*Washington Post* survey said that they did have a clear idea on the matter. Further, at no point during the buildup and debate about military action did Bush's approval ratings for handling the crisis fall below 55 percent.[14]

The polls also provided a track record of the impact of the two most significant steps the administration took to secure public approval. First, by seeking and obtaining a UN Security Council vote that set a deadline for Iraqi withdrawal from Kuwait, the administration transformed public opinion about the use of force. As the report observed, the Gallup Organization polls did the best job in tracking the impact of the UN decision on American public opinion. "Prior to the decision, 51 percent of the American public opposed going to war against Iraq if it did not meet the deadline. After the decision, majorities favored going to war every time Gallup asked the question."[15]

Just as Gallup's CNN/ *USA Today* poll captured the impact of multilateral support on American attitudes, so the ABC/*Washington Post* poll provided a clear record of the extent to which Bush's desire to seek congressional approval bolstered the argument for going to war rather than waiting for economic sanctions to discourage Saddam. Using a daily tracking poll over the course of the congressional debate, the poll found the percentage of respondents favoring the use of force immediately or within a month rose from 48 percent during the January 2–6, 1991, period to 58 percent by January 13.[16]

Ultimately, the Gulf War enjoyed public support because it was brief and ended well. But it also illustrated the extent to which leadership could address and educate a public concerned about the use of force in an era in which the legacy of Vietnam was still much in evidence. And it showed the extent to which the media's reporting of public opinion served as the backdrop for coverage of the debate about when and whether to go war.

The Public Saves President Clinton's Job

Of all the opinions that polls have tracked in the modern era, none has been more remarkable than President Bill Clinton's approval ratings rising on the news of allegations that he had carried on an affair with a White House intern, Monica Lewinsky. A Pew Research Center poll in mid-January 1998 found that 61 percent of its respondents approved of the way the president was handling his job.[17] Two weeks later, Clinton's ratings spiked to 71 percent, reflecting public outrage over the way the media had prejudged Clinton's guilt.[18] The same trend was recorded in Gallup and other national surveys. The Pew poll analysis found the public more discontented with the president's accusers in the news media than upset by Clinton's alleged misbehavior.

Sympathy for a president beleaguered by a press perceived as biased and inaccurate is an important element in Clinton's support.... Strikingly, 69% of Pew's respondents think that most reporters presume Clinton is guilty of perjury, while only 9% of the public think this is definitely true.

In an unusual twist, the controversy has broadened Clinton's base, at least for now. Fully 57% of Americans who now approve of the president, but had not prior to the controversy, are Republicans and Independents. An equal share of these new supporters (59%) say they do not like Clinton personally, but do like his policies. These new supporters are not alone in drawing a distinction between Clinton the man and Clinton the president: 39% of Americans like both the man and his policies; 30% like his policies but dislike him; while 23% like neither. Put another way, 53% of Americans do not like the president personally, but 70% like his policies.[19]

The public's unexpected rallying to Clinton's side led to a transformation of the Washington establishment's judgment of his political viability. Before news of Clinton's polling boost, political insiders had all but written him off. Public support for the president allowed, if not encouraged, congressional Democrats to rally to his side. On the PBS *Newshour*, on January 30, Paul Gigot and Jim Lehrer discussed the changed political climate.

Paul Gigot, *Wall Street Journal:* Well, the view inside Washington this last week was that he was Andrew Johnson on his way out to impeachment. This week he's Abraham Lincoln about to get up on Mt. Rushmore. Neither is right. What is true this week was also true last week. Two processes are in motion. One was legal.... And the other is the media, where it's—you know, a lot of publications and broadcast media ... throwing in a lot of resources. ...

Jim Lehrer: Huge backlash against them on that too as we're—according to the polls.[20]

The impact of Clinton's standing in the polls along with growing antipathy toward the president's accusers were also potent factors in the impeachment debate and the broader politics of that contentious midterm year. The *Washington Post*'s Guy Gugliotta captured the interplay between parties and public.

And finally, say House lawmakers and aides, an inquiry of impeachment will likely depend as much on the tide of public opinion as it will on the case against Clinton. "Go ahead, make my day," said Rep. John Conyers Jr. (Mich.), ranking Democrat on the Judiciary Committee, where any impeachment inquiry would begin.

"A foolhardy attempt to impeach an overwhelmingly popular and successful president on inconsistent and highly suspect circumstantial evidence is one way to ensure a Democratic congressional majority next November," Conyers said.

Indeed, surveys continue to demonstrate unprecedented levels of popularity for Clinton since the scandal broke. A *Wall Street Journal*/NBC News poll last weekend showed him with a towering 79 percent approval rating. More typical was the latest *Newsweek* poll, which found a 66 percent approval, with 49 percent saying the president shouldn't be impeached even if he told Lewinsky to lie about the alleged affair.[21]

So it went for the rest of the year. Official Washington was obsessed with a scandal that rolled off the backs of the American people. The public stood by Clinton through each chapter of the saga: his grand jury testimony, his admission of lying, the revelations of the Starr report, and ultimately the Republican vote to impeach him. He ended the year with a 71 percent approval rating. His party actually picked up eight seats in the House of Representatives—an unusual occurrence for a second-term president, let alone one about to be impeached.

The subsequent Senate trial attracted little public attention and had virtually no impact on opinions of the president or the state of the nation. Writing at the conclusion of this chapter in history, Ron Brownstein of the *Los Angeles Times* summed it up:

No one is listening. Like cannons laying siege to a stubbornly resistant fort, the Washington media barraged Americans for a year with the message that they ought to be outraged about this case. Despite the fusillade, public opinion never wavered from the conclusion it reached within weeks of the scandal's disclosure: Clinton's behavior, while inexcusable, was not a sufficient cause to remove him from office.

From the start, most Americans have viewed this as a political rather than legal or moral confrontation. . . . There's a message larger than hypocrisy in that pattern. What it shows is that the use of ethical allegations has become so integral to the parties' political strategies that the public and the participants now tend to view these charges principally as a form of partisan warfare.[22]

It is not an exaggeration to say that these judgments saved Clinton's presidency. And, it is inconceivable to think that public opinion could have had such an impact in an era prior to the emergence of the media polls.

The Public Changes Its Mind about Privatizing Social Security

In December 2004 President George W. Bush proclaimed that he was "armed with political capital" that he had earned in his reelection victory, and he planned to spend some of it to reform the Social Security system. The main idea was to give younger workers the option of depositing part of their Social Security contributions into private accounts. The polls at the time indicated that the president might well be successful. Americans for years had given high priority to steps to secure the Social Security system, and polls found broad conceptual support for the idea of allowing younger workers to have a private accounts option.

Anticipating opposition from many quarters, including the powerful AARP, the president announced he would personally lead a campaign to ensure public backing. As the White House revved up on the issue, however, the public's response grew more negative. A March 2005 Pew survey noted:

President George W. Bush is losing ground with the public in his efforts to build support for private retirement accounts in Social Security. Despite Bush's intensive campaign to promote the idea, the percentage of Americans who say they favor private accounts has tumbled to 46% in Pew's latest nationwide survey, down from 54% in December and 58% in September. Support has declined as the public has become increasingly aware of the president's plan. More than four-in-ten (43%) say they have heard a lot about the proposal, nearly double the number who said that in December (23%).[23]

The reaction of the Bush administration to the feedback from the polls was a lack of reaction. The president continued to promote the plan in meetings across the country. As a result, growing numbers of Americans became aware of the idea, fewer supported it, and more expressed overall disapproval for Bush. He was spending his political capital, but not getting much for it.

By May the *Washington Post*'s Peter Baker was writing the first drafts of the epitaph of this chapter of Bush's second term, noting the weakened public support for the private accounts idea observed in Pew polls:

Bush ignores the bad news and keeps hopping across the country on Air Force One, betraying no fear of failure. "I think we're going to get something done," he said Thursday. "I really do. I think the American people understand we've got a problem."

Still, the half-empty press charter and filing center Thursday spoke to the dwindling news media interest. None of the networks sent its regular White House correspondent. *USA Today,* the *Washington Times* and other papers that usually cover presidential trips saw no reason to cover this one. Even some White House aides weary of the barnstorming privately roll their eyes and groan at the notion of yet another Social Security trip.[24]

The administration's continued push on this issue in the face of public opposition resulted in its first setback of the second term. Moreover, it also began a process in which the public reconsidered Bush more generally. His personal favorable ratings tumbled, and the percentage of people regarding Bush as a strong, trustworthy leader who could get things done declined dramatically. By ignoring public response to an important issue, Bush set in motion a climate of opinion about him that would feed into public reactions to other policies. As Jim VandeHei and Peter Baker observed in a September 2005 *Washington Post* article, the spillover included attitudes toward the administration's Iraq war plan, which had been losing support even among Republicans, and its handling of the aftermath of Hurricane Katrina. The *Post* quoted conservative commentator Bill Kristol, editor of the *Weekly Standard,* as saying, "The negative effect of the Social Security [campaign] is underestimated. Once you make that kind of mistake, people tend to be less deferential to your decisions."[25]

Lessons and Limits

These cases should not be viewed as a celebration of the power of public opinion or the importance of polls. Rather, they illustrate the extent to which public views have played a central role in the course of national affairs since the 1980s. They also provide an opportunity to consider how the emergence of an empowered public has altered the relationship both between the people and the press and the people and its leaders.

As to the people and the press—or, more broadly, the media—the polls have made clear in reactions to the Clinton case, as in many other instances, how great a capacity the public has for ignoring the media. In the Clinton-Lewinsky episodes, press condemnations and pronouncements that the president was finished were flatly rejected. The consequence was not worsened opinions of Clinton, but backlash against the media and the president's Republican prosecutors.

The Clinton episode is certainly not an isolated incident of public opinion polls coming in with a different verdict from the one proclaimed by the media. One stunning turnabout occurred in the 1988 presidential campaign, when candidate Bush picked Dan Quayle as his running mate. The press let out a hoop and a holler from the convention in New Orleans, predicting that the junior senator from Indiana's reputation as a "lightweight" and his National Guard service during the Vietnam era would doom Bush's chances of winning the fall election. The polls came in quickly and in unison—they said yes, the public did not have a high regard for Quayle, but his presence on the ticket made not a whit of difference to potential support for Bush's candidacy.

Another high-stakes example of the public ignoring press exhortations occurred in 1995 following the Republican takeover of Congress. While the media, and the political community more generally, were extolling the new House Speaker Newt Gingrich's political success and hyping how conservative the country had turned, the polls came in very quickly to say *wait—this is not the case.* We voted against the Democrats. We did not vote for undermining the school lunch program, shutting down the Department of Education, or weakening the Environmental Protection Agency, and the like.

Gingrich was going too far, too fast, for the public's tastes. Public opinion polls were the first to reveal this truth, and they did so at a time when the media were still enthralled with Gingrich's political genius. So, although polling has done what Phil Meyer wanted in the 1970s in providing the press with a more comprehensive and accurate portrayal of public opinion, at critical junctures it also serves as reality check for the media when they prematurely and inaccurately pronounce what conventional wisdom is emanating from the American public.

But polling has played an even more important role in national affairs by illuminating and specifying the complex relationship between the people and their leaders. Consider President Reagan's case. The public liked him personally and approved of many of his policies, but that did not mean it was willing to follow him everywhere he might want to go. There were clear limits to how far the public trust extended even to such a popular president as Reagan. In another era, with much less polling available, those limits might not have been as clear as they were in the 1980s.

Time and again, the polls have illustrated that at no point does the public suspend judgment of its leaders. In the Clinton years, the public gave its assent to many major policies, including quiet approval of welfare reform and grudging approval to NAFTA (North American Free Trade Agreement). Yet the polls also illustrated the public's capacity to ultimately reject a major reform proposal even though it addressed an area of great concern. In September 1993 when the Clinton health care plan was first announced, the polls initially found at least tepid support for it. But ultimately the public soured on a managed competition proposal that appeared too complicated and injected too large a dose of government into the health care system. Public reactions changed from cautious enthusiasm to strong rejection over a six-month period as the public learned more or, at least, heard more.

The case of G. H. W. Bush's marshalling of public opinion during the buildup to the Gulf War reminds us that the public responds to leadership—give people a rationale for national sacrifice by seeking international and congressional endorsements, and they will follow. But it also reminds us that leaders cannot own public support; they can only rent it. Bush had the highest approval ratings of any president in polling history in March 1991, yet he lost a bid for reelection eighteen months later.

More recently, George W. Bush's experience with Social Security reminds us that although a president may have the bully pulpit and a nation that responds to leadership, there is a serious risk to ignoring public opposition to policy issues that engage the citizenry. Bush not only lost backing for his privatization proposal, he severely undermined the public's confidence in him. As Bill Kristol noted, the interaction with the public over the Social Security plan engendered broader doubts about the president's abilities and judgments.[26]

This effect came home most dramatically in a Pew survey in spring 2005 that showed public opposition to proposals with Bush's name specifically attached to them, even when the public favored their thrust. For example, the poll found broad support for Bush's suggestion of limiting the growth of Social Security benefits for wealthy and middle-income retirees, while keeping the current system intact for lower-income people. By a margin of 53 percent to 36 percent the public liked the idea—that is, as long as the plan did not have the president's name on it. When Pew tested it as a "Bush proposal," public reaction to the same idea was quite different: 45 percent in favor, 43 percent opposed.[27]

The severity of the backlash against Bush in response to the Social Security proposal may well have resulted from how doggedly he pushed a program that seemed wrongheaded to ordinary Americans. The Bush/Rove strategy of hard campaigning for public support worked in the years immediately after the September 11, 2001, attacks, when Americans were more favorably disposed to the administration, as well as in the 2004 presidential election campaign when his opponent, Sen. John Kerry, served as a foil. In 2005, however, with another policy floundering that Bush stubbornly promoted—the war in Iraq—the polls recorded the unraveling of public confidence in the administration that ultimately led to its party losing control of the Congress one year later.

t us consider what can be concluded about public opinion itself in
era. Yes, through media polls, public opinion has become an
t factor in national affairs. As we have shown, it has a direct bear-
ons between the people and the media and between the people and
. But, what inferences can be drawn about the nature of the role of
public opinion in national affairs, as a consequence?

First, the public plays a passive, not active role in shaping public policy. The polls show assent or opposition to policies that the media know or suspect are on the agenda of national leaders. For any number of reasons, the news media are unlikely to conduct polls on policy options that are not under current consideration. One reason is they do not want to be accused of manufacturing news through polling. Even so, this is one of the frequent complaints about civic journalism, which is primarily concerned with local affairs. But polling that asks ordinary citizens about policy options they have not heard about often produces dubious results. Polls provide a good sounding board for public reactions, but they are not a fount of specific suggestions for public policy.

Second, polling has influenced the techniques and strategies of leadership, rather than hamstrung leaders. Coping with what the polls show about public opinion is one of the things that leaders now have to do. Yes, previous generations of leaders could not ignore public opinion altogether; certainly not on the biggest questions of the day. FDR knew he had to bring the public around to enter World War II. But such instances were the exception, not the rule. Harry Truman did not have to worry about constant reminders that he lacked public support for the Marshall Plan or the Berlin airlift or other early cold war policies. In four years (1950–1953), the Gallup poll asked only 135 questions about Korea. In contrast, Gallup has asked 1,021 questions about Iraq in three and a half years. And that is just what Gallup has asked—not to mention all of the other public polls that did not exist in the early 1950s.[28]

Modern leaders cannot avoid public opinion as measured in the polls. They need to know how to use polls or they end up being used by them, to quote historian Garry Wills.[29] In some cases, they are successful, as was G. H. W. Bush during the buildup to and execution of the Gulf War. In other instances they are not, as shown by the younger Bush's handling of Social Security reform.

In addition, the registration of public support or lack of it becomes an issue in itself. Backers of President Clinton in 1998 could point to public opinion polls to show how wrongheaded Republicans in Congress were when it came to attempting to remove the president from office because of his affair with

Monica Lewinsky. At almost the same time, the Clinton administration had a public relations problem with the findings of polls showing lack of support for the interventions it would undertake in the Balkans and Haiti.

Third, although the prominence of polls gives greater voice to the people, other competing voices can still trump public opinion or, at a minimum, tone down the impact of what the polls are showing. A notable example is found in the general public's consistent calls for greater gun control. After the Columbine school shooting, support for greater restrictions reached a crescendo.[30] Yet, broad public opinion was no match for the power of the National Rifle Association. The NRA can marshal voting support for candidates of its choice far more effectively than can supporters of gun control, despite their far larger potential constituency. Similarly, public opposition to free trade is often blunted by effective lobbying by business interests, which in the modern era are often more effective than labor unions and other like-minded groups.

Fourth, the great empowerment of public opinion raises questions about the potential for manipulation. The American public is noted for the limited attention it pays to public affairs.[31] Critics of the public's judgments charge that an ill-informed public is easily pushed and pulled by advocates. For example, some supporters of the Clinton health care plan would argue that the public change of heart on the proposal was not a result of learning, but a consequence of an opposition media campaign that scared the American public into opposition.

It is certainly not unreasonable to think that the public is susceptible to undue persuasion on occasion, but there is a long history of failed attempts to manipulate public opinion. Further, scholars Benjamin Page and Robert Shapiro found considerable evidence that, on the big questions of the day, public opinion is stable and rational.[32] The work of political scientist Samuel Popkin and others on the concept of "low information rationality" may further assuage fears about the public's aptitude for judgment.[33] Perhaps the best way to think about public opinion and its relationship to politics and policymaking is that the American public is typically short on facts, but often long on judgment.

To conclude, by adopting polling, the news media not only improved their reporting, as Meyer urged long ago, but also they fashioned a tool that has empowered the press and given it a source of information useful in planning and anticipating news coverage.[34] Another unintended consequence has been to give greater voice to the American public in national affairs. In so doing, the media have increased the chances that broad public sentiments can influence national affairs.

Notes

1. George Gallup and Saul Forbes Rae, *The Pulse of Democracy* (New York: Simon and Schuster, 1940).

2. Kathleen Frankovic, "Public Opinion and Polling," in *The Politics of News: The News of Politics*, ed. Doris Graber, Denis McQuail, and Pippa Norris (Washington, D.C.: CQ Press, 1998).

3. David Halberstam, *The Powers That Be* (New York: Knopf, 1979), 596.

4. Philip Meyer, *Precision Journalism: A Reporter's Introduction to Social Science Methods* (Bloomington: Indiana University Press, 1979), 1–3.

5. Ibid., 1.

6. Frankovic, "Public Opinion and Polling," 156.

7. Gallup Organization survey, July 11–14, 1986, based on in-person interviews with a national sample of 1,539 adults.

8. Robert Merry, "Reagan's Foreign Policy Gaffes on Nicaragua," *Wall Street Journal*, April 24, 1985.

9. Ibid.

10. David Ignatius and Michael Getler, "Reagan's Foreign Policy: Where's the Rest of It?" *Washington Post*, November 16, 1986.

11. Ibid.

12. ABC News/*Washington Post* survey, August 8, 1990, based on telephone interviews with a national sample of 769 adults.

13. Gallup Organization survey, August 23–26, 1990, based on telephone interviews with a national sample of 1,010 adults.

14. Andrew Kohut and Robert C. Toth, "The People, the Press, and the Use of Force," The Aspen Strategy Group, August 14–19, 1994, Aspen, Colo. (Washington, D.C.: The Aspen Institute, 1994).

15. Ibid.

16. Ibid., 142.

17. Pew Research Center for the People and the Press survey, "Spending Favored over Tax Cuts or Debt Reduction," January 23, 1998.

18. Pew Research Center for the People and the Press survey, "Popular Policies and Unpopular Press Lift Clinton Ratings," February 6, 1998.

19. Ibid.

20. Paul Gigot, interview, *The NewsHour with Jim Lehrer*, Public Broadcasting Service, January 30, 1998.

21. Guy Gugliotta, "Impeachment Inquiry Discussed in House; Leaders Consider Logistics of Probe but Link Decision with Caveat on Stronger Evidence," *Washington Post*, February 10, 1998.

22. Ronald Brownstein, "National Perspective with Impeachment Book Closed; Here's What We've Learned So Far," *Los Angeles Times*, February 15, 1999.

23. Pew Research Center for the People and the Press survey, "Bush Failing in Social Security Push," March 2, 2005.

24. Peter Baker, "Bush Continues Social Security Campaign; Polls Show President's Roadshow Failing to Drive Up Support for his Plan," *Washington Post*, May 20, 2005.

25. William Kristol, quoted in Jim VandeHei and Peter Baker, "President Struggles to Regain Pre-Hurricane Swagger," *Washington Post*, September 24, 2005.

26. Ibid.

27. Pew Research Center for the People and the Press survey, "Economy, Iraq Weighing Down Bush Popularity," May 19, 2005.

28. Gallup question numbers come from a Roper Center for Public Opinion Research Ipoll search of Gallup surveys, between the identified dates. Terms searched were *Korea* and *Iraq*.

29. Garry Wills, "Read Polls, Heed America," *New York Times Magazine,* November 6, 1994, 49.

30. Andrew Kohut, "Gore, Bush and Guns," *New York Times,* May 12, 2000.

31. Pew Research Center for the People and the Press survey, "The Age of Indifference," June 28, 1990.

32. Benjamin I. Page and Robert Y. Shapiro, *The Rational Public: Fifty Years of Trends in Americans' Policy Preferences* (Chicago: University of Chicago Press, 1992).

33. Samuel L. Popkin, *The Reasoning Voter: Communication and Persuasion in Presidential Campaigns* (Chicago: University of Chicago Press, 1991), 9.

34. Frankovic, "Public Opinion and Polling."

Section IV   The Changing Context of Political News

*transformation from
loss leader to profit center*

10 The Challenges of Public Functions and Commercialized Media

Robert G. Picard

We expect a great deal of media companies. We expect them to inform us about our communities, the nation, and the world. We expect them to serve public interests by creating the means for the aspirations and concerns of citizens to be conveyed and acted upon in society. We expect them to self-finance their operations through commercial activities. We expect them to behave without self-interest. We expect them not to disappoint us. They often do.

The roots of that disappointment can be found in ourselves and an all-too-often uncritical belief that that the market system will produce the media products and services society wants and needs. This belief emanates from a general satisfaction with competitive markets for other goods and services and from the underlying conviction that too much government involvement in society—especially in the media—is undesirable and harmful.

This environment creates significant challenges in producing public benefits from media because markets are not necessarily free or fair, and they cannot produce beneficial outcomes for all individuals. Moreover, media are not like other products. In our ideal notion of media, they perform many tasks necessary for the functioning of mass society: they convey and create culture and norms of society; they help us define and create our individual, professional, community, and national identities; they apprise us of events and developments of significance; and they link us to our political representatives and monitor their performance. These public functions of media support social cohesiveness, democratic activities, and public education. They also create tensions between the desire to ensure that media actually do serve these functions and the belief in private media and limitations on government ability to require less self-interested behaviors from media companies.

Those tensions combine with the competitive and commercialized nature of media markets to create an environment in which it is difficult for media to

211

fulfill expectations of public service. These include: providing a wide range of information, opinions, and perspectives on developments that affect the lives of citizens; mobilizing members of the public to participate in and carry out their responsibilities in society; helping citizens identify with and participate in the lives of their community, their state, and the nation; serving the needs and representing the interests of widely differing social groups; and ensuring that government, economic, or social constraints do not narrow information and ideas.

The conflict between public functions and private media creates a paradox because commercially funded media cannot pursue economic self-interests without harming their public service roles.[1] Because market-based media face levels of competition never before experienced and their markets are more unstable than in the past century, and because they operate in a system in which the primary driver is self-interest and heavy commercialization of content, the movement away from serving public functions is clearly evident and is breeding discontent among social observers and citizens. Understanding that conflict and finding appropriate ways to respond are crucial if society is to deal with the paradox of public functions and commercialized media content.

Market Changes Drive Media Behavior

The history of market-based media reveals a strong relationship between market stability and media behavior. When conditions are stable and companies are financially secure, they tend to exhibit more willingness to attend to public functions than when conditions are turbulent and their financial performance is poor.

The sensationalism and lurid behavior of the penny press at the end of the nineteenth century, for example, was driven by an industry financially dependent upon circulation income and vigorous competition among papers to attract readers. That dependence increased until the 1920s when extreme levels of cutthroat competition led to the kind of chaotic and unprincipled media behavior immortalized in Ben Hecht and Charles McArthur's 1931 play *The Front Page*. The market ultimately produced a shakeout in competitors, which—combined with the need to advertise finished consumer goods—improved the financial situations of publishers and helped settle the market; it also supported the development of professionalism in journalism and newspapers. During the second half of the twentieth century, the rise of branded consumer goods tripled advertising income (in real terms) for publishers making them less dependent upon circulation income and more willing to resources in news coverage.[2]

Television news and public affairs coverage operated in a unique si when it developed in the 1950s and 1960s because network news was r of the *business* of television. Large amounts of money were being made from entertainment, and the time devoted to pursuing public functions was considered a cost of broadcasting and a loss leader. Ultimately, developments in communications technologies altered how news was gathered and broadcast, leading the networks to expand their broadcasts and lure large audiences from news in print. By the 1970s advertisers were finding the network evening news broadcasts highly attractive, and the news became financially beneficial to the networks. The success of network news served as a template for local stations, which expanded their news operations significantly, duplicating the financial benefits that had accrued to networks. At leading local stations, news broadcasts became the largest source of revenue.

The increasing competition between network and local news, between local stations, and between broadcast and cable channels that developed in the late 1980s and early 1990s reduced the profitability of all television news operations, creating instability, heavy commercialization of content, and movement away from serious public affairs content. The stresses of the television environment were explored in Sydney Lumet's 1976 film *Network*, which explored the impact of ratings on news and news personnel, a problem that journalists and social observers have explored.[3]

Today, the media environment for print and television news is characterized by even more market complexity and market turbulence than before.[4] Market complexity results from the greater amount of effort and difficulty media companies face operating in the environment, and turbulence results from the instability and the lack of clear direction in media markets that is creating uncertainty and business risks. Because their survival is at stake, media companies respond by placing greater emphases on their self-interests than on the public interests.

Five trends drive the pressures the media experience: media abundance, audience fragmentation and polarization, product portfolio development, the eroding strength of media companies, and a power shift in the communications process.

Abundance is seen in the dramatic rise in media types and units of media. The growth of media supply is far exceeding the growth of consumption in terms of both time and money. The average number of pages in newspapers tripled in the twentieth century; the number of over-the-air television channels has quadrupled since the 1960s—supplemented by an average of about fifty-six cable channels in the average home. In addition, there are four times as many magazines available as in 1970s, and newly created and stored information is growing at a rate of 30 percent a year. We used to think of competition among newspapers or competition among television channels, but this media abundance has fostered competition not only among media but also between media and other leisure time activities such as sports, concerts, and socializing at cafés and bars.

The abundance has created fragmentation and polarization of the audience because people are spreading their media use across more channels and titles (newspapers, magazines, and Web sites).[5] The plethora of choices produces extremes of use and nonuse among available channels and titles. In television, for example, individuals tend to focus most use on three or four channels. Increasing channel availability does not create an equal amount of channel use. For example, if twenty channels are received in a household, the average viewed is five. When fifty channels are received, the average rises to twelve, and if one hundred channels are received, the average viewed by all members of the household is only sixteen.[6] Advertisers understand this development and have responded by spreading their expenditures and paying less for smaller audiences. The audience-use changes mean that competition is no longer institutionally and structurally defined but is being defined by the time and money audiences/consumers spend with media, and the competitive focus is now on the attention economy and the experience economy.

The difficulties faced by individual units of media have led the parent companies to create and operate portfolios of media products.[7] This response occurs because declining average return per unit makes owning a single media product problematic. The portfolios are efforts to reduce risk and obtain economies of scale and scope. These portfolios can increase return if they involve efficient operations and joint cost savings.

Despite the growth of portfolios and large media companies, their strength is eroding. Today media companies rarely are in the top one hundred companies in the United States or in the top five hundred worldwide. Moreover, the reach of these companies is declining, even though they have grown bigger. Each has less of the viewers', readers', and listeners' attention than in the past, and their difficult strategic position concerns many investors. As a result, media companies are struggling with their major investors, and all major media companies fear they may become takeover targets.

Underscoring all of these problems is a fundamental power shift in communications. The media space was previously controlled by media companies; today, however, consumers are gaining control of what has become a demand market. This shift is apparent in the financing of contemporary initiatives in cable and satellite, TV and radio, audio and video downloading, digital television, and mobile media, which is based on a consumer payment model. Today, for every dollar spent on media by advertisers, consumers spend three.[8] Advertisers are cutting back on traditional types of advertising—already only about one-third of their total marketing expenditures—and spending their money on personal marketing, direct marketing, sponsorships, and cross-promotion.

The result is that media today experience commercial pressures that are reducing their willingness to invest significantly in news and public affairs content and that they commercialize the content they provide to an extent that—although it attracts some audience—it only marginally serves public functions. News and public affairs choices and presentations are affected by an emphasis on their entertainment value rather than their value as information and for provoking thought. News focuses on conflict, accidents, deviance, and celebrity, often presented in a sensational and salacious manner. Much public affairs programming has degenerated into forums for sound bites and polarized attacks on participants with other views.

Commercial Media and Concentration

Media companies tend to face less direct competition than other types of businesses, and despite complaints of concentration,[9] U.S. media are far less concentrated than media industries in Europe[10] and other parts of the world. Nevertheless, many observers are concerned about the growth of media company portfolios by their increased ownership of multiple titles and channels and their operations of multiple types of media in individual communities. The trend toward concentration has led to calls for greater regulation of ownership.

It needs to be recognized, however, that the U.S. government's ability to regulate concentration and media ownership differs between print media and electronic media. The U.S. Constitution limits government regulation of print media, and only laws and regulations that apply to all businesses or individuals are permitted. The government may not make special laws regarding print media ownership and concentration.

The government, however, has the ability to create specific laws and policies for electronic media, and to apply other laws and regulations that apply to all businesses or individuals. It has done so to varying degrees since it began regulating broadcasting at the beginning of the twentieth century. Since the 1980s significant policy shifts have occurred in electronic and telecommunication regulation, and they have affected concentration and commercialization.

Congress and regulatory agencies, most notably the Federal Communications Commission (FCC) and the Federal Trade Commission (FTC), are responsible for creating national communications policies. When conflicts arise between Congress and regulatory agencies, or someone alleges that the policies or developments in the industries violate other laws or the Constitution, courts make decisions regarding the conflicts and charges.

The history of the development of telecommunications and electronic media in the United States differs from that in other Western nations in that U.S. media have been commercial since their inception. Because of geographic and demographic distribution factors and the absence of a strong federal government with significant taxing ability during the early development of modern media and their regulation, government policy typically allowed private monopolies or oligopolies in telecommunications and broadcasting as a means of encouraging investment.

As a result, economic concentration and—in some cases—concentration of ownership was evident in these industries from the start. Since the 1980s, however, the government, with the backing of both major political parties, began efforts to reduce the power of that concentration and introduce more competition. In the process, the old monopolies in telecommunications were ended, and the government began to alter its regulation of broadcasting and cable services.

Four principles traditionally guided the regulation of electronic media: (1) protecting military and intelligence interests in electronic communications; (2) protecting the financial investments of existing companies; (3) locating media in as many cities as possible; and (4) increasing the media units in each market to the extent that existing companies' survival was not threatened.

The first principle stemmed from the development of broadcast communication for naval use and its initial regulation in the United States by naval authorities. The second principle stemmed from the lobbying by early communication companies to gain regulation that reduced risk in investing in radio and then television. The third principle emerged from the desire to create localism in electronic media to ensure that local as well as national interests were served. The final principle was based in the belief that competition was good for both the economic market and the market for ideas.

These principles stood as the foundation of electronic communication regulation for most of the twentieth century, but since the 1980s they have undergone significant change as the approach to regulation changed. Today, four contemporary principles are apparent: protecting military and intelligence interests in electronic communications; increasing competition among existing companies; allowing the market to determine where and what services are provided; and allowing the market to determine the number of media units available in each market.

When the lists of traditional and contemporary principles of regulation are compared, what becomes immediately evident are the greater reliance on the market to make choices and the rejection of government as the arbitrator of what services should be provided in which locations. The policy changes significantly loosened government control and protectionism of existing companies and helped spur the rise in media outlets, which in turn has produced not only lower concentration levels than in the past but also competition previously unknown in the industries.

Those developments led to perhaps the most sweeping policy changes in the industry. The Telecommunications Act of 1996 permits local telephone companies to provide long distance service when they face competition in the local market and permits long distance companies to enter the local market at that time; permits phone companies to offer video services but not buy cable systems in their markets; permits cable companies to provide local phone services; permits broadcasters to own TV stations that reach 35 percent of all viewers (up from 25 percent); permits a party to own no more than five radio stations in a market of fourteen or fewer stations, or eight in a market of forty-five or more stations; and provides that local TV-newspaper-cable system cross-ownership prohibitions may be reviewed on a case-by-case basis.[11]

The Telecommunications Act was primarily intended to introduce more competition into telephone and cable services and to rationalize a great deal of separate regulation that had been the responsibility of several different regulatory agencies, Congress, and the courts. One result, however, is that the law has allowed some mergers and acquisitions not previously permitted. It was believed that the increased concentration would be fully offset by increased competition, but developments since 1996 have not borne out that prediction.

Although the trends in policy and the Telecommunications Act are to remove government control, they do not exempt mergers and acquisitions from antitrust concerns. Because the size of many mergers and acquisitions in the communications industries in the United States today meet the threshold requiring scrutiny, they are subject to review by government antitrust authorities. If regulators believe laws are violated, they can force rescission of the sale or merger or require actions to eliminate the antitrust concerns. Stringent enforcement of antitrust measures in the media and communication markets has not been observed since the late 1990s, however.

One of the most serious problems related to the regulation of large media companies and their concentration results from the subtle erosion and alteration of public policies and interests and a shift toward the purposes, convenience, and interests of the conglomerates. This is not to say that the media companies have always been happy with regulations promulgated, but that in the long term regulators have been generally more supportive of industry interests than public interests. This development should not be surprising because regulation of electronic media industries was spawned by major companies such as RCA and Westinghouse at the beginning of the twentieth century, when they sought protections for their investments. Since that time, most regulation has been strongly influenced by and supportive of the interests of those regulated.

It must be noted, however, that communications businesses do not share a monolithic approach to regulation; nor do all the businesses and their media share the same interests simultaneously. Because of differences in their structures and properties, they sometimes diverge in terms of what policies are important. This is true for every type of industry, and, as Doris Graber points out, "a conglomerate heavily involved in export industries will not share the same view of tariffs as a conglomerate invested primarily in domestic manufacturing. Even within conglomerates, the interests of various components may clash." [12] Because leading communications companies have separate divisions for print, electronic, and recorded media, and their economic and public policy interests often differ dramatically, there can be and are conflicts within companies. These divisions are exacerbated even further when a company owns communications and noncommunications properties.

Even when such differences exist, corporate management will attempt to use and co-opt public policies in ways that provide the best overall situation for the company. Part of the success of industry in co-opting much regulation has been the result of well-funded industry associations and lobbyists and legions of communications company attorneys taking part in legislative and regulatory processes and hearings, while broader social concerns have been represented by small, underfunded public interest groups and only a few active legislators and regulators.

One of the continuing targets of communication companies and industry organizations has been regulations aimed at halting or controlling concentration or its effects. After successes by the broadcast, cable, and telecommunications industries in loosening regulations in the Telecommunications Act of

1996, the Newspaper Association of America, which represents the interests of large media companies and newspapers, began urging the FCC to repeal newspaper-broadcast cross-ownership regulations, which prohibited simultaneous ownership of newspapers and broadcast stations in the same market, calling them "anachronistic" because of growing competition in media.

In 2003 the FCC under the Bush administration promulgated regulations that liberalized ownership rules, loosening controls on the number of broadcast stations permitted to a single owner and cross-ownership rules. The move created a public and congressional protest, and a federal appeals court blocked the rules on grounds that they had not been adequately justified. The commission in 2006 reopened its consideration of the rules, and opponents have begun a vigorous campaign to block changes.[13]

The problems evident in the United States are compounded when media companies operate in more than one country. As these businesses become global in their operations, conflicts over content may occur as they enter markets with different cultures, political structures, and regulations. To accomplish their goals, media businesses develop contacts and friendships with political figures in nations where they do business or wish to do business in hopes of currying favor and beneficial policies. When conflicts occur, some companies are willing to behave amorally or immorally to ensure that their relationships and interests are protected.

Although European Union and domestic European laws that require a majority of local production have provoked angry outcries from U.S. motion picture, television, and cable industries, U.S. companies have altered their operations to gain access to those markets. NBC, for example, began local content production for news and public affairs programming to meet the European content requirements when it purchased SuperChannel and gained access to much of the wealthy European market.[14] The Disney Channel, which wanted to enter the attractive French market, gave up its objections to the laws by agreeing to produce 40 percent French content when it began distribution in that country in 1997.

These developments show that large companies can be persuaded to follow rules they dislike if regulators are willing to establish and enforce content and other regulations but leave economic incentives in place. Nevertheless, the ability to fashion workable policies to halt media consolidation and preserve media that provide pluralism and diverse voices even in Europe has been limited by internal disagreements and antiregulatory forces and by barriers to entry that have made it difficult for new entrants in newspaper markets.[15]

tate-owned media encompass and convey the interests of the state,
owned media are built upon and disseminate the interests of their
owners and the media themselves. Setting aside egregious examples of self-interest for the moment, it is clear that the content of privately owned media nearly universally and continually convey probusiness, antiregulatory biases. Given that such media in developed societies operate in capitalist environments that are promoting laissez-faire capitalism or capitalism with only minor constraints, the private enterprise–oriented biases of media operated by communications companies can hardly be unexpected.

When it comes to general political and social issues, biases favoring lower unemployment, lower taxes, and crime control are generally evident in private media, as they are in developed societies as a whole. On most issues commercial media—which usually try not to unduly antagonize their audiences or advertisers—typically avoid being seen as highly supportive of one policy or another. They tend to be centrist and amoral in their coverage and portrayals, but often show progressive biases favoring clean environment, individual freedom, justice, and the like.

Portrayals and coverage by media companies are often convoluted when it comes to issues involving workers. Although they have a progressive bias toward good working conditions, reasonable salaries and benefits, and workers' rights, self-interests come into play when they face issues of employment and benefit costs and union activity. They often have an antiunion bias in coverage and are suspicious of government policies regarding salaries, benefits, and working conditions.

Among the main problems associated with concentration and commercialization are the use of media for the political purposes of their corporate owners, the homogenization of news and emphasis placed on mainstream voices, cross-promotion of communication products and services, and the increasing reliance on celebrity even in news and public affairs. It is also recognized that media companies use their communication to favor and support their individual political interests. Because the media have spent a great deal of effort wrestling with the government over regulations, associations and coalitions funded by media companies lobby feverishly to promote the interests of the private commercial companies. These groups—especially the National Cable Television Association and the National Association of Broadcasters—have produced campaigns and advertisements supporting the media companies' policy interests. The messages have been distributed nationwide for their members to broadcast and cablecast on their stations and systems, urging support for the associations' positions and asking viewers to contact Congress and the FCC with that support.

At times, however, media do not find it beneficial to widely cover and disseminate public policy proposals and legislation so as not to engender interest or opposition. Such was the case with the Telecommunications Act of 1996, where most coverage was buried in the business news pages and the political and public interest elements were not well explored.[16] The paucity of coverage was also obvious for the passage of the Newspaper Preservation Act and efforts to amend it to benefit monopolist newspapers even further.[17]

Many of the contemporary news processes and practices produce a significant homogenization of news and opinion. Dominant ideologies governing the definition of news and how it should be covered create the opportunities for economies of scale in the collection and distribution of news. This trend has led to the development of commercial companies designed to collect news and information and then sell it to media, providing services to any media that will buy. These news and feature syndicates now supply the bulk of materials of newspaper and magazines, although many readers believe that their favorite publications produce their own materials. Similar services now serve broadcasters in the United States and globally.

A growing number of businesses link print, broadcast, on-line, and other properties in the production of information programming. In doing so, they exchange information and/or stories and cooperate or coordinate coverage to avoid duplication of labor. The result is that fewer journalists or other observers cast an eye on events, and the coverage is similar in every medium involved. When fewer independent eyes are needed to view domestic and international events, fewer journalists are needed and bureaus close down. At its extreme, the buying or re-reporting of news and information leads to situations of journalists and media personalities interviewing each other and relying on each other as sources rather than finding the facts first hand. Ultimately, such practices lead to the major media reporting rumors, gossip, and false information because lesser media already did it.

The result of these interactions between media companies is that a large proportion of news and information comes from the same sources and is merely packaged and reused by various media, creating a homogenization of material. Even when major commercialized media create their own material, they do so with the same ideologies of news and information, thus limiting the perspectives and breadth of coverage.

Commercialized mainstream media do not behave much better in the area of opinion and ideas. Newspapers acquired by groups typically eschew partisan positions out of fear of offending readers and advertisers, particularly if the views are out of the mainstream or on controversial subjects such as abortion, the death penalty, or immigration. As a result they become minor equal-opportunity offenders, carrying syndicated columnists who express various accepted political viewpoints. In reality, the spectrum of views provided by the major commercial media companies is rather limited because terms such as *the left* and *the right* are used loosely. The left today is represented in most mainstream media by, at best, liberal voices, and the right is represented by the conservative branch of the Republican Party.

Media groups therefore promote dominant or acceptable frameworks of society and politics by focusing on political debates among easily accessible political figures and dominant organizations while generally ignoring political concerns outside those parameters. This indexing of opinion limits the range of debate by comparison to opinions throughout the society.[18]

Because political reality for the citizens is created by mediated communications, because most of what is communicated through media are "fantasies" contrived by those politicians and interest groups who wish to manipulate opinion, and because media convey these fantasies in ways designed to produce profit, the public is left with a distorted picture of politics that is designed to entertain, reassure, and manipulate by providing more style than substance.[19]

This manipulation of the public is compounded by market-driven approaches to television and print news that are designed to select and convey information that primarily entertains and diverts rather than informs the user or analyzes significant issues and problems in society. News that "sells" becomes an overriding concern, and companies make extensive efforts to find and convey news in ways that keep ratings high and support their financial goals.[20]

In news of politics, the emphasis on ratings leads to a scandal-driven, destructive style of journalism in which minor issues are blown out of proportion at the expense of coverage of more significant but less provocative issues. Political news therefore emphasizes the sensational: scandals, conflicts, mud-slinging, allegations, and investigations that produce little results. Many nongovernmental organizations now regularly exploit these emphases by feeding information that perpetuates the practice and supports their positions.

The problem also manifests itself in televised political talk shows, which have played a significant role in reducing much political discourse to extreme rhetoric, partisanship for the sake of conflict, and incivility. In pursuit of ratings, the talk shows pit parties against each other in what often degenerates into shouting matches. Policy opponents exchange verbal blows rather than discuss and exchange ideas. These self-serving approaches to news and discourse ultimately result in public distrust and resentment of politics and the media.

Implications of Concentration and Commercialization for Democratic Participation

Political theorists and media scholars recognize that preconditions for the establishment and preservation of democratic governance include freedom of expression for individuals and groups with divergent views. The basic tenets of democracy hold that through an airing of such views citizens will be able to choose the most meritorious from among the ideas and that society will be advanced.

In the realm of media theory and policy, this concept has been manifest in the idea that media plurality—in other words, multiple media outlets—is a primary goal for providing the opportunity for diverse voices to be heard and for ideas to circulate. The number of views about a particular event and the amount of information that units of each medium can carry are already limited by time and space constraints. Without plurality, the number of voices heard is further restricted. Although the existence of multiple media outlets makes it theoretically possible for a larger number of views and opinions to be communicated, the mere existence of media plurality does not ensure message pluralism—the diversity of viewpoints. Most studies of media content have shown that different units of a medium and different media tend to provide relatively similar content, programming, and views because of commercial concerns, the adoption of standard industry norms and business practices, and dependence on a small number of similar sources of news and opinion.

Because of these problems it does not matter greatly if a television station is owned by a large conglomerate such as Time Warner or by a smaller—but similarly motivated—media firm such as Hearst Corporation. In both cases the operations of the station, programming, and news choices will be decided on generally similar bases. The solution to such problems therefore must come not in the form of competition laws and regulations limiting ownership, but in policies and regulations that encourage the establishment of additional competing media. And, more important—because of the homogenization problems—policies are needed that provide for access to nonmainstream voices and alternative means of coverage of social and political issues.

In the United States and most of the developed world, the first goal of establishing additional competing media has been and continues to be accomplished. Much of the world has had a history of state-owned or state-controlled telecommunications and broadcasting supplemented by a commercial and party press. The primary commercial medium in many countries was the magazine. In Europe and some other developed parts of the world, the government monopolies in broadcasting and telecommunications were broken in the 1980s and 1990s, and they are now being supplemented by commercial systems subject to the same pressures as those seen in the United States.

The United States never had government monopolies, but the government supported monopolies in telecommunications and limited competition to protect broadcasting companies' investments. As in Europe, those monopolies and protections were diminished in the 1980s and 1990s.

The development of additional competing media, however, has engendered new forms of private ownership and commercial operation. Because they tend to follow the same practices that led to limitations on the marketplace of ideas, they have raised a great deal of interest about their effects. This is especially true where the deregulation and increasing commercialization of media and communications systems has been accompanied by the growth of large companies serving domestic and foreign markets worldwide. In their growth, these companies have bought up family-owned media and smaller enterprises.

But these changes in media ownership and communications systems cannot be universally condemned because they have created both more and less opportunity for political discourse and action. Changes in technology and deregulation have resulted in a larger number of broadcast stations, cable and satellite distribution systems, and broadcast and cable/satellite networks in the United States and throughout the world. These media changes, along with telecommunications developments that have made possible the wide diffusion of fax, e-mail, and related Internet services, have created more opportunities and means for communications, but at the same time have resulted in communications to smaller audiences and fewer individuals than were reached by traditional mass media.

As this chapter has shown, there is a tendency among observers of media to confuse the effects of commercialization and the private interests of media firms with concentration. Many of the complaints about media operations result not from there being fewer owners of few media; rather, they result from the proliferation of commercial firms that are willing to overtly act in their own self-interest.

In media that produce the largest audiences, commercial pressures dominate decisions. At the same time, such media are subjected to decreasing regulatory requirements and oversight. Consequently, they behave in ways designed to generate large audiences with little regard for social or cultural effects.

No nation has perfect mechanisms to respond to media concentration and commercialization. Each country faces unique circumstances and has different abilities to respond through legal and policy mechanisms. Concentration and/or commercialism can be seriously addressed, however, only when governments have a vision for the national, provincial, and local communications and media market structures and are vigilant in efforts to halt and reduce concentration and limit the harmful effects of a commercial media structure. They can pursue these goals by pursuing antitrust and other policy initiatives that limit or reverse concentration. They can also do so by working to reduce barriers to entry and promoting the entry of new noncommercial competitors. And they can do so by finding methods to promote content not determined by commercial needs alone. To achieve results, the initiatives of controlling concentration, promoting new competition, and countering commercialism need to operate simultaneously.

Private media companies, like all corporations, exist primarily to serve the economic self-interest of their owners. When that self-interest is at stake, the companies cannot be expected to remain guardians of the social interests. It is up to society, through government, to ensure that the self-interest does not continue to result in the types of harm that media concentration and commercialism produce.

Some communications executives argue that concentration is necessary to provide the strength that will permit their companies to compete domestically and internationally. This argument is sophistry but is heard more often as media and communication products and services are privatized around the world. The argument is erroneous for two important reasons. First, competitive ability is not merely a function of size but of the overall management and structure of the business. This is not to say that size is unimportant, because it can provide resources and economies of scale that are useful. But those resources and economies can be achieved even without concentration by diversification. Second, executives who use the argument that concentration is necessary for competitiveness ignore the fact that nearly all the businesses with whom they wish to compete have faced and continue to face significant limits on concentration in their home countries and many other countries in which they operate.

Voices heard in communications policy debates in the United States and elsewhere are predominantly those engaged in the business of communications. It is critically important for advocacy groups and other social organizations to become involved by monitoring the degrees of concentration and commercialism and by seeking regulations that control the behavior of media companies in ways that ensure that social and cultural interests are not harmed. The use of public policies and antitrust laws to protect or respond to harm must be increased, but most nations are not setting into place policies that adequately protect against abuses and countering those problems with positive measures.

Unless significant efforts are directed further than slowing the growth and abuses caused by commercial ownership and concentration, the situation will not improve. Until policies address the types and kinds of content provided, ensure access for a broader spectrum of producers and voices, and find ways to allow groups and smaller companies without great financial resources to become owners or operators of media, complaints about the contemporary media system will continue without seriously changing the existing situation or trends.

Commercial media are obligated to pursue profit and maximize company value, so they can be expected to voluntarily temper their self-interests only if offered incentives to do so. In the past intangible benefits such as prestige and influence were effective, but they are rarely valued today. The primary incentives today are economic—profits, growth in company value, and minimal requirements to obtain or retain broadcasting licenses.

The challenge of persuading media entities to provide content that serves social functions is significant because most content that supports public interests and democratic processes—news, commentary, and political discussions—does not attract large audiences and is often more expensive to produce and less profitable than other types of content.

Despite our convictions about the importance of media in democratic society, we must recognize that media are not a necessary and sufficient condition for democracy. Although media—especially those with news and public service operations—create public forums for discussion and review of public life that are important in large-scale societies, those functions are not exclusive to media. A lack of effective options made news organizations the focus of such activity in the nineteenth and twentieth centuries, but changes in communication technologies and abilities have made other forums possible.

Given the poor performance of many news organizations in serving public needs and the rising possibilities presented by new technology, we may need to seriously consider whether the conditions that led the nation's founders to grant the press constitutional protection still exist or whether the diminished role that many news organizations play today will make them irrelevant in the future.

The classic roles of news organizations in the past were based on coordinating activities and representing interests among citizens and all the institutions of society, informing citizens of developments, overseeing the actions of government and other powerful institutions and entities, and ensuring citizens' views and interests were effectively represented. The press became an intermediary between the public and governments when democratic societies grew to the point that it was not possible for individual voices to be widely heard or to carry significant influence. The public opinion concept—linking citizens to governors—developed in an era when the speed of communication and the technical ability of individuals to communicate were severely limited. Although the need for such linkage remains, new technologies are empowering individuals to do it themselves by means such as talk radio, Web sites, blogs, and discussion groups—all avenues of e-citizenship. Unless society and news organizations reemphasize the position of media in social functions, the significance of media in the processes of democratic participation and governance will continue to decline and other communication functions and institutions will take their place.

Notes

1. Robert G. Picard, "Money, Media, and the Public Interest," in *The Institutions of Democracy: The Press,* ed. Geneva Overholser and Kathleen Hall Jamieson (New York: Oxford University Press, 2005), 337–350; James T. Hamilton, "The Market and the Media," in *Institutions of Democracy.*

2. Robert G. Picard, "U.S. Newspaper Ad Revenue Shows Consistent Growth," *Newspaper Research Journal* 23 (Fall 2002): 21–33; and Robert G. Picard, "Evolution of Revenue Streams and the Business Model of Newspapers: The U.S. Industry Between 1950–2000," Discussion Papers C1/2002, Business Research and Development Centre, Turku School of Economics and Business Administration, 2002.

3. See Tom Fenton, *Bad News: The Decline of Reporting, the Business of News, and the Danger to Us All* (New York: Regan Books, 2005); James T. Hamilton, *All the News That's Fit to Sell: How the Market Transforms Information into News* (Princeton: Princeton University Press, 2004); Thomas E. Patterson, *Doing Well and Doing Good: How Soft News and Critical Journalism Are Shrinking the News Audience and Weakening Democracy—And What the News Outlets Can Do About It* (Cambridge: The Shorenstein Center for the Press, Politics, and Public Policy, John F. Kennedy School of Government, Harvard University, 2000); James Fallows, *Breaking the News: How the Media Undermine American*

Democracy (New York: Pantheon, 1996); and Philip Gaunt, *Choosing the News: The Profit Factor in News Selection* (Westport, Conn.: Greenwood Press, 1990).

4. Robert G. Picard, ed., *Strategic Responses to Media Market Changes* (Jönköping, Sweden: Jönköping International Business School, Jönköping University, 2004).

5. Lee Becker and Klaus Schönbach, *Audience Response to Media Diversification* (Mahwah, N.J.: Lawrence Erlbaum, 1999); Robert G. Picard, *The Economics and Financing of Media Companies* (New York: Fordham University Press, 2002); Philip Napoli, *Audience Economics: Media Institutions and the American Marketplace* (New York: Columbia University Press, 2003).

6. Nielsen Media Research, National People Meter sample, 2003.

7. Robert G. Picard, ed., *Media Product Portfolios: Issues in Management of Multiple Products and Services* (Mahwah, N.J.: Lawrence Erlbaum, 2005).

8. PriceWaterhouseCoopers, *Global Entertainment and Media Outlet, 2005–2009* (New York: PriceWaterhouseCoopers, 2005).

9. See Ben Bagdikian, *The Media Monopoly*, 5th ed. (Boston: Beacon Press, 1997); Erik Barnouw, ed., *Conglomerates and the Media* (New York: The New Press, 1997); Anthony Smith, *The Age of the Behemoths: The Globalization of Mass Media Firms* (New York: Priority Press, 1991); Alfonso Sànchez-Tabernero, *Media Concentration in Europe: Commercial Enterprise and the Public Interest* (London: John Libbey, 1993); and Robert G. Picard, James Winter, Maxwell McCombs, and Stephen Lacy, eds., *Press Concentration and Monopoly: New Perspectives on Newspaper Ownership and Operation* (Norwood, N.J.: Ablex Publishing, 1988).

10. Gillian Doyle, *Media Ownership: Concentration, Convergence and Public Policy* (London: Sage Publications, 2002); Alfonso Sànchez-Tabernero and Miguel Carvajal, *Media Concentration in the European Market: New Trends and Challenges* (Pamplona, Spain: University of Navarra, 2002).

11. The Telecommunications Act is Public Law #104-104 (1996), 110 Stat. 56 (codified in 47 U.S.C.).

12. Doris A. Graber, *Mass Media and American Politics*, 3rd ed. (Washington, D.C.: CQ Press, 1989), 36.

13. Federal Communications Commission, "2006 Review of the Media Ownership Rules," available at *www.fcc.gov/ownership/*; last reviewed/updated December 29, 2006. A coalition of organizations has joined together to oppose any liberalization of media ownership rules. See *www.stopbigmedia.com/*.

14. SuperChannel was subsequently morphed into a platform for MSNBC and CNBC.

15. For discussions of these developments and problems, see Sophia Kaitatzi-Whitlock, "Pluralism and Media Concentration in Europe: Media Policy as Industrial Policy," *European Journal of Communication* 11 (December 1996): 453–483. The significant contributions of barriers to entry to the concentration problem are explored in Colin Sparks, "Concentration and Market Entry in the UK National Daily Press," *European Journal of Communication* 10 (June 1995): 179–206; and Karl Erik Gustafsson, "Government Policies to Reduce Newspaper Entry Barriers," *Journal of Media Economics* 6 (Spring 1993): 37–43.

16. For criticism of the coverage, see Neil Hickey, "So Big: The Telecommunications Act at Year One," *Columbia Journalism Review* (January/February 1997): 23–28.

17. Self-interest and bias in the coverage of these policy debates are documented in John C. Busterna and Robert G. Picard, *Joint Operating Agreements: The Newspaper Preservation Act and Its Application* (Norwood, N.J.: Ablex Publishing, 1993).

18. Indexing refers to the hypotheses associated with Robert Entman and Lance Bennett that a relationship exists between the opinions expressed by political leaders and elites and that expressed in major media. The views expressed in the media thus serve as an "index" to the views expressed by those dominant forces. For how the indexing of opinion occurs, see Robert M. Entman, *Democracy Without Citizens: Media and the Decay of American Politics* (New York: Oxford University Press, 1989); and W. Lance Bennett, "Toward a Theory of Press-State Relations in the United States," *Journal of Communication* 40 (1990): 103–125.

19. These processes of distortion are developed in Dan Nimmo and James E. Combs, *Mediated Political Realities,* 2nd ed. (New York: Longman, 1990); Kathleen Hall Jamison and Karlyn Kohrs Campbell, *The Interplay of Influence,* 2nd ed. (Belmont, Calif.: Wadsworth, 1988); and W. Lance Bennett, *News: The Politics of Illusion,* 2nd ed. (New York: Longman, 1996).

20. How the emphasis on the market directly effects choices and content is explored in John McManus, *Market-Driven Journalism: Let the Citizen Beware?* (Thousand Oaks, Calif.: Sage, 1993); Doug Underwood, *When MBAs Rule the Newsroom* (New York: Columbia University Press, 1993); and Philip Gaunt, *Choosing the News: The Profit Factor in News Selection* (Westport, Conn.: Greenwood Press, 1990).

11 Globalization and the New Media

W. Russell Neuman

Provocative predictions follow new technologies like a shadow: Satellite television will usher in a global village. The Internet will transform broadcasting into narrowcasting. Well-known journalists and columnists will be able to communicate independently and profitably on the Web, no longer dependent on corporate MegaMedia to convey their insights to an interested audience.

In my view these prognostications are not without merit and are based on a relatively sophisticated understanding of changing technology, media economics, corporate strategies, and audience expectations. But they may well miss the mark because there are so many more ways to get it wrong than right. Furthermore, most scenarios for the future tend to highlight one change (such as the explosive growth of the World Wide Web or the dramatically declining cost of global communication) and assume that everything else will remain constant—a demonstrably flawed modeling strategy.

Skeptics are quick to point out incorrect predictions and ridicule the effort, often criticizing what they view as a naïve technological determinism.[1] I am inclined to encourage the speculation, however, precisely because I am a skeptic of technological determinism. The pace of change in the technologies of human communication is particularly rapid now. We are in the process of designing and building a global digital communications infrastructure. The architecture and cost structure of that global electronic grid is subject to human control and not determined unilaterally by the nature of the technology itself. So, to speculate about the "effects of technology" on news, news institutions, the role of the journalist, journalism economics, news flows, and possible changing public perceptions of the political realm is to think about how to design technology to serve human ends, a worthy enterprise indeed.[2]

Technology does not determine, but it can make a difference. New technologies are too often engineered to do what preceding technologies did. They just do it a little better, faster, or cheaper. As a result, failure to speculate shortchanges imaginative thinking about new functions and opportunities, precludes arguments about the viability of alternative structures, and diminishes debate about the social value of evolving institutions.

Another shadow is following technical change—the economic self-interest of the major institutions profiting from existing technologies. Newspapers watch the evolution of news Web sites with pained fascination.[3] Television network news executives track developments in cable and satellite programming the way gamblers follow results from the racetrack.[4] They too are gamblers, and they understand that their corporate stake is at risk.[5]

Since 1998, when the previous edition of this volume was published, an outburst of scholarship on news and the new media has occurred. My informal monitoring of the new books in this field yielded a list of more than twenty-five full-length books and edited volumes devoted specifically to this issue.[6] Given the informal character of the search, these titles may represent only a fraction of the new work in book form. Moreover, many if not most of the new general volumes and textbooks on journalism and news media will contain a chapter (usually the last one) discussing the new media. An electronic search in scholarly journals for work on new media and news generates about three hundred citations for the same period. Are there some convergent findings emerging in this fast-growing literature? In this chapter, I try to make the case that there are, starting with four hypothesized "positive" outcomes of the digital revolution that scholars have been struggling to understand.

Many analysts feel that the dynamism of the new media environment serves to (1) *engage*, (2) *inform*, and (3) *empower* the public to address issues in the public sphere better than "old" media do, and that the public sphere itself is becoming more (4) *global* in scope as the boundaries of the traditional nation state become less constraining. And, predictably, analysts point to at least two potentially "negative" outcomes: greater (1) *polarization* of public opinion and knowledge and a subtle increase in (2) *monopolization* of control of media enterprises.

Tallying Up the Digital Difference

In the developed world the Web has become a critical channel for the flow of news. The Pew Center for the People and the Press reports that 50 million people turn to the Internet for news in the United States on a typical day. Among broadband households, people are more likely to get news from the Internet (43 percent) than a local newspaper (38 percent), and among top 40 percent of heavy Web users in broadband households the Internet is the primary news source (71 percent) compared to only 59 percent turning to TV news.[7] Always-on broadband connections appear to be critical for Web-based news content to be defined more or less interchangeably with television, radio, newspapers, and magazines. And broadband adoption continues on a steep curve, growing 33 percent in Organisation for Economic Co-operation and Development countries in 2006.[8] An equivalent impact in the developing world is likely to require another generation or two in the development of wireless and low cost access technologies.[9] MIT's Nicholas Negroponte, for example, has developed a $100 Web-oriented computer in a project called One Laptop per Child.[10]

But technical availability and even active use of the Web does not necessarily lead to changes in political knowledge and behavior. The earnest expectation that the new media might engage, inform, and empower citizens has met with a sobering modesty of empirical results. It may be that we are witnessing yet another example of what Robert Merton dubbed the "Matthew effect" after the biblical observation that it is so often the rich who get richer.[11] Those already interested and active in the public sphere are the most likely to take advantage of the new media to pursue their interests. The so-called NASCAR dads and soccer moms, for the most part, have other matters that come first. Among the many studies that come to this conclusion is Richard Davis's *Web of Politics*. Davis says that voters "will not become different people just because there are resources at their disposal to follow politics quite closely."[12] Pippa Norris uses the phrase "activating the active" to characterize the phenomenon in her more internationally focused study.[13]

David Tewksbury's research suggests that the Internet may have a negative rather than a positive effect on political knowledge. His study of news-seeking on the Internet reveals that rather than rely on the editorial judgment of broadcast and print journalists who use placement in time (broadcasting) and space (print) to signal journalistic importance of various stories, citizens use search engines and related techniques to find topics of special interest. As often as not, sports and celebrity trump political significance.[14] Eszter Hargittai reminds us that the most popular news sites on the Web are not new institutions; rather, they are emblazoned with the logos of very large and very familiar media companies.[15] Jared Waxman reports that 80 percent of Web visits are concentrated in a mere .5 percent of the sites available.[16]

Doris Graber posits that "media user empowerment" may be the major outcome of the interaction of new media and politics.[17] Indeed, a greatly expanded menu of political thought and opinion confront the citizens, and some ravenous activists dig in with gusto. Roza Tsagarousianou and colleagues document a fascinating set of case studies of "civic networking movements" in the United States and Europe.[18] They conclude that for these activists, the participatory character of the Web really does facilitate a meaningful and effective electronic public sphere. Kevin Hill and John Hughes examined a large sample of UseNet discussions, chat rooms, and political Web sites and found a rich diversity of discussion, most of it quite civil, informative, and, at the time of their analysis, slightly leaning to the right.[19] But political activists continue to represent a tiny minority of the citizenry. Perhaps that was true as well in the salons and coffeehouses of Europe that inspired Jürgen Habermas's notion of an active public sphere. In the end, Graber acknowledges, "While available food for political thought has grown . . . the appetite for it and the capacity to consume it remain limited."[20]

On the negative effects side, especially the posited polarization effect, the evidence is quite convergent. Cass Sunstein's imaginings of an electronically segregated world in which different political and ethnic groups consume only news and information configured especially for them to reinforce their existing beliefs are false fantasies.[21] The work of Kelly Garrett and Paul Resnick with the Pew Internet and American Life Project makes the strongest case. They combine survey and experimental research to reveal that although people do enjoy reinforcing existing beliefs, they do not avoid oppositional information. In fact, they may frequently seek it out to better understand the "other side's" arguments if only to refute them.[22] Bruce Bimber and Richard Davis concur— the "Daily Me" is technically straightforward, but such an approach does not resonate well with human psychology. Citizens want to know what others know. Furthermore, they point out that the Web is never the only information source for citizens.[23] It may be that the polarization hypothesis resonates with analysts because it coincides with a more pervasive cycle of partisanship, particularly in American politics.[24]

Finally on the monopolization hypothesis, we find a continuing concern among critical scholars that the number of megamedia conglomerates appears to be getting smaller despite a growth of media outlets. It is indeed ironic. The growth of new competitive media has made traditionally profitable old media very nervous and has led to binge conglomeratization. Ben Bagdikian makes the case dramatically. Writing in the 1980s he traced the fifty largest media companies that dominated the airwaves and newsstands and their interlocking boards of directors. Bagdikian raised questions about the diversity of news and public affairs they were likely to produce. His stunning finding in 2004 was that large companies still dominated the media, but, instead of fifty, there were only five—Time Warner, News Corp., Disney, Viacom, and Bertelsmann.[25] The work of other scholars and the Pew Project for Excellence in Journalism confirm this trend.[26] The ironic conclusion of careful analyses of actual news content diversity, however, is that although the ownership has changed, the news coverage for the most part has not. We have no evidence to date that conglomeratization has led to less diverse news coverage.[27]

The Technology of Creating and Delivering News

Edward Jay Epstein in *News from Nowhere*, published in 1973, explained with considerable flourish and insight how the ungainly technologies of television news of that era affected how news got on the air. For example, he describes how the rollout of a new Boeing plane in "remote" Seattle, Washington, was difficult to cover on network newscasts based in New York because of the time needed to shoot and edit film and to fly it back to New York while it was still news. Naturally, this was the situation before electronic news gathering and satellites. Today instantaneous live coverage of news events virtually anywhere on the globe is routine. Furthermore, amateurs with video cameras and cell phone cameras can capture unfolding events and become news cameras for the world. The Rodney King video is but one example.

But what ultimately may be most disruptive to traditional news practice is that audience members may well take it upon themselves to decide what is news and not just provide the raw materials to the news professionals. YouTube.com and related video sharing sites are becoming particularly popular and influential. A widely circulated video of Sen. Conrad Burns of Montana sleeping during a congressional hearing important to the citizens of his home state, with "Happy Trails" musically enlivening the sound track (among several other well-captured miscues) may have contributed to his defeat in 2006. A mixture of amateur and professional commentaries and Op-Eds generally referred to as blogs (short for Weblog) further blur the line between professional and grassroots news and commentary. Attentive bloggers, for example, were credited with drawing attention to Mississippi senator Trent Lott's insensitive racial remarks at a public gathering. They persisted until the issue caught on in the mainstream media and contributed to his resignation as majority leader. It is not unusual for journalists to cite the blogosphere and for bloggers to quote, critique, and sometimes repurpose traditional news text and video. Although concerns are expressed about how amateur journalists both inadvertently and purposefully violate various journalistic norms, most analysts have welcomed the development because do-it-yourself newscasting tends to supplement rather than replace mainstream news.[28]

The traditional definition of a news marketplace was a newspaper-television-defined metropolitan area supplemented by weekly local newspapers and an occasional community cable television channel. That definition turns out to be a historical-technological artifact.[29] The definition of a communications "market," as any politician or news professional will confirm, is an important political entity. Changes in the overlap (or lack thereof) between a political district and a commercial market could have profound political effects. Previous attempts have been made to use technology to break down the local programming monopolies. What plagued public-access cable television, for example, was that community programming was shown at a fixed time, available to only a small fraction of those who might be interested.[30] Furthermore, without a tradition of promotion or outreach, these programs attract little attention.[31] The new digital options, such as podcasting and e-mail lists, however, permit communication unconstrained by the technical limitations of fixed-format broadcasting. Small audience and special interest programming can be provided on demand. In addition, viewers are free to pass along the digital video file to potentially interested friends and neighbors, as they would pass along a news clipping. The economics of capture and transmission do not necessarily require large audiences and commercial production values.[32] What evidence do we have that the new digital media may succeed in stimulating special interest news and citizen communication even though their analog forebears may have failed? Evidence is tricky here; it is still early in the diffusion of technologies and in the evolution of their use. Enthusiasts and skeptics both have their assemblage of anecdotes. But some lessons might be drawn.

In research conducted at the MIT Media Lab, we posited that the early adopters of home computer technology, by dint of their technical interests and background, would have patterns of Web use systematically different from the large mass of midterm adopters as penetration rates increased (by all indications, quite quickly) from 30 percent to 60 percent of American homes.[33] So we recruited early Internet enthusiasts through local Internet service providers in two locations and matched them up with a special sample of friends, coworkers, and family who had heard about the Web but had not yet used it much at work or at home. We provided them with loaned laptop computers and modems and, with their permission, tracked their usage patterns and content predilections, which we then compared with our parallel early-adopter cohort.

Although the early adopters spent more time looking at Web sites and were more facile at making their Web browsers behave, we found to our surprise that their content tastes and usage patterns were not distinctly different from the novices. Both samples used the Web primarily for special interest information and entertainment seeking, not just monitoring some of the many mass media Web outlets. We concluded that the flexible and interactive nature of the Web is suited to an active style of information-seeking in contrast with the more passive "monitoring" of traditional print and broadcast news media. It is not technological determinism; rather, it is evidence that technologies interact in distinct ways with different domains of human curiosity and interest.

A similar field trial was conducted in Pennsylvania.[34] In that study researchers at Carnegie Mellon University found that the difficulty of adapting to new technology greatly limited Internet use, especially for older users. The teenagers, notably male teenagers, used the home-based personal computers provided by the experimenters six to ten times more often than their parents. This finding may not be generalizable, however. The study was based on high school students who brought computers home, but the parents had little incentive to experiment with the computers, and no peer support was provided for the older users. Nevertheless, the patterns of use for all subjects were similar to those in the MIT study. The interactive nature of the Web led even novice users to quite diverse subject matter. The researchers report that 55 percent of the Web sites hit were visited by only one user of the one hundred households participating, and only 10 percent of the Web pages viewed were visited by ten or more study participants.[35] Eszter Hargittai, who has been pursuing this question, makes a persuasive case that a "digital divide" dichotomy of access versus nonaccess to the Web is unhelpful and must be supplanted with a richer notion of digital literacy based on evolving behaviors rather than the simple presence of online laptops.[36]

Journalistic experiments with community-oriented, small-scale news projects online have suffered many frustrating failures. Therefore, some skepticism is due, especially if the proposed system depends on sustained labor by volunteers. But earlier experiments on the Web promise new formats, new flexibility, indeed new definitions of what news could be, only part of which is derived from traditional media streams and formats. The new formats of news involve audience discussion and commentary not easily incorporated in the broadcast domain, and detailed coverage of specialized topics not ordinarily found outside of specialty magazines. Perhaps a fresh mixture of amateur enthusiasm and quasi-professional and fully professional journalism will produce a different definition of news and the economic model to sustain it.[37]

The Changing Economics of the News Business

The spate of new books on the state of the fourth estate has a demonstrable tendency, first, to celebrate a golden age of Western journalism peaking in the recent past and, second, to decry the current and presumably evident decline of serious journalism.[38] Television, the new media, and the new media economics represent the usual suspects, the convenient bête noire as these narratives unfold. This critical perspective would probably be in evidence absent the invasion of new technologies, but it is nevertheless worthwhile to explore the logic of these inquiries.

Critiques of modern media resonate with three central themes: autonomy, format, and funding. The first theme is the need to protect the independence and unapologetic honesty of reporters and editors as they chronicle the issues and events that swirl around their employers' corporate empires. Expanding corporate cross-ownership, joint ventures, and ever-larger corporate command structures inevitably challenge that tradition of journalistic independence.[39] Numerous case studies of potential abuse circulate in the academic journals and professional trade press. From the media executives' point of view, the need to reduce the risk of new competitors and to control technology expenditures drives the merger mania. From the critic's point of view, these pressures have important unanticipated effects on journalistic integrity.[40]

The second theme revolves around the evolution of news formats. In the newspaper world, the audience-research–derived model for *USA Today* is derided as McPaper. This format—short, simple, colorfully printed, with cute graphics and universally bland content—tastes best to the largest number of readers. But it is not necessarily nutritious. In television news, the growth during prime time of the magazine format mix of news and entertainment is a product of the competitive battle for viewership in a multichannel environment.[41] It is decried as a sure sign of journalistic decline. The format's emphasis on soft news, personality, and celebrity allegedly weakens the tradition of hard-hitting serious journalism in the dinner-hour window for network news. Network news viewership is down, primarily as a result of the competition from cable and satellite entertainment programming.[42]

The third and related theme is funding constraints—the pressure on print and broadcast news operations to be more efficient and to grow profits. During the 1990s media companies cut back on international travel, closed down foreign bureaus, placed new pressures on reportorial efficiency, and funded fewer long-term and high-cost investigative assignments.[43] One might characterize the golden age of serious journalism as primarily a golden age of near-monopoly profits.[44]

In the United States the three dominant networks used to draw in 90 percent of the viewing audience in prime time for entertainment programming. That audience share provided a healthy cushion in advertising revenues to support a high-profile and high-status news operation. In other industrialized nations during the 1990s, spectrum scarcity and government-sanctioned monopolies generated equivalently large audiences and (in commercial systems) profitable operations to support news programming. Metropolitan newspapers in the industrialized world, the medium of choice for regional retail advertising, also found themselves in a profitable position. Although some have argued that the pressures on the costs of quality journalism are primarily the outcome of a new management culture, the link of the evolving corporate norms in the news business to new competition and new media is in all likelihood highly significant.

How should we respond to the collision of new technology and the hard-won values of independent journalism? The playing field is divided between outrageous enthusiasts with roots in technology and capitalism and outraged critics with roots in cultural theory and the political left. The abandoned middle may prove to be the high ground here. It is important not to equate structural change with an abandonment of basic values or selling out. What are now the revered principles of the independent fourth estate were largely crafted by capitalists.[45] The most significant danger to independent journalism is capture by monopoly or oligopoly interests or, in this case, the recreation of artificial scarcity. American academics and news professionals have dominated the dialogue thus far. European, especially Scandinavian, media have different editorial traditions—political party–based and more ideologically oriented. Will the new media offer a new lease on life to these traditions or instead reflect an Americanization and commercialization of news practices around the world, as many fear?[46]

One of the defining characteristics of the critical literature is a concern about pandering to the lowest common denominator. The electronic media give rise to instantaneous and two-way communication. Unlike magazines and newspapers, what people like and dislike is immediately apparent. They like the local, the visual, the human perspective, the concrete example; they dislike abstract political rhetoric and institutional perspectives. The mass audience's proclivity is well known but not necessarily well understood. For good or for ill, the ratings game of today's television programming will intensify in the next generation of digital video. Consider it a challenge to research-based professional creativity rather than a test of ethical and political will.

The Global Village

Some of the most stimulating speculation on the impact of new media on news centers on the potential "death of distance."[47] Walter Lippmann's 1922 classic, *Public Opinion*, is an examination of the public's understanding of distant events, in that case Americans' perceptions of the Great War in Europe.[48] In his own way, Lippmann introduced the globalization issue. He puzzled over how Americans could be expected to make sense of such structurally complex events half a world away and in such unfamiliar contexts. Undersea cables connected Europe and North America by the time of the First World War, so up-to-date telegraphic reports from the battlefields were featured in the newspapers of the day. But radio was not yet in common use, and television and satellites were a long way off. Lippmann's book is still frequently assigned in classrooms, even after Vietnam, the first televised war, and the Gulf War, the first war televised live. The questions he raised are no less relevant today than they were when *Public Opinion* was first published.

There are indeed increased flows of news across international boundaries through satellites, data networks, and the interconnection of new and traditional news media.[49] The United States may be a world leader in new technology, but it exhibits the lowest levels of foreign news content in its media and the lowest levels of foreign news interest and foreign news knowledge among the publics of industrialized nations. Is there evidence that the increasing global media flows may nudge public opinion toward a new worldliness? The answer would have to be: not yet. Electronic connectedness cannot be equated with global interest, attention, and most important, understanding.

The quadrennial—now biennial—survey of the Chicago Council on Foreign Relations consistently reveals that only one-third of Americans express interest in news about other countries.[50] The Pew Center studies of news interest also reveal an unchanging disinterest in international political news, a pattern especially pronounced among young U.S. citizens. Only one person in ten under thirty years of age follows such events closely.[51]

But the digital day is young. Although it is trumpeted that CNN is available in nearly one hundred nations around the world (a fact acknowledged by those world travelers who stay in the better hotels), CNN has not yet reached a penetration of 1 percent of the world's population despite the wide availability of cable in Europe, North America, and Japan.[52] In the industrialized world it took nearly seventy-five years for the telephone to reach near universal penetration.[53] Although the diffusion of new media is moving more quickly, it is too early for a definitive assessment.

The technical drivers of this diffusion are, as before, relatively straightforward. The migration to electronic communications has prompted a robust international competition among undersea optical-fiber cables, satellite transmission companies, and, to a lesser extent, terrestrial microwave networks. The technical challenge is to get greater amounts of information through an existing infrastructure while new and even more sophisticated electronic links are constructed. Such are the tests by which capitalism demonstrates its vitality. There are numerous competitors, each with a legacy in the traditional communication industries, invested in digital networks desperately looking for business.[54] The prices of international voice, video, and data are dropping dramatically. The lower costs become evident to the average consumer in international long-distance telephone rates.[55] The pervasive impact of lower costs is also seen in the greater flow of financial data, international news, and entertainment programming across international boundaries.

But cost is only part of the picture. As massive flows of digital communication surge across national boundaries, patrolling and protecting political boundaries becomes more difficult.[56] A truckload of news magazines at a border crossing is easy to identify and, if necessary, to seize. In earlier eras those few broadcasts that spanned borders could be jammed if found to be politically offensive.[57] But how is it possible to police the Internet? Some authoritarian regimes around the world will doubtlessly hunt down an offending Web site or impolitic e-mail message, and the offenders will be pilloried with appropriate ceremony. The pretense of control will be resolutely proclaimed, but in truth the authorities of the industrialized nations are losing the capacity to censor or even to monitor the internal and international communications of their citizenry. The Chinese experimentation with an economically vibrant but politically muted Internet is a closely watched case study.[58] It is simply impossible to monitor every electronic utterance. With a few keystrokes on a personal computer, citizens can encrypt messages, resulting in a digital stream that would call for months of analysis engaging banks of government supercomputers to decrypt (if the authorities could find the digital fragment in the first place).[59]

Because the Internet blurs the distinction between an interpersonal and a broadcast communication network, it blurs the distinction between private and public speech. Authoritarian nations' restrictive regulations, designed to prevent speech deemed contrary to national security, focus on mobilization appeals and incitement-to-riot concepts of public speech. A rabble-rouser on a street corner with a bullhorn is, by definition, easier to locate and silence than, say, a thoughtful but anonymous critic at a computer terminal.

Have the new media nurtured a global village? Not yet. The new media make such a phenomenon possible. But in the post-9/11 world, a lot will have to evolve in the beliefs and behaviors of the world's citizenry before the village metaphor even begins to fit. Hill and Hughes point to the newsgroup, *alt.politics.French,* which appears to be a forum for hurtling insults back and forth across the English channel between the British and the French.[60] Al Jazeera has used direct satellite broadcasting with great effect and some profit by vilifying Israel and to some extent the West in general for an attentive Arab viewership.[61] As Jonathan Zittrain points out, the nation state, if it chooses to, can exert significant control over the content of the Internet and broadcast channels, even satellite broadcasts.[62]

The Public Sphere

In authoritarian media systems the official line of public rhetoric is often viewed with appropriate skepticism. There is a long-standing tradition of sophisticated audience members reading between the lines to catch subtle changes in policy and strategy. One could point to numerous examples when officially decreed falsehoods are widely understood by the public to be lies and sometimes are even freely acknowledged so in private discussion.[63] This rich dynamic between the official and grassroots public sphere is what Jürgen Habermas focused on in his celebration of nineteenth-century salon society in Europe.[64] By most measures, the evolving media, including talk radio and especially the Internet, have the ability to energize that tradition of a vibrant public sphere. The critical literature in mass communications research argued for decades that the rhetoric of official news obscured the links between public policy and the daily circumstances of private life. We may expect that the dominant public language of the media will continue to interact with the private language of the street. But if, as predicted, the new media truly enhance small group communication, new forms of private speech will migrate forcefully from the street into the surviving mass media. The new media are still young additions to the global institutional complex. Despite numerous constraints, a virtuous circle of political progress is still possible. Modest expectations and a knowing reliance on activists and not just the mass public may yet generate some interesting new models.[65]

Michael Schudson's study of the evolution of the American news industry has, like Lippmann's study, become a classic and is widely used in teaching journalism, press politics, and public opinion.[66] It is a book with a message, especially for young readers who grew up with mass mediated news and may think they know what news is. It is, Schudson demonstrates powerfully, a socially constructed phenomenon. The idealized objectivity of the fourth estate has its roots in the economics of newspaper competition at the beginning of the twentieth century. And, as a socially, politically, and economically constructed phenomenon, the definition of news may yet evolve further in response to future needs and future incentives.

Professional journalists squinting ahead at the news industry's economics, technologies, and competition may be inclined to circle the wagons to protect old principles and old ways of doing business. Indeed, they have much of value to protect. But in times of dramatic change, there also is an opportunity to affect the definition of news in positive ways, to explore the subtle dynamics of public and private speech in other ways, to examine policy agendas in more depth, and to discover different news communities. Judging from recent history, we have reason to expect that digital news will be much more than yesterday's headlines on a computer screen.

The Bottom Line

We have reviewed four hypothesized positive outcomes of the digital revolution found in the recent literature. Although scholars have eagerly sought out evidence that the new media may serve to *engage, inform,* and *empower* the public to address issues in the public sphere, the evidence is sparse and in some cases negative. It is also argued that the public sphere is expanding—becoming *global* in scope as the boundaries of the traditional nation state are less constraining. Here the evidence is stronger, but it is still too early in the game to draw a firm conclusion. Among the potentially negative outcomes, such as greater *polarization* of public opinion and knowledge around a self-filtered "Daily Me," we find that research thus far contradicts the hypothesis, as people prefer to keep tabs on both sides of most issues. And the concern about the growth in *monopolization* of media by a shrinking number of media conglomerates is indeed evident in the literature, but surprisingly has not manifested itself in less diverse content, at least not yet. The monopolization-megamedia issue has been a continuing concern for many decades and is likely to be resolved, if at all, by policy and political decisions independent of the character of the new technical media themselves.

The real bottom line is the explosion of new media information sources and the much-expanded menu of ideas and opinions about public affairs when the Internet is close at hand. But for the most part, the public uses its newfound freedom of choice to seek out entertainment rather than civic edification. It is a familiar pattern in the development of new media. Those who already have an interest in and knowledge about public affairs are those most likely to take advantage of new resources. As a result, any "effects" of the new media tend not to be very dramatic; rather, they are highly constrained by psychological, cultural, and economic forces—phenomena we were just beginning to understand as we struggled to make sense of the "old media."

Notes

1. Daniel Bell, "Technology, Nature and Society," in *The Winding Passage* (New York: Basic, 1980), 3–33; Ithiel de Sola Pool, *Technologies of Freedom* (Cambridge: Harvard University Press, 1983); Geoff J. Mulgan, *Communication and Control: Networks and the New Economies of Communication* (New York: Guilford Press, 1991).

2. Denis McQuail, "Research on New Communications Technologies: Barren Terrain or Promising Arena?" in *Wired Cities: Shaping the Future of Communications,* ed. William H. Dutton, Jay G. Blumler, and Kenneth L. Krammer (Boston: G. K. Hall, 1987), 431–445.

3. Pablo J. Boczkowski, *Digitizing the News* (Cambridge: MIT Press), 2004.

4. Benjamin Compaine and Douglas Gomery, eds., *Who Owns the Media? Competition and Concentration in the Mass Media Industry* (Mahwah, N.J.: Erlbaum, 2000).

5. W. Russell Neuman, Lee McKnight, and Richard Jay Solomon, *The Gordian Knot: Political Gridlock on the Information Highway* (Cambridge: MIT Press, 1997).

6. Matthew A Baum, *Soft News Goes to War: Public Opinion and American Foreign Policy in the New Media Age* (Princeton: Princeton University Press, 2003); Yochai Benkler, *The Wealth of Networks: How Social Production Transforms Markets and Freedom* (New Haven: Yale University Press, 2006); Daniel Bennett and Pam Fielding, *The Net Effect: How Cyberadvocacy Is Changing the Political Landscape* (Merrifield, Va.: e-Advocates Press, 1999); Bruce Bimber, *Information and American Democracy: Technology in the Evolution of Political Power* (New York: Cambridge University Press, 2003); Bruce Bimber and Richard Davis, *Campaigning Online* (New York: Oxford University Press, 2003); Michael Cornfield, *Politics Moves Online: Campaigning and the Internet* (New York: Century Foundation, 2004); Richard Davis, *The Web of Politics: The Internet's Impact on the American Political System* (New York: Oxford University Press, 1998); Richard Davis and Diana Owen, *New Media and American Politics* (New York: Oxford University Press, 1998); William H. Dutton, *Society on the Line: Information Politics in the Digital Age* (New York: Oxford University Press, 1999); Kirsten A. Foot and Steven M. Schneider, *Web Campaigning* (Cambridge: MIT Press, 2006); Barry N. Hague and Brian D. Loader,

Digital Democracy: Discourse and Decision in the Information Age (New York: Routledge, 1999); Kevin A. Hill and John E. Hughes, *Cyberpolitics: Citizen Activism in the Age of the Internet* (Lanham, Md.: Rowman and Littlefield, 1998); Philip N. Howard, *New Media Campaigns and the Managed Citizen* (New York: Cambridge University Press, 2006); Thomas J. Johns, Carole E. Hays, and Scott P. Hays, eds., *Engaging the Public: How Government and the Media Can Reinvigorate American Democracy* (Lanham, Md.: Rowman and Littlefield, 1998); Elaine Ciulia Kamarck and Joseph S. Nye Jr., eds., *Democracy.Com? Governance in a Networked World* (Cambridge: Harvard University Press, 1999); Robert J. Klotz, *The Politics of Internet Communication* (Lanham, Md.: Rowman and Littlefield, 2004); Robert Latham and Saskia Sassen, eds., *Digital Formations: It and New Architectures in the Global Realm* (Princeton: Princeton University Press, 2005); Sonia Livingstone, *Young People and New Media* (Thousand Oaks, Calif.: Sage, 2002); Pippa Norris, *A Virtuous Circle: Political Communications in Post-Industrial Societies* (New York: Cambridge University Press, 2000); Pippa Norris, *Digital Divide: Civic Engagement, Information Poverty, and the Internet Worldwide* (New York: Cambridge University Press, 2001); John V. Pavlik, *Journalism and New Media* (New York: Columbia University Press, 2001); Peter M. Shane, ed., *Democracy Online: The Prospects for Political Renewal Through the Internet* (New York: Routledge, 2004); Cass Sunstein, *Republic.Com* (Princeton: Princeton University Press, 2001); Chris Toulouse and Timothy Luke, eds., *The Politics of Cyberspace* (New York: Routledge, 1998); Roza Tsagarousianou, Damian Tambini, and Cathy Bryan, eds., *Cyberdemocracy: Technology, Cities, and Civic Networks* (New York: Routledge, 1998); Jan A. G. M. van Dijk, *The Deepening Divide: Inequality in the Information Society* (Thousand Oaks, Calif.: Sage, 2005); and Anthony Wilhelm, *Democracy in the Digital Age: Challenges to Political Life in Cyberspace* (New York: Routledge, 2000).

7. Pew Center for the People and the Press, "Online News" (Washington, D.C.: Pew Research Center for the People and the Press, 2006). See *www.pewinternet.org/*.

8. OECD Broadband Statistics to June 2006, *www.oecd.org/sti/ict/broadband*, released October 13, 2006.

9. United Nations, *The Wireless Internet Opportunity for Developing Countries* (New York: United Nations Publications, 2004).

10. See One Laptop per Child at *www.laptop.org*.

11. Robert K. Merton, "The Matthew Effect in Science," *Science*, January 5, 1968, 56–63.

12. Davis, *The Web of Politics*, 183.

13. Norris, *A Virtuous Circle*.

14. David Tewksbury, "What Do Americans Really Want to Know? Tracking the Behavior of News Readers on the Internet," *Journal of Communication* 53, no. 4 (2003): 694–710.

15. Eszter Hargittai, "Content Diversity Online: Myth or Reality," in *Media Diversity and Localism: Meanings and Metrics*, ed. Philip M. Napoli (Mahwah, N.J.: Erlbaum, 2006).

16. Cited in Paul DiMaggio, Eszter Hargittai, W. Russell Neuman, and John Robinson, "Social Implications of the Internet," *Annual Review of Sociology* 27 (Palo Alto, Calif.: Annual Reviews, 2001): 307–336.

17. Doris Graber, "The New Media and Politics: What Does the Future Hold?" *PS: Political Science and Politics* 29, no. 1 (1996): 33–36.

18. Tsagarousianou, Tambini, and Bryan, *Cyberdemocracy*.

19. Hill and Hughes, *Cyberpolitics*.

20. Ibid., 34, quoting Graber.

21. Sunstein, *Republic.Com.*

22. Pew Internet and American Life Project, *The Internet and Democratic Debate* (Washington, D.C.: Pew Research Center for the People and the Press, 2004); R. Kelly Garrett, "Exposure to Controversy in an Information Society," PhD diss., University of Michigan, 2005.

23. Bimber and Davis, *Campaigning Online.*

24. Morris P. Fiorina, Samuel J. Abrams, and Jeremy C. Pope, *Culture War? The Myth of a Polarized America* (New York: Longman, 2004).

25. Ben H. Bagdikian, *The New Media Monopoly* (Boston: Beacon Press, 2004).

26. Pew Internet and American Life Project, *State of the News Media* (Washington, D.C.: Pew Research Center for the People and the Press, 2006); Mara Einstein, *Media Diversity: Economics, Ownership, and the FCC* (Mahwah, N.J.: Erlbaum, 2004).

27. Einstein, *Media Diversity;* Napoli, *Media Diversity and Localism.*

28. Cornfield, *Politics Moves Online;* A. Michael Froomkin, "Technologies for Democracy," in *Democracy Online.*

29. Leo Bogart, *Commercial Culture: The Media System and the Public Interest* (New York: Oxford University Press, 1995).

30. Ithiel de Sola Pool, ed., *Talking Back: Citizen Feedback and Cable Technology* (Cambridge: MIT Press, 1977); Carol Davidge, "America's Talk-Back Television Experiment: Qube," in *Wired Cities,* 75–101; Carrie Heeter and Bradley S. Greenberg, *Cableviewing* (Norwood, N.J.: Ablex, 1988).

31. David Waterman and August Grant, "Cable Television as an Aftermarket," *Journal of Broadcasting* 35, no. 2 (1991): 179–187.

32. Chris Anderson, *The Long Tail: Why the Future of Business Is Selling Less of More* (New York: Hyperion, 2006).

33. W. Russell Neuman, Shawn R. O'Donnell, and Steven M. Schneider, *The Web's Next Wave: A Field Study of Internet Diffusion and Use Patterns* (Cambridge: MIT Media Lab, 1996).

34. Sara Kiesler, Robert Kraut, Tridas Mukhopadhyay, and William Scherlis, *Homenet: A Field Trial of Residential Internet Use* (Pittsburgh: Carnegie Mellon University, 1997).

35. Ibid.

36. Eszter Hargittai, "Second Level Digital Divide: Differences in People's Online Skills," *First Monday* 7, no. 4 (2002); Eszter Hargittai, "The Digital Divide and What to Do About It," *New Economy Handbook,* ed. Derek C. Jones (San Diego: Academic Press, 2003); Eszter Hargittai, "Toward a Social Framework for Information Seeking," *New Directions in Human Information Behavior,* ed. Amanda Spink and Charles Cole (New York: Springer, 2003).

37. Raul Fernandez, "Uploading American Politics," *Washington Post,* December 9, 2006.

38. Benjamin C. Bradlee, *A Good Life: Newspapering and Other Adventures* (New York: Simon and Schuster, 1995); Lawrence Grossman, *The Electronic Republic* (London: Penguin, 1995); James Fallows, *Breaking the News* (New York: Pantheon, 1996).

39. Ben Bagdikian, "The Lords of the Global Village," *The Nation,* June 12, 1989.

40. Anthony Smith, *The Age of Behemoths: The Globalization of Mass Media Firms* (New York: Priority Press, 1991).

41. Fallows, *Breaking the News.*

42. Shanto Iyengar and Jennifer A. McGrady, *Media Politics: A Citizen's Guide* (New York: Norton, 2006), 54.

43. Stanley E. Flink, *Sentinel Under Siege: The Triumphs and Troubles of America's Free Press* (Boulder, Colo.: Westview, 1997).

44. Bagdikian, *The New Media Monopoly*.

45. Michael Schudson, *Discovering the News: A Social History of American Newspapers* (New York: Basic Books, 1978).

46. George Gerbner, Hamid Mowlana, and Kaarle Nordenstreng, eds., *The Global Media Debate: Its Rise, Fall and Renewal* (Norwood, N.J.: Ablex, 1993); Sandra Braman and Annabelle Sreberny-Mohammadi, eds., *Globalization, Communication, and Transnational Civil Society* (Cresskill, N.J.: Hampton Press, 1996).

47. Frances Cairncross, *The Death of Distance* (Boston: Harvard Business School Press, 1997).

48. Walter Lippmann, *Public Opinion* (New York: Free Press, 1922).

49. Walter B. Wriston, *The Twilight of Sovereignty* (New York: Scribner's, 1992).

50. Chicago Council on Foreign Relations, "General Population Survey" (1994). The new name is Chicago Council on Global Affairs. Surveys are published in even-numbered years.

51. Kimberly Parker and Claudia Deane, *Ten Years of the Pew News Interest Index* (Washington, D.C.: Pew Research Center for the People and the Press, 1997). The *Index* has been continuous, adding attention data for contemporary stories.

52. Richard Parker, *Mixed Signals: The Prospects for Global Television News* (New York: Twentieth Century Fund Press, 1995).

53. Ithiel de Sola Pool, ed., *The Social Impact of the Telephone* (Cambridge: MIT Press, 1977).

54. Neuman, McKnight, and Solomon, *The Gordian Knot*.

55. Telegeography Report and Database (Washington, D.C.: TeleGeography Research, 2006).

56. Ithiel de Sola Pool, *Technology Without Boundaries* (Cambridge: Harvard University Press, 1990).

57. Ithiel de Sola Pool, "Future Perspectives on Communication," Speech to the Honda International Symposium, Tokyo, Japan, 1978.

58. Francoise Mengin, ed., *Cyber China: Reshaping National Identities in the Age of Information* (New York: Palgrave Macmillan, 2004); Yongming Zhou, *Historicizing Online Politics: Telegraphy, the Internet, and Political Participation in China* (Stanford, Calif.: Stanford University Press, 2005); Jack Goldsmith and Tim Wu, *Who Controls the Internet?* (New York: Oxford University Press, 2006).

59. Pool, "Future Perspectives on Communication."

60. Hill and Hughes, *Cyberpolitics*,184.

61. Hugh Miles, *Al Jazeera: How Arab TV News Challenges America* (New York: Grove Press, 2005).

62. Jonathan Zittrain, "Internet Points of Control," in *The Emergent Global Information Policy Regime*, ed. Sandra Braman (New York: Palgrave Macmillan, 2003), 203–227.

63. William A. Gamson, *Talking Politics* (New York: Cambridge University Press, 1992).

64. Jürgen Habermas, *The Structural Transformation of the Public Sphere*, trans. Thomas Burger with Frederick Lawrence (Cambridge: MIT Press, [1962] 1989).

65. Pippa Norris, *A Virtuous Circle*; Benkler, *The Wealth of Networks*.

66. Schudson, *Discovering the News*.

12 Press Freedom and Democratic Accountability in a Time of War, Commercialism, and the Internet

W. Lance Bennett and Regina G. Lawrence

When Americans think of a free press, they generally think of the First Amendment and its long tradition of protecting journalists and citizens from government censorship. This hallowed and well-traveled democratic ideal is widely believed to be a standard that gives American news a protective shield and a public compass that will keep the people informed, even when government may not be fully transparent in its activities. Although the protective shield aspect of the First Amendment does seem generally to guard journalists against government censorship, the public compass that points news organizations toward the most useful citizen information is not well established by the mere principle of press freedom.

What news organizations do with their freedom is pretty much left to them to decide, with only the check of audiences and weak government guidelines to guide their direction. This state of affairs raises some important questions: Should the public be the main check and direction mechanism on news organizations? Do most members of the public really know what they need to know? Should news organizations be trusted to set their own standards of reporting when it is tempting to sacrifice expensive quality journalism for more profitable soft news and handouts from official sources? In the absence of clear democratic standards, what happens to press independence when a climate of fear favors safe reporting that does not challenge audiences?

In the current era of mistrust toward the media and politicians, confounded by fear in a threatening post-9/11 world, challenging the public may be particularly risky. People do not always have coherent and consistent expectations of the press. Many Americans expect the press to behave as a "watchdog," but they also expect the press to be "neutral" or "objective." Media coverage that is critical of government can therefore seem to violate the neutrality standard or appear motivated by partisan bias.[1] Yet media coverage that conforms too closely to official government positions may downplay critical information and lead people to accept information that has been distorted or misrepresented for political purposes, as happened in reporting Bush administration claims about weapons of mass destruction that led to the U.S. invasion of Iraq. After such incidents, the feeling of being misinformed or deceived adds to the mistrust of politicians and the press. Having clear standards of press accountability might help reverse the downward spiral of confidence and confusion.

Most democracies struggle with questions of how the press should hold those in power accountable and how journalism should be responsible to the public. These difficulties turn out to be inevitable companions to the ideal of press freedom.[2] If government defines how the press should report on events or how it should regard its responsibilities to the public, the ideal of freedom is compromised. On the other hand, the absence of shared social and journalistic norms for press accountability can result in the press becoming too close to government in times of crisis and public fear and perhaps unable to gauge a proper distance afterward. These problems have become major dilemmas during a time when the American press is rocked by many forces, from patriotic pressures to corporate takeovers, and from citizen distrust to the rise of alternative Internet channels for information. These factors all challenge a free press to find its democratic compass.

A Press System in Search of a Democratic Standard

The American public information system is in crisis. News audiences are shrinking, and confidence in journalism has declined steadily over nearly two decades. For example, media scholar Thomas Patterson shows that steep declines in audiences for the most common news formats (local and national television, newspapers, and newsmagazines) have occurred since the early 1990s. These declines follow a shift in news content that began in the mid-1980s, when so-called hard news about political issues and policies began to be displaced by soft news on scandals, personalities, crime, disaster, and human interest features—news forms that audiences often report as negative and unsatisfying.[3] During the same period, news organizations have been bought and consolidated by large corporations that believe their primary responsibilities are to their investors, not the public interest. News divisions have been pushed to conform to profit demands and audience demographics, often at the expense of quality and independence. The acceleration of mergers has been made possible by a political climate in Washington favoring government deregulation of media ownership requirements and lowered standards for public affairs content traveling over the airwaves.

At the same time, the Internet, where users can find information that is often produced independently of news organizations, has heightened the crisis in journalism. Indeed, many Internet sites and technologies enable the production and sharing of information at a citizen-to-citizen level, without having to pass the test of editorial review or other standards of trustworthiness. At the same time, the low levels of confidence that many citizens express in conventional journalism suggest that the ideal of truth in a heavily spun mainstream press may have been replaced by what Comedy Central anchor Stephen Colbert has termed "truthiness."

Finding a common solution to the challenges currently facing the press is made even more difficult by the prevailing popular view that the main problem is that most journalists are too liberal. This belief is something of a "default" view that is easy to adopt without much thinking because so many politicians and pundits serve it up on a regular basis. In addition, conservative cable outlets such as Fox News have branded themselves as more balanced alternatives to the liberal press. Letting the political tastes of the times drive the mainstream media to the right (and then perhaps to the left in the future) may not be the ideal conditions for thinking about clearer standards of journalistic accountability.[4]

If we can see beyond the conventional wisdom about liberal bias, the greatest problem with the free press in America may be its general conformity and dependence on official (usually government) versions of events. When reporting on political and policy issues, major news organizations, with occasional exceptions, conform to the prevailing currents of opinion among leading political elites, replacing objectivity with political authority and official pronouncements. This media conformity is such a regular finding of academic research on the news that scholars have begun referring to the media as an "institution." The media act as an institution in the sense that different news organizations seem to operate by remarkably similar rules of what "news" is. Scholar Timothy Cook calls this "the abiding paradox of newsmaking: News professes to be fresh, novel, and unexpected, but is actually remarkably patterned across news outlets and over time. Rather than providing an unpredictable and startling array of happenings, the content of news is similar from day to day, not only in featuring familiar personages and familiar locales, but also in the kinds of stories set forth and the morals these stories are supposed to tell."[5]

The media have also become institutionalized in terms of their relationship to government. In the American system, the media are formally independent from government. Yet they have become so embedded in the power relations that define conventional politics that their independence is highly constrained— what Cook describes as an "ever-closer linkage of newsmaking and policy-making to the point that they are all but indistinguishable."[6] The result is that the press has become something like a branch of government—without which the other branches would have trouble functioning, yet toward which many people have developed considerable doubt and mistrust. The American press, in other words, is formally "free" but is also dependent upon the government it is supposed to monitor in the public's behalf.

One irony of this system is that people who seek perspective on the heavily spun information coming through official channels into the news often turn to late-night comedy and other entertainment programming.[7] Many observers decry the idea that citizens might be informed by comedians such as Jay Leno or Jon Stewart, but it is more likely that such satire serves the same purpose that it has for ages: enabling skeptical publics to find common ground to think about the often limited information provided by those in power. Moreover, it is unlikely that most viewers of these programs are substituting them for real news. As *Daily Show* host Jon Stewart put it: "The truth is I know [most kids] are not [getting their news from us] because you can't—because we just don't do it. There's not enough news to get . . . If [kids] came to our show without knowledge, it wouldn't make any sense to them."[8] (Stewart's remark is similar to the point made by Jim Lehrer in chapter 3.) Indeed, research by Dannagal Young and Russell Tisinger shows that audiences for late-night comedy are among the best informed about politics and have high levels of mainstream news consumption.[9] These findings point to the conclusion that when the default standard for journalism becomes an unreflective reporting of official versions of events, some publics seek perspective in other places. For example, in the run-up to the Iraq war, the leading news organizations downplayed evidence that conflicted with Bush administration claims about weapons of mass destruction (WMDs) and links between Saddam Hussein and the terrorist attacks of September 11, while Stewart pointed out the foibles of the press and officials, alike, in nightly reports under the running head "Mess-o-Potamia."

A Conformist Press in Time of War

Perhaps the greatest lesson from the post-9/11 experience is that government can exercise tremendous pressure on public communication. This pressure can range from publicly condemning news organizations and individual journalists who depart from approved coverage, to offering tempting and dramatic exclusives to cooperative organizations that take the bait and cover important events just as government press-minders script them. In such an atmosphere of fear and news management, the government may get its story covered at the expense of other points of view. For example, even the nation's leading newspapers, such as the *New York Times* and the *Washington Post,* ran news much as manufactured by the White House—aimed at selling a war in Iraq based on claims of WMD and connecting Iraq to the events of 9/11. These papers later issued apologies to their readers for getting so caught up in the Bush administration's determination to go to war that they lost focus on competing perspectives on the necessity and wisdom of that war. As the *Times's* editors put it: "Looking back, we wish we had been more aggressive in re-examining the claims as new evidence [of WMD] emerged—or failed to emerge.... Articles based on dire claims about Iraq tended to get prominent display, while follow-up articles that called the original ones into question were sometimes buried. In some cases, there was no follow-up at all." [10]

Those apologies came far too late to affect the debate about whether to go to war; they also came after the papers had cooperated in reporting the administration's blatantly staged, made-for-Hollywood "ending" to the war in May 2003. When President George W. Bush gave his "Mission Accomplished" speech after landing in a *Top Gun* flight suit aboard an aircraft carrier converted to a big-screen movie set, nearly every major U.S. news organization reported the story just as it was scripted. Despite the news organizations' later apologies, the compliant news coverage of the war continued, as the press largely avoided covering the most potentially explosive aspects of the treatment of Iraqi detainees at Abu Ghraib and other facilities. [11]

Abu Ghraib and the Limits of Press Freedom

Although the memories may have begun to fade, images from inside Abu Ghraib prison were hard to escape as they flooded the airwaves and the Internet in spring 2004. Using personal digital cameras, U.S. soldiers had snapped hundreds of photographs, some showing Iraqi detainees in various states of humiliation and suffering. Most of the photos never became public, but those that did quickly became sickening icons of something gone wrong inside the U.S.-controlled prison: detainees being terrorized by unmuzzled dogs, male detainees forced to wear women's underwear, naked detainees forced to simulate masturbation and homosexual acts, hooded detainees attached to wires in either real or simulated electrocution—all with U.S. soldiers standing by, even joining in. The infamous photos of young Spec. Lynndie England grinning while she pointed at the detainees' exposed genitals and led them by leashes like dogs perhaps captured most pointedly the sense of chaos and degradation the Abu Ghraib photos conveyed. The photos showed not only humiliations inflicted for the entertainment of the low-ranking soldiers present, but also the use of interrogation techniques that higher military and civilian officials had approved, such as hooding, forced "stress positions" such as prolonged squatting, and the use of dogs to frighten prisoners. These distinctions were rarely made clear in the news coverage.[12]

The Abu Ghraib case illustrates just how hard it is for the press to exercise independence from government, even after admitting to being deceived by official spin on earlier aspects of the war. Despite having considerable independent information at its disposal about the nature and extent of problems in U.S. detention facilities in Iraq and Afghanistan, the nation's leading media found it difficult to offer a coherent alternative to the Bush administration's claim that Abu Ghraib was an isolated incident of poorly supervised low-level soldiers committing regrettable crimes. Challenging this official story was ample evidence that the administration had knowingly authorized practices in U.S. detention facilities in Iraq, Guantánamo Bay, Cuba, and elsewhere that many legal experts and much of the rest of the world's news coverage depicted in terms of government-authorized cruelty and torture.[13] There was also evidence that many inhabitants of these prisons were innocently caught in U.S. military sweeps and had little intelligence information, no matter what interrogation procedures they suffered, but this evidence received little press attention. In addition to contradicting the Bush administration's claims of democracy and decency in the conduct of the war, the practices in U.S. prisons also may have broken U.S. and international laws.[14] All in all, these would seem to be big stories worth exploring.

No one doubts that the photos were newsworthy. Indeed, leading news media gave them big play. The question is, what larger story did they tell? Some of the nation's top news organizations already had, or soon began to acquire, an impressive set of documentary evidence strongly suggesting that the photographed abuses were part of a larger story of how U.S. forces were capturing and detaining suspected terrorist and insurgent forces. In the months before and after the Abu Ghraib photos became public, the *Washington Post*, for example, reported at least fourteen different sources of evidence that suggested connections among Abu Ghraib, a pattern of inhumane treatment of U.S. detainees in other facilities, and high-level policy decisions about detention and interrogation procedures. But because the government spun those bits of evidence in different directions, they were not coherently tied together in the news to challenge the administration story.

The evidence available to the press included military reports, leaked internal government memos, testimony before the Senate Armed Services Committee, reports by independent human rights organizations, and the early stories from a few intrepid reporters documenting inhumane treatment of prisoners in other U.S. detention facilities. Perhaps most damning were the Pentagon and Justice Department memos that came to light shortly after the Abu Ghraib story broke. They brought the possibility of a high-level torture policy directly into the picture. The memos included a list of interrogation techniques—some shown in the photos from Abu Ghraib—approved by Secretary of Defense Donald Rumsfeld for use at the U.S. detention camp at Guantánamo Bay, techniques that had somehow "migrated" to Iraq; a 2002 Justice Department memo that made a case for exempting prisoners in the war on terror from U.S. and international legal restraints on torture; and an earlier memo written by White House counsel (later U.S. attorney general) Alberto Gonzales telling the president that he could declare members of the Taliban and al Qaeda to be outside the protection of the Geneva Conventions to allow more coercive interrogation techniques. The *Washington Post* reported Gonzales as advising the president: "In my judgment, this new paradigm [of the war on terrorism] renders obsolete Geneva's strict limitations on questioning of enemy prisoners and renders quaint some of its provisions."[15]

Despite this battery of evidence that seemed to contradict the administration's story, critical reports were left scattered, often in the back pages, without much interpretation or emphasis. Meanwhile, the front pages were dominated by administration spin that turned the story into a drama of appalling criminal acts by a cast of pathetic low-level soldiers. Given the volume of evidence to the contrary, one might have expected the Abu Ghraib photos to touch off a major national debate on the role of torture in U.S. policy—that is, the use of threats, humiliation, and physical pain against detainees, particularly to acquire information from them.[16] Instead, the national media largely avoided the term *torture* altogether, or buried it within stories on the inside pages. As a result, the most prevalent interpretation of the photos was that offered by President Bush, administration officials, and other Republican leaders who called the events at Abu Ghraib isolated cases of "mistreatment" and "abuse" at the hands of low-ranking soldiers. One study found that in the *Washington Post*—the same newspaper that had access to so much evidence suggesting a systematic U.S. policy of coercive interrogation—*abuse* was the primary term used in connection with the Abu Ghraib story in 81 percent of news stories. The word *torture*, by contrast, was primary in only 3 percent.[17]

The ironic epilogue to the Abu Ghraib story is that eventually, long after the photos had faded from the airwaves, the word *torture* became almost a household word as the media focused on an effort led by Arizona senator John McCain and other congressional leaders to pressure the White House to support an amendment limiting the cruel and inhuman treatment of war detainees. Of fifty-four articles mentioning the McCain amendment in the *Washington Post* between October and December 2005, 77 percent included the term *torture*—a dramatic contrast from the predominant pattern in coverage of Abu Ghraib. It was only when a powerful member of government (backed by enough Senate votes to challenge the president) "authorized" the discussion of torture in U.S. policy that the press finally focused on it as well. If the public had been looking to the news for ways of understanding the situation, it had to wait until some government insiders tried to correct its wrongdoing.

A Free and Dependent Press?

The twisted path of torture in the mainstream news illustrates perfectly the dependence of the institutional media upon government: until major congressional leaders forced a high-profile showdown with the president, the topic of torture was not high on the media agenda. Before the public airing of the issue during the McCain amendment fight, some credible sources were available to tell another side of the story. The problem was that these sources (independent journalists, legal experts, and the Red Cross and other humanitarian organizations) work outside of the government power hierarchy and so lack the institutionalized access and legitimacy the mainstream press commonly extends to prominent government officials.

The irony is that the press seems unable to sustain challenges to official versions of events unless and until those challenges come from government itself. As a large body of research has indicated, when leaders from the opposing party do not challenge an administration's policies (particularly regarding national security and war), the press is unlikely to raise challenges on its own.[18] Yet in the absence of critical press coverage, critics in either party have even less incentive to step forward. With Democrats out of power and unwilling to challenge a president who was still popular (and who was himself buoyed by supporting news coverage), the press was also unwilling to question his policies, even though many credible sources and considerable evidence raised doubts about the president's decisions and conduct of the war.

The lesson from Iraq is that despite freedoms guaranteed by the Constitution, the press operated largely in conformity with government spin, which resulted in many citizens becoming disillusioned about a war they initially supported based on dubious information. The point is not whether a more robust discussion in the media could have prevented a misguided war, but whether citizens might have become more engaged in discussing and expressing reasonable concerns. The press alone does not have the power to change the course of policy. In a fragmented, pluralist political system that values press "neutrality," we cannot expect the media alone to bring about major policy changes. The press can, however, engage and motivate citizens, experts, and officials from all quarters to enter public debates about policy, and such involvement can shape the course of events. Media scholar Robert Entman has proposed a reasonable standard for how the news could cover politics:

The media should provide enough information independent of the executive branch that citizens can construct their own counterframes of issues and events. It is not enough for the media to present information in ill-digested and scattered morsels. Rather, what citizens need is a counterframe constructed of culturally resonant words and images, one that attains sufficient magnitude to gain wide understanding as a sensible alternative to the White House's interpretation.[19]

In the absence of reliably independent coverage of important events, many citizens are turning to other sources of information, in particular, the Internet, which offers a broad spectrum of ideas and perspectives, ranging from the Web sites of leading news organizations from around the world to direct citizen observations in the form of blogs. But does the Internet really expose the public to different and better information patterns, and can such parallel, fragmented channels of information be as effective as the mainstream media in shaping public debate?

Is the Internet the Answer?

Many observers argue that with the rise of the Internet and its proliferating information sources, people have more information sources than ever before. Digital media technologies enable citizens to sample from great volumes of information, and even to produce their own content. For example, citizen news monitors used their blogs to expose a CBS News story based on documents alleging that Bush dodged his duties in the Air National Guard. The bloggers showed that the documents were likely to have been fabricated. Ultimately, the story led to the resignation of venerated news anchor Dan Rather.

The reach of the Web enables broad distribution of information that goes well beyond scrutiny of mainstream news and that would otherwise be limited in its reach. In 2005 when a small Danish newspaper issued a challenge to cartoonists to spoof the Prophet Mohammed in the name of protecting free speech, the resulting cartoons spread widely through newspapers, the Internet, and other digital media and angered much of the Islamic world. More than a year after the incident occurred, a Google search for "Danish Mohammed cartoons" still produced nearly 1 million Web hits, a remarkable number. Many of those Web sites were clearly intended to inflame already tense relations between the West and the Islamic world. Indeed, this small assertion of press freedom by an obscure Danish paper touched off riots and protests throughout Islamic communities from Denmark to Pakistan, resulting in more than one hundred deaths. The damage to strained political relations during a time of war raises questions about the responsible use of press freedom, particularly when local communication can quickly become globally accessible. The Danish cartoons remind us in a different way that press freedom in the absence of clear public standards does not guarantee responsibility or accountability, particularly when dealing with inflammatory images.

For better or worse, the Web is alive with experiments in citizen-produced information from the mixed bag of YouTube.com to OhMyNews.com, a Korean online paper with tens of thousands of citizen journalists who produce a daily flow of news, features, and reviews. Can we say anything about credibility and focus in these new media? Despite the many different sites and the resulting fragmentation of audiences, numerous examples suggest that these digital media channels are affecting the mainstream news agenda.

An example of Web-driven news occurred during the 2006 election campaign when Sen. George Allen of Virginia, running for reelection, derided a young man working for his opponent, James Webb. The Webb campaign staffer was engaged in the common practice of videotaping a rally to try to catch the candidate in a gaffe. (Allen's campaign engaged in similar practices.) At one point in the rally, Allen pointed out the taping activity and referred to S. R. Sidarth, the person with the camera, as a "macaca," and suggested that he was an immigrant who should be welcomed "to America and the real world of Virginia." Sidarth, a student at the University of Virginia, is of Indian heritage and a Virginia native. The Webb campaign posted the video on You Tube.com, where it became one of the most viewed videos on the site. From there, it made the mainstream news and became an issue in the election, which Webb, who was considered a long shot, won by a narrow margin. Naturally, other factors influenced the election, but surely the production and distribution of the tape of this damaging incident helped to close the gap and play a part in Webb's unexpected victory, which resulted in a Democratic takeover of the U.S. Senate. Allen's imprudent remarks dealt a blow to his political career and the possibility of a presidential bid in 2008. This sort of information flow suggests new possibilities for the future of news as the conventional media interact with new communication technologies.

Before Allen and his videotaper, the presence of citizens with cameras had already changed the news game. In 1991 a bystander's videotape of Los Angeles police officers beating black motorist Rodney King dominated the airwaves and led to the resignation of LAPD chief Daryl Gates and, later, to fiery riots when the officers were acquitted of criminal charges. The images from inside Abu Ghraib prison were taken by American soldiers with their digital cameras. These incidents, however, involved citizens giving the images to conventional news organizations to publicize. In contrast, George Allen's gaffe and Dan Rather's documents began as stories in the alternative public spheres of blogs and YouTube, then quickly migrated to the mainstream media when they caught journalists' interest. One thing that all of these examples suggest is that the Internet may change the microdynamics of the game, but it is unlikely to replace conventional media's ability to focus public attention in ways that bring scrutiny and accountability—however imperfect—to those in public life.

Why Mainstream Media Still Matter

Mainstream media continue to matter because they constitute the common meeting point for political ideas and a main arena for the formation of public opinion. Even as alternative media channels proliferate, the conventional media provide the connecting material that helps active publics form. For all the diversity of information that lies beyond the mainstream, those second and third tiers of media reach only small factional audiences and do not speak with the agenda-reinforcing voice that emanates from the top tier media. The mainstream media are regularly fed, monitored, and targeted with information, albeit seasoned with spin, by influential elites. They share the same networks of wire feeds and news beats. They look to the same leading organizations (such as the *New York Times, Washington Post,* and *Wall Street Journal*) for determining the top stories and news frames. They also cling to the same enduring, if fraying, commitment to the ideal of objectivity—an ideal that ironically supports their reliance on officials as the most legitimate sources for authoritative information.[20]

Despite the diversity of information channels available to Americans, most alternative media, from small magazines to Webzines, play a secondary role in the process of shaping mass opinion about political issues or reinforcing the policy agendas set by influential members of government and special interest networks. Indeed, the great irony of public information in America is that the spectrum of information available to citizens may be unsurpassed by any other nation, given the profusion of alternative publications, niche cable and radio, and the extraordinarily high rates of broadband and general Internet access. But it is the institutionalized mainstream press that matters most for public opinion regarding politics, because it speaks with such a singular voice (often the voice of government itself) and still commands the attention of mass audiences. For these reasons, the public interest standards and responsibilities of the mainstream press need reexamination. No matter how pressing this need may be, the trend toward corporate mergers and government deregulation makes it difficult to address it.

Commercial Media Versus Social Responsibility

The Telecommunications Act of 1996 was presented to the public by politicians from both parties as opening the marketplace of ideas to greater diversity by freeing corporations to own more media outlets such as television and radio stations and newspapers in the same markets. The thin argument behind this implausible notion was that media companies surely would not buy new properties that produced content that competed with properties they already owned. As it turned out, many newly acquired properties were merged, stripped, reformatted, or simply killed. The result was more generic, formula-driven newspapers and broadcast channels to sell recycled products to targeted demographic audiences. Around the edges, small and less-profitable audiences (for ethnic programming, classical music, or in-depth news coverage) were generally lopped off and lost in the corporate logic. Cable systems packed in more shopping and religion channels. Newspaper chains added more papers and TV channels, as they slashed reporting resources and added promotional lifestyle features on travel, home, and fashion for upscale readers.

Large media companies lobbied heavily for these reforms and contributed to the political funds of both parties. It is no surprise that this landmark legislation was barely reported in the news and received almost no critical coverage. The resulting levels of media concentration—which were already staggering by the 1990s—became breathtaking as the new millennium began.

Just how well has the free market worked to realize the ideals of a free press? Today, most local radio stations are owned by distant corporations that pump formula music and other content from afar, while cutting news and public affairs down to near nothing in many cases. Most of these stations have no news staff and cannot report on local affairs. Today, many once-excellent newspapers such as the *San Jose Mercury* and the *Los Angeles Times* have been stripped of resources, inflated with lifestyle features, and milked for profits. These trends suggest that leaving a free press to the forces of the free market is ideal only for investors—and even they are beginning to sour on their own excess. Former claims about how the public interest is served by deregulation now seem little more than public relations fodder.

We are currently looking at a media system in which the ideal of press freedom is becoming a shield to defend corporations against pressures to be more responsible in the public interest. For example, as the content of news on local television deteriorates, companies hide behind the First Amendment to defend their right to free speech. On most local news programs, that means more mayhem and less reporting on government and civic affairs. In 1998, when the media merger mania was at full roar, an activist group called Rocky Mountain Media Watch challenged local television license renewals of four stations in Denver. The citizens' group charged that the levels of sensational news—spawned by the "if it bleeds, it leads" local TV formula—made local news "toxic" and hazardous to public health. Yet the Federal Communications Commission (FCC), which presides over license renewal hearings, ruled in favor of the Denver stations on First Amendment grounds.[21]

The use of constitutionally guaranteed freedoms to defend practices that arguably undermine the public interest presents a serious dilemma. Press freedom as understood by most large corporations (and by many Americans who have been taught to oppose government regulation) seems to require that no strings be attached to First Amendment protections. This view begs the question of where news organizations will find standards of public responsibility to guide them in dealing with ongoing government attempts to manage the news, and to help them resist the pressures of the economic marketplace. In the absence of such standards, press decisions about what is news have become ever more anemic—deteriorating into mere echoes of government consensus and the lowest common denominator of public taste.[22] This situation calls for renewed public discussion of how the press should exercise its freedom in the public interest. One place to start is with a look back at a time not so long ago when the press had precedents for setting clearer and stronger standards.

Perhaps even more surprising, we see that people once trusted the government to help develop and monitor those standards.

Can Government Regulation Help?

One obvious solution to the problems of formulaic, commercially driven news is government regulation—that is, deciding through broad public input what kind of information serves democracy well, and then providing government policies to monitor and enforce greater competition and independence in the media. Beyond legislating requirements for some minimum amount of public affairs content, most democratic nations have far stronger provisions for independent public service broadcasting than does the United States, and some even have subsidies for newspapers in areas where there would be no competing press otherwise.

Even broaching the subject of government regulation of the media is difficult these days in the United States, partly because of the prevailing climate of opinion—particularly among business and political elites—against regulation. This equation of freedom with avoidance of government involvement in setting standards means that the history of public interest broadcast regulation in the United States has been weaker than in other countries such as Canada or England. Still, at times the United States has had stronger media regulation, including the now defunct fairness doctrine, a set of FCC policies that in theory, at least, guided the agency's decisions about renewing the licenses of broadcasters. By the terms of the fairness doctrine, broadcasters were understood to have a public obligation to air controversial topics and to provide more than one viewpoint on those issues, both during election campaigns and at other times.

Perhaps the most dramatic instance of the use of the fairness doctrine occurred when the FCC decided that President Richard Nixon had used the airwaves so extensively to promote his Vietnam War policies that the networks needed to grant critics of the war equal time to respond. But that level of government intervention was rare. As media scholar Robert McChesney points out, the fairness doctrine "was never enforced to require commercial broadcasters to do ample public affairs and controversial programming."[23] Even though the fairness doctrine was not pushed very hard to create clearer public standards, the sentiments against regulation that accompanied the rising conservative tide of the 1980s began to push it even farther back. By 1987 FCC chairman Mark Fowler had vowed to kill the doctrine, and the federal courts declared that it did not have to be enforced. In response, Congress attempted to write the fairness doctrine into law, but President Ronald Reagan vetoed the legislation. Since then, broadcasters no longer are held to the doctrine's formal obligations to the public.

The fairness doctrine is not the only example of public interest media regulation in U.S. history, and the 1970s were not the only time that American elites considered what might be done if a nominally free press seemed to slight the public interest. The media's public interest obligations were debated in the 1930s with the establishment of the regulatory framework for the emerging radio industry.[24] They were debated again in the 1940s, when a blue-ribbon panel called the Hutchins Commission reviewed the media industry and found problems stemming from media consolidation. The commission considered a number of standards for the social responsibility of the press.[25] If we fast-forward to the present, these topics were barely debated by the Congress that passed the 1996 Telecommunications Act.

But not everyone has forgotten the possibility of greater public discipline over the press. A coalition of citizens and interest groups led an unprecedented public reaction to proposed FCC rules changes in 2003 that would have allowed even greater consolidation of media ownership. Despite the dearth of news coverage about those proposed changes, citizens of many political stripes helped pressure Congress to block them.[26] Today an active citizen media reform movement is attempting to raise public discussion of media responsibilities and standards that would help address them.[27]

It is not surprising that this movement is not led by public officials because politicians may have benefited most from a commercially focused, politically docile press. For example, as hard news coverage of elections has declined, political advertising has become more important than news in introducing candidates and airing issues during campaigns. This trend suits the broadcast media industry, which now earns a huge chunk of its revenues from political ads, and it suits the candidates, who can control the messages in their ads more directly than they can control the "free media" of the news. And so, as government has been pushed out of the regulatory picture, many politicians actively attack the press in ways that further undermine its independence and critical edge. Indeed, attacking the press has become a core strategy within the conservative social movement that rose to power during the 1980s and 1990s.

Few have worked harder than members of the Bush administration to discredit the press and undermine its role in the political system. The administration's techniques, often attributed to communications chief Karl Rove, have included an eye-opening array of tactics, including bullying reporters who raise critical questions, doing an end run around the press by producing its own "news" segments to promote domestic and foreign policies, and infiltrating the press corps at briefings and press conferences with supporters disguised as reporters.[28] As longtime media observer Jay Rosen describes it, the Bush White House did not "settle for managing the news—what used to be called 'feeding the beast'—because there is a larger aim: to roll back the press as a player within the executive branch, to make it less important in running the White House and governing the country."[29]

Rather than wait for politicians to consider new standards for the news (especially because it is politicians who have helped turned the public against the press in the first place), perhaps we should consider other ways to foster public debate and dialogue with journalists on the role of the media in democracy. We offer several possible starting points for such a debate.

Three Models of Press Responsibility

Luckily, we do not have to invent new standards of press performance entirely from scratch. Several models already exist in the history of U.S. journalism to suggest how press freedom can be used in socially responsible ways. They are the watchdog, the marketplace of ideas, and civic journalism. Each offers standards worth considering and reinvigorating.

Two of these standards, the watchdog and the marketplace of ideas, are widely accepted ideals within American journalism—even though they are currently honored more in theory than in practice. The ideal of watchdog journalism envisions the media as the eyes and ears of the public, continually scrutinizing government and other social institutions such as business for signs of malfunction and malfeasance. As Supreme Court justice Potter Stewart once described this ideal, it is the obligation of the free press to provide "organized, expert scrutiny of government" and to "create a fourth institution outside the Government as an additional check on the three official branches."[30]

Today's mainstream media do occasionally rise to that challenge, but substantive watchdogging does not seem to be the norm. Occasional investigative reports do crop up, and some are quite consequential, such as those in 2005 that revealed the National Security Agency's domestic surveillance program and the administration's secret complex of "black sites" for detaining and interrogating suspected terrorists. But more common are stories focusing on politicians' campaign tactics, gaffes, and scandals, stories that provide a political scorecard in the game of Washington politics rather than a steady, independent-minded scrutiny of issues of wide public concern.[31] As media scholar Thomas Patterson observes, the sensationalized soft news that "passes for watchdog journalism . . . needs to give way to a more credible form of journalism" that neither ignores official wrongdoing nor "turn[s] the media agenda over to the newsmakers."[32]

The marketplace ideal, in which the media provide robust public debate among a diversity of views so that the best or "truest" ideas can rise to the top, also has deep roots in American political thought and jurisprudence.[33] It was this ideal that the fairness doctrine was designed to achieve: to ensure that the media organizations that dominate the airwaves presented more than a single perspective. But like the watchdog ideal, this ideal is honored more often when government is already doing its job of vigorously debating issues and alternatives. When a high-level government debate breaks out, as happened in the case of the McCain antitorture amendment, the news gates swing open to admit a wider range of voices and views.[34] Whether government debate is vibrant or broadly representative of views and voices in society, the daily norm is news that sticks closely to the press releases and public performances of leading politicians, producing those remarkably similar news stories across the vast media landscape.

It is the marketplace ideal that many fans of the Internet implicitly refer to when they celebrate its possibilities for diverse information channels. Enhancing the marketplace of ideas by adding numerous idea boutiques would seem to be one of the Internet's strengths. As noted, however, those small sites do not displace the dominant mainstream news organizations that are most readily encountered by most visitors to the media marketplace, whether they read newspapers, watch television, or go online. With the major press so often offering essentially the same narrow range of ideas, the marketplace of ideas today looks more like a standardized shopping mall filled with big-name chain stores.

The third news standard that could inform a new public debate about the role of media in democracies is the more controversial civic journalism that some news organizations have experimented with. Civic journalism advocates argue for shifting away from conventional journalism that simply depicts "both sides" (usually official) of any given political controversy toward explanatory news stories that provide greater context and a wider range of viewpoints. They also advocate allowing the public, through opinion polls, focus groups, and town hall meetings, to tell journalists what issues they want to see covered. Like the watchdog and marketplace models, the civic journalism ideal purports to derive from the Constitution. According to one of its leading advocates, the press "is singled out for special protection because its independent status is what keeps a free people free."[35]

Despite its potential for empowering citizens and restoring their confidence in news, mainstream news organizations have not widely embraced civic journalism. Many leading journalists have objected that allowing the public to set the news agenda compromises their professional integrity, an argument that reveals some of the primary assumptions on which mainstream journalism rests. Experiments with civic journalism also began to decline when one of its major promoters, the Pew Center for Civic Journalism, curtailed its funding. Despite its sometimes chilly reception by many leaders in the press and its uneven financial support, the civic journalism ideal raises a useful question: Is journalistic integrity better upheld by allowing government spin to set the news agenda, or by inviting citizens to set some of the news agenda based on issues they care about?

Time for a National Discussion

Any of these models for a well-functioning press needs support from a variety of sources to be more fully realized. Reversing the direction of recent media regulation seems a crucial first step to stop further media consolidation and encourage greater diversity in media ownership, bringing us closer to the marketplace of ideas model. News organizations must also be released from the intense economic pressures experienced from competition by entertainment and other industries—something that can happen only through a combination of government regulation, citizen pressure, journalistic resistance to crude market demands, and revised industry practices and standards.

In the meantime, the watchdog ideal can perhaps best be reinvigorated from within journalism itself. At present, watchdog reporting seems to occur most reliably when spurred by other groups, such as political parties, interest groups, and bloggers, who also try to play a watchdog role.[36] But a consistent desire to achieve the watchdog tradition of independent-minded scrutiny must come from reporters, the journalism schools that train them, and the news organizations that employ them.[37]

Embracing something closer to civic journalism would require wholesale changes in the present norms of the journalistic profession. Such changes would take a combination of internal agitation by dissatisfied reporters and external pressures from citizens tired of the news-as-usual, and perhaps the support of private foundations such as those that spurred the initial experiments in civic journalism across the country.

Although each ideal is somewhat distinct, together they suggest a starting place for media reform: Americans (officials, journalists, and citizens) must take more seriously the idea that the First Amendment protects more than the freedom of corporate media to maximize profits and play it safe politically. The notion is simple and yet radical: the press enjoys its constitutional protections from government censorship in order to serve democracy and the public interest. Just as public pressure introduced the First Amendment into the Constitution, it is pressure from the people today that will restore the spirit of a free press.

Many signs of popular interest in media reform have surfaced, starting in 2003 with the public protest that stopped the FCC from allowing further ownership deregulation. Since then increasing numbers of people have joined local media watchdog groups and linked nationally to organizations such as freepress.net to keep informed about issues and think about ways to promote national discussion of press reform. The sentiment is growing that press freedom should not merely enhance the press's ability to do whatever it wishes. Freedom with responsibilities attached would enable the press to be the eyes and ears of the public, even to be the public's voice, while providing a robust forum for public debate. These ideals are as American as apple pie.

Notes

1. Regina Lawrence, "Daily News and First Amendment Ideals," in *Freeing the Presses*, ed. Timothy Cook (Baton Rouge: Louisiana State University Press, 2005), 87–108.

2. Denis McQuail, *Media Accountability and Freedom of Publication* (Oxford; New York: Oxford University Press, 2003).

3. Thomas Patterson, "Doing Well and Doing Good: How Soft News and Critical Journalism Are Shrinking the News Audience and Weakening Democracy—And What News Outlets Can Do About It," Kennedy School research report, Shorenstein Center on the Press, Politics, and Public Policy, Harvard University, 2000, 14.

4. For a more detailed discussion of the issue of press bias, see W. Lance Bennett, *News: The Politics of Illusion*, 7th ed. (New York: Longman, 2007).

5. Timothy Cook, "Afterword: Political Values and Production Values," *Political Communication* 13 (October–December 1996): 469.

6. Timothy Cook, "The News Media as a Political Institution: Looking Backward and Looking Forward," *Political Communication* 23 (April–June 2006): 160.

7. See Michael X. Delli Carpini and Bruce A. Williams, "Let Us Infotain You: Politics in the New Media Environment," in W. Lance Bennett and Robert M. Entman, eds., *Mediated Politics: Communication in the Future of Democracy* (New York: Cambridge University Press, 2001), 160–181.

8. Quoted in Dannagal G. Young and Russell M. Tisinger, "Dispelling Late-Night Myths: News Consumption Among Late-Night Comedy Viewers and the Predictors of Exposure to Various Late-Night Shows," *Press-Politics* 11 (Summer 2006): 115.

9. Ibid.

10. *New York Times*, "The Times and Iraq: From the Editors," May 26, 2004, *www .nytimes.com/2004/05/26/international/middleeast/26FTE_NOTE.html?ex=1400990400& en=94c17fcffad92ca9&ei=5007&partner=USERLAND*, accessed April 12, 2006. For other accounts of the administration's faulty claims about WMD in Iraq and the press's failures to counter them, see Michael Massing, *Now They Tell Us: The American Press and Iraq* (New York: New York Review of Books, 2004); Paul R. Pillar, "Intelligence, Policy, and the War in Iraq," *Foreign Affairs* (March/April 2006): 15–27; and Bob Woodward, *State of Denial* (New York: Simon and Schuster, 2006).

11. W. Lance Bennett, Regina G. Lawrence, and Steven Livingston, *When the Press Fails: The News Media and Political Power from Iraq to Katrina* (Chicago: University of Chicago Press, 2007).

12. See Mark Danner, "Abu Ghraib: The Hidden Story," *New York Review of Books*, October 7, 2004, 44–50.

13. This evidence is reviewed in Bennett, Lawrence, and Livingston, *When the Press Fails*, chaps. 3 and 4. See also Mark Danner, *Torture and Truth: America, Abu Ghraib, and the War on Terror* (New York: *New York Review of Books*, 2004); Jane Mayer, "The Memo," *New Yorker*, February 27, 2006, 32–41; and Seymour Hersh, *Chain of Command: The Road from 9/11 to Abu Ghraib* (New York: HarperCollins, 2005).

14. Kathryn Sikkink, "U.S. Compliance with International Human Rights Law," paper presented at the annual meeting of the International Studies Association, Honolulu, Hawaii, 2005; and United Nations Commission on Human Rights, "Situation of Detainees at Guantánamo Bay," February 15, 2006, *www.ohchr.org/english/bodies/chr/ docs/62chr/E.CN.4.2006.120_.pdf*, accessed February 16, 2006.

15. Glen Kessler, "U.S. Releases Human Rights Report Delayed After Abuse Scandal," *Washington Post*, May 18, 2004, A15. After these memos were leaked to the press, Gonzales told reporters that the president did not actually consider adopting those more aggressive measures. He added, "All interrogation techniques actually authorized have been carefully vetted, are lawful and do not constitute torture." The president, when asked, said what he continued to say even when he was eventually forced politically to accept Sen. John McCain's legislation banning cruel and inhumane treatment of prisoners: "We do not condone torture. I have never ordered torture. I will never order torture."

16. The International Convention Against Torture includes the purpose of gathering intelligence or extracting information as one element in its definition of torture. See United Nations Commission on Human Rights, "Situation of Detainees at Guantánamo Bay."

17. Bennett, Lawrence, and Livingston, *When the Press Fails*, chap. 3.

18. See Bennett, Lawrence, and Livingston, *When the Press Fails*.

19. Robert Entman, *Projections of Power: Framing News, Public Opinion, and U.S. Foreign Policy* (Chicago: University of Chicago Press, 2004), 17.

20. See David T. Z. Mindich, *Just the Facts: How "Objectivity" Came to Define American Journalism* (New York: New York University Press, 1998).

21. For a more detailed discussion of this case, see Bennett, *News: The Politics of Illusion*, 19.

22. On media "uncertainties" that encourage cautious news coverage of political issues, see Bartholomew Sparrow, *Uncertain Guardians: The News Media as a Political Institution* (Baltimore: Johns Hopkins University Press, 1999).

23. Robert McChesney, *The Problem of the Media: U.S. Communication Politics in the 21st Century* (New York: Monthly Review Press, 2004), 44.

24. See Robert McChesney, *Rich Media, Poor Democracy: Communication Politics in Dubious Times* (New York: New Press, 2000).

25. See Stephen Bates, "Realigning Journalism with Democracy: The Hutchins Commission, Its Times, and Ours," Annenberg Washington Program of Northwestern University, 1995, *www.annenberg.northwestern.edu/pubs/hutchins/*, accessed June 14, 2006.

26. See McChesney, *The Problem of the Media*, chap. 1.

27. See *freepress.net* for an example.

28. See Bennett, Lawrence, and Livingston, *When the Press Fails*, chap. 5; Michael Massing, "The End of News?" *New York Review of Books*, November 15, 2005, *www.nybooks.com/articles/18516*, accessed January 15, 2006.

29. Jay Rosen, "Rollback," *Pressthink*, July 16, 2005, *http://journalism.nyu.edu/pubzone/weblogs/pressthink*, accessed July 20, 2005.

30. Potter Stewart, "Or Of the Press," *Hastings Law Journal* 26 (1975): 631. Although Stewart's description may have been historically inaccurate, he was articulating a powerful idea in American culture. See Timothy Cook, "Freeing the Presses: An Introductory Essay," in *Freeing the Presses*, ed. Timothy Cook (Baton Rouge: Louisiana State University Press, 2005), 1–28.

31. W. Lance Bennett and William Serrin, "The Watchdog Role," in *The Press*, eds. Geneva Overholser and Kathleen Hall Jamieson (New York: Oxford University Press, 2005), 169–188.

32. Patterson, "Doing Well and Doing Good."

33. Philip M. Napoli, "The Marketplace of Ideas Metaphor in Communications Regulation," *Journal of Communication* 49 (Autumn 1999): 151–169.

34. W. Lance Bennett terms this dynamic "indexing" in "Toward a Theory of Press-State Relations in the United States," *Journal of Communication* 40 (Spring 1990): 103–127.

35. Jay Rosen, *What Are Journalists For?* (New Haven: Yale University Press, 1999), 187.

36. See Bennett and Serrin, "The Watchdog Role."

37. Ibid., 182.

Conclusion: Contemporary Challenges in Journalism and Democracy

Denis McQuail, Doris A. Graber, and Pippa Norris

The connection between news and democratic politics is an intimate one, even though the relationship varies and changes according to time and place. The connection is based on two ideas: (1) that news is a primary determinant of public opinion as well as an indicator of public opinion, and (2) that public opinion is ultimately translated into votes. These assumptions have proved difficult to establish definitively and precisely, and the linkages are somewhat uncertain. Even so, we can find sufficient evidence to justify the view that the health of democratic politics depends on the general quality of journalism and the effective working of the press as an institution of public life. Judgments of quality are also not easy to arrive at and depend on evidence reflecting different and competing perspectives in the political process. The essential elements in the assessment have always centered on the freedom and independence of the press in a given political system and the volume, variety, and adequacy of the information provided by news media, according to varying criteria of truth. In a freely competitive political environment, all participants seek to maximize benefits and advantages with the means at their disposal. The guiding assumption within the liberal model of politics is that pluralistic competition works to the benefit of all participants.

The contributors to this book all speak with a certain amount of consistency about the current situation, especially its more problematic aspects. Although the material mainly relates to the United States, many of the same features have been observed in other Western democracies or are anticipated in varying degrees before too long. Developments in post-Soviet Eastern and Central Europe suggest that interactions there between media and political actors are taking on quite familiar forms with respect to the needs of democratic processes, the pressures on the press, and the tensions between political actors and journalists. In this case, however, a fault line seems to have opened between the countries that have rejoined the "West" and Russia and some other states that have to a degree rejected the liberal model.

The relationship between politics and news is dynamic and involves pressures, restraints, and demands for access on the side of politicians and counterclaims from the media, especially where their independence, professional integrity, or commercial interests might be at stake. Generally, the news media have de facto control over the "gates" giving access to the public and are supported in this by democratic theory, but access is still a perennial source of tension. In practice, mutual assistance may be as common as conflict, although the one is not necessarily more healthy for democracy than the other. Both have their dangers. Democratic politics certainly needs the news, even if not all news is good news for politicians. Disputes over news access are mitigated by the potential assimilation of the media and political and press roles. For the media, news of politics has always been a staple commodity—relatively cheap, plentiful, and in demand. Ritual complaints of public satiation are soon forgotten at times of crisis and heightened awareness; fears that the audience for political news is gradually dwindling and aging are never quite realized. Young people as they grow up tend to discover the relevance of politics, and new forms of media are compensating for the limitations of traditional channels.

These remarks indicate that the problems in the relationship between news and politics, in the age of mass democracies, are perennial but ameliorated by the normal operation of the media market in conjunction with the "free marketplace of ideas." According to a relaxed view of the case, the chief problems that affect the state of news are attributable either to the rather low requirements of most citizens as news consumers and their failure (or inability) to make use of the information on offer, or to the unrealistic judgments of elites about the true information needs of citizens. These requirements are assessed according to the standard of the committed political activist rather than the average voter, who needs only the equivalent of a "burglar alarm," for problematic eventualities.[1] Within these terms, the problems appear to be soluble by the traditional means of better education and by gradually closing residual "knowledge gaps," aided by improved journalistic professionalism and more volume and diversity of news systems. Arguably, however, more fundamental diagnoses are called for, and essential continuity and self-correction cannot be counted on as a matter of course. Such doubts have varied origins and take varied forms, but add up to a fear that the current dynamics of the relationship between politics and news are aggravating rather than alleviating the situation. Among the underlying causes of the malady are three primary and interrelated factors: (1) gradual public disengagement from, and disillusion with, mainstream politics, as part of more general social and cultural changes; (2) stronger commercial pressures on global and national news media; and (3) emerging forms of political campaigning (and even of governing) that rely on manipulation, marketing, and the management of opinion. This last factor is associated with the further secularization of politics, increased media leverage, and a burden of cost that gives an advantage to the wealthy.

It cannot be claimed that between the first and second editions of this book, we have witnessed a fundamental shift in the forces involved and the factors at work. Nevertheless, certain trends that are germane to these general issues have continued or accelerated.[2] And democratic political systems have been put to the first severe test since the euphoria and complacency that followed the collapse of communism and the supposed "end of history." In addition, the institutions in which news is produced for public consumption are changing, possibly quite profoundly, for technological and market reasons. Speaking first of the global geopolitical changes, we have entered a period of more active military intervention and response in relations between states, centered most immediately on the newly perceived threats to the United States and the West, even to the established international order and its value system. For present purposes, the main point is that these threats can only be handled in a democratic political process by way of journalism that provides the public with a great deal of information and with convincing frameworks of interpretation. In the circumstances of international conflict and crisis, the demands made from all sides on news are higher, and in a quasi-war situation the news media find it is more difficult than usual to deviate far from the perspectives and wishes of elected governments. The routine demands and constraints on mass mediated news are accentuated, reducing sources of independent news and making independent news judgments more risky, organizationally and commercially.

Quite apart from the changing environment of critical events, there has been, and continues to be, an accretion of practices of news (and opinion) management and control, by way of staged events, close surveillance of opinion, and all the usual devices of public relations and political marketing. These trends are legitimate, mainly informal in manifestation, and often exposed to view by journalism itself, but they contribute to a cynicism about news as well as about politics. Although it is not yet possible for free media to be fully controlled, nor for free populations to be brainwashed en masse, traditional inhibitions on interference in the work of news media have been reduced, along with other liberties. At present the chance is quite remote that the mainstream media will adopt outright oppositional news policies and agendas on sensitive issues, even when they express contrary editorial opinions. The context of (probable) greater submission of news media to agencies of national power is influenced by the trends of media industry conglomeration and commodification. The need to make a profit also plays an inhibiting role, where independent reporting and commentary of quality carry a high price and have an uncertain yield if they go against dominant opinion. The argument that economic independence can sustain freedom of journalistic expression applies only under certain conditions and can be negated when the final criterion has to be profitability in the larger media marketplace.

Democratic News Models

Alternative versions of the ideal relationship between news and democratic politics are still part of the discussion. The most conventional version sees news as an objective and trustworthy account of reality, provided by expert observers and reported in a disinterested and professional manner, coupled with a willingness to adopt an adversary role vis-à-vis government. This version gained ground steadily during the twentieth century on the basis of the professionalization of journalism. It is the model most suited to serving large national and international markets for news as a commodity. It makes a strong claim for the independence of journalism from political power, valuing the former far above the latter; it also asserts a clear separation between the facts of the news and any opinion, interpretation, or argument. The credibility of news derives from conventions of objective reporting and from the professional integrity of journalists, which should set limits to manipulation for political ends.

In an older, but declining tradition of democratic politics the news (ideally) is not independent of politics but is politicized on behalf of competing parties in a transparent way. This tradition survives in a number of northern Europe's democracies. The two models, one of professional objectivity and the other of political commitment, are both still extant, although they are often found in hybrid forms. They depend upon and foster a distinctive relationship among journalism, politics, and society that is further embedded in a particular political culture and resistant to change.[3] It is clear from cross-national comparisons, for example, Thomas Patterson's chapter in this volume and David Weaver's book, *The Global Journalist,* that journalists' attitudes toward their professional roles often contain elements of both models.[4] It is not hard to support the view that democratic process requires not only the detached observation of events and persons as well as critical engagement but also the representation of basic political values and beliefs.

Both versions of the democratic news model rely on certain conditions and assumptions. Most important is the precondition that political news be in demand and that audiences see it as relevant and useful. In the "neutral" model of journalism, the continued supply of news has to be "paid for" by audience interest and attention, notably via advertising. Without this support, the resources of the media would be diverted away from politics or might have to be derived from other sources that could undermine the credibility and integrity of the news. The "partisan" model would, by definition, lose its raison d'être without the continued existence of actively engaged and ideologically committed publics.

These versions of news and politics, generally in mixed forms, still dominate the spectrum of news in democratic political systems. We can, however, identify other bases for a relationship, with historical examples, that tell us at least that nothing is fixed and that alternative values and institutional forms for journalism do exist besides those that reflect either the principles of determination by market or by political ideology. Among these alternatives are (1) the social responsibility model, as exemplified in regulated public broadcasting, that adopts the objective news standard, without any adversarial stance; (2) the radical oppositional press of resistance movements and action groups that rejects objectivity; (3) the communitarian model in its various forms—including "civic journalism"—that rests on shared values of local citizenship and community; and (4) the development model, which accepts a role for journalism in national economic and social development. Such alternatives are also dependent on favorable conditions of political culture and practical feasibility and cannot simply be adopted at will as solutions to the kinds of problems indicated.

A Crisis of Political News?

The contributors to this book all share a sense that something new is at hand in the relations between the press and political actors. It has long been clear that ideology is a declining force in political behavior and that partisanship has been weakening, even in the most favorable national circumstances. The news media still have a unique value for politicians just because most voters see them as more independent and trustworthy sources than parties and their propaganda. In addition, there is plenty of evidence that voters look to the news media for guidance, perhaps more than to politicians directly. These elements are enough to promote a symbiotic relationship between media and politics that benefits the democratic process.

New strains, however, are arising from changes in politics and the media. Political actors change because they must respond to developments in society and in political culture. The media also respond to social change, and they must adapt to new conditions created by revolutionary progress in information technology. This technology intensifies media competition and destabilizes established media structures and relationships. The balance between the media's traditional public role in democratic society and their private commercial imperatives is being severely disturbed. The media are no longer, if they ever were, primarily institutions of public life but profit (or loss) centers for large corporations.

Two aspects of the crisis described in the foregoing remarks are particularly noteworthy. First, it seems that whatever the aims or expectations of the news media, they never seem to inform adequately, according to their numerous critics. Second, what passes for news of politics is often an inextricable mixture of messages from different sources as well as a soup of information and entertainment. Advertising, public relations, reports of opinion polls, gossip, scandal, and propaganda are blended into the news product along with facts and editorial opinions in ways that can confuse or mislead as well as engage the unwary news consumer. This mixing is neither random nor casual. It often combines the covert aims of political agencies and interests with the self-interests of the media. The media follow a logic of entertainment and story-telling designed to catch the attention of an audience that is typically not deeply interested in, or discerning about, routine political events. Politicians silently conspire with news media to maximize audience exposure at almost any price. Audience reach and ratings also seem to matter more to participants in the political "game" than do any measures of news depth or intrinsic quality. It certainly tends to undermine any simple faith in the reliability and independence of news.

The news is also an arena of competition between interest groups of numerous kinds, for whom access to the news space on favorable terms is an important goal or a means to achieve their other organizational ends. These would-be sources and voices are often just as political as are the candidates for political office or other major party political and government actors. They represent minority groups or special interests as well as sponsors of various single issue campaigns. The great appeal of news is not only that it reaches people who would disregard overt propaganda, but also that it can put a stamp of legitimacy on causes and movements. However much journalists recognize and try to escape the consequences of these activities, the news is inevitably tarred to some degree with the brush of manipulation.

These features of the news-politics relationship do not necessarily mark the sure demise of the neutral and partisan models of political news outlined above. They do suggest, however, that the reality of journalistic practice is not well captured by either traditional model.

Decline of a Modernist Paradigm?

Some of the elements noted above have been apparent for quite a long time; others are open to dispute. It would be foolish to say that journalism has not manifested improvement as well as decline in volume, variety, and quality. Moreover, without agreement on the appropriate standards of political knowledge for the average citizen, we cannot really assess the adequacy for the political process of the information the news typically provides. Recent critiques of news performance can fairly be said to stem from an essentially modernist outlook and set of assumptions.

The underlying assumption is that citizen-electors should receive enough information and be stimulated enough to participate actively in politics. The role assigned to the media is to provide the information, opinions, and guidance to inform citizens' rational choice and to encourage interest and involvement. Furthermore, it is assumed that there is a single "public sphere" of society in which all can symbolically meet and exchange views and information. This ideal-typical modernist vision can equally accommodate either the neutral or the committed model of press roles in a democracy.

In the new century, it is arguable that politics has less claims than it once had to precedence in setting news values, and politicians have less access to the news on their own terms. This shift is a logical consequence of the continued secularization and privatization of society. The social world is less clearly structured by ideology and belief, and the average citizen has many more interests and ways of spending free time. Our social and symbolic environment can be thought to contain more significant and fascinating objects than are provided by conventional party politics. These include new consumer products, new forms of entertainment, and the stars and luminaries of the world of sports, fashion, and entertainment, as well as social elites.

Politics more than ever appears to be a minority sport, not a uniquely compelling subject of interest for all. Its efficacy for changing things that matter in everyday life is subject to doubt. Polls provide evidence to suggest that politicians are less trusted and respected than they once were. Attitudes toward politics have changed as have the media's news priorities, which leads to the supposition that a new model of relations between press and politics has emerged—one of disassociation rather than neutral surveillance of politics by the media or ideological assimilation. Perhaps such a model already exists in that part of the media community that claims to report on "reality"—not the reality of public office and politics, but of personal concerns, sensational events, scandal, and the private lives of celebrities.

Politicians, inspired by their own marketing and publicity experts, are determined to manipulate the media. Their attempts do not endear them to journalists and editors; rather, they perpetuate a vicious cycle of strained relations. For its part, institutional politics has failed to find effective alternatives for reaching out to the mass followers that it still needs. If anything, it has become even more dependent on mass media to carry its messages, if need be by paid advertisements.

The new electronic media, the Internet in particular, do open up alternative channels for citizens to reach politicians and each other. Quite apart from their valued interactive potential and other novel aspects, the new media are attractive to politicians because they are not controlled by media owners, editors, and journalists. They have created significant alternatives for the revival and democratization of politics, in principle seeming to counter a number of the tendencies toward the homogenized, controlled, and manipulated society sketched above. So far, however, these media do not promise a great deal for the flow of communication from politicians to citizens, either because the new media are poorly used or simply because contact is easily avoided, unless actively sought out. Fears have also been expressed that a society shaped by the highly fragmented and complex networks fostered by the Internet will lack any common political agenda, shared knowledge, or meeting point.[5] The benefits of diversity can easily be portrayed as the ills of atomization. The real degree of open access and freedom enjoyed by would-be voices on the Internet may conceal the equally new real possibilities for indirect control and surveillance that new technology has brought. To put it more mundanely, it can be argued that the availability of new media as a means of communication to all can provide an excuse for traditional press and broadcast media to shirk some of their "social responsibility" duties of public information, outside the special circumstances of national crisis, major elections, and public scandal.

Under ever-increasing competitive pressure, these traditional media have to take care of their own priorities in the changing media marketplace. They adapt, not by ignoring politics, but by changing their style of coverage and by making new demands on politicians to supply what will interest audiences no longer clearly identifiable in terms of political allegiance or belief. Democratic politics runs the risk that the majority will be cut off from the will or capacity to participate in an informed way in political life.

In Conclusion

The changes in media and politics described in this book may not constitute a fundamental discontinuity from the past, but they do signal a growing tension between the needs of democratic institutions and the media, which sporadically claim to be the guardians of democracy but just as often neglect or deny the responsibility that goes with the job. This tension has deep roots and is connected with far-reaching social and cultural changes. These changes are not confined to one country or one political system, and their incidence and severity vary. Moreover, a national political culture does not shift overnight, and the tools of intervention by public policy are largely blunt or obsolete.

In Europe, the problems might once have been tackled by interventions in the media market to secure better performance or to limit concentration and commercialization. This line of action is no longer viable or efficacious and has no relevance for the United States. Control or regulation can do little to ensure that positive informational tasks will be successful. The old policy tools were designed to deal with monopoly and loss of diversity, not the current malaise. Although the incorporation of traditional press and broadcasting into global multimedia corporations is certainly part of the problem, this too is an outcome of larger forces at work.

Whatever is done will have to be gradual and long term and will depend on the ability of democratic institutions to solve their own problems of communication effectively with diverse publics by continual adaptation. It will involve the combined efforts of active citizens, politicians who take a wider view of their responsibilities, and journalists and other media people who recognize a professional and institutional task of informing citizens. Rather than changing the content of news to make it more appealing by featuring trivia over serious politics, the media must change the often dull and convoluted presentation format to make serious politics more attractive.

The new media (especially Internet Web pages, blogs, chat rooms, news groups, and whatever comes next) have yet to find a clear definition or task in the democratic process, and it is still too early to estimate their actual or likely impact on politics. It is, however, not too early to conclude that in themselves they are unlikely to constitute a new dawn for a political life that will be better informed, participant, and democratic, with an answer to the fears expressed here for political journalism. The new media have inherent limitations in their potential to fulfill the role that news journalism plays. They can be an important supplement to, and extension of, the spectrum of mass media, especially by providing a platform for greater diversity and quantity of opinions and ideas that mainstream channels ignore. Their presence limits the monopolization of news sources and creates the possibility of challenge and subversion.

Nevertheless, the value of Internet news in politics, leaving aside its main form in the replication of existing media on a different platform, is limited by several obstacles, which include (1) the variable and often uncertain reliability of information provided, as distinct from opinions expressed; (2) the limited professionalism of most content; (3) the lack of independence of many sources and the general lack of accountability; (4) the absence of a known or knowable audience for political messages; and (5) the limited guarantees of freedom of expression enjoyed, despite the lack of regulation. The new media will certainly increase in relative importance for political communication and will be incorporated in all campaigns, with a particular appeal for the most engaged citizens. Some partial solutions may emerge for current limitations, but it is unclear whether they can involve a majority of citizens in public debate and do what "old media" on the whole still aim to do. The shape of political communication in an information society is still very hazy. The essays in this book are not intended as a jeremiad, but as a contribution to problem diagnosis and solution.

Notes

1. John Zaller, "A News Standard of News Quality: Burglar Alarms for Monitorial Citizens," *Political Communication* 20, no. 2 (2003): 109–130; W. Lance Bennett, "The Burglar Alarm that Just Keeps Ringing: A Response to Zaller," *Political Communication* 20, no. 2 (2003): 131–138.

2. Jay G. Blumler and Dennis Kavanagh, "The Third Age of Political Communication: Influences and Features," *Political Communication* 16, no. 3 (1999): 209–230.

3. Daniel C. Hallin and Paolo Mancini, *Comparing Media Systems* (Cambridge; New York: Cambridge University Press, 2004).

4. David Weaver, ed., *The Global Journalist: News People Around the World* (Cresskill, N.J.: Hampton Press, 1998).

5. See, for example, Cass Sunstein, *Republic.com* (Princeton: Princeton University Press, 2001).

Index

ABC News Internet site, 179
ABC News/*Washington Post* polls, 193, 197
ABC's *World News Tonight*, 166
Abelson, Robert P., 115*n*
Aberbach, Joel D., 93*n*
Abraham Lincoln, USS, 81
Abrams, Samuel J., 245*n*
Abu Ghraib story, 251–254
Action repertoire, for media-centered
    political message production, 75–76
Active-advocate journalists, 35, 37
Active-neutral journalists, 35, 37
Activists, political, 232–233, 241–242, 269
Adversaries, journalists as, 34, 79, 88–89,
    271
Advertising
    audience size, democratic accountability
        and revenues from, 184
    audience size, news operations and, 238
    of branded consumer goods, media
        enterprise profitability and, 212–213
    demand market for media and reductions
        in, 215
Advertising, campaign. *See also* Political
        marketing methods
    agenda-setting using, 148–153
    direct, ethical issues with, 7
    direct effects on voting behavior,
        156–157
    early research on effectiveness of,
        142–144
    hard news coverage of elections vs., 261
    learning about the candidates through,
        144–148
    lessons learned about, 157–158
    political polarization and effectiveness
        measures of, 141–142
    priming and defusing by, 153–156
    theories on influence of, 14
Advocates
    journalists as, 34
    news producers as, 5
"Ad Watch Database: Election 2004,"
    130–131
Affective campaign ads, voter choices and,
    144–145
Afghanistan, war in, agenda-setting ads in
    2004 campaign and, 150
AFL-CIO, 111
Agenda-setting. *See also* Framing of news;
        Government news management; News
        shapers
    in election campaign of 1988, 149
    in election campaign of 2004, 149–151
    polls and, 194

prioritizing issues for, 151–152
    television and, 148
Agnew, Spiro T., 191
Al Jazeera, 241
Allen, George, 152, 256–257
Alliance building, for framing of news, 107
Alterman, Eric, 38*n*
Althaus, Scott L., 15–16, 186*n*, 189*n*
American Idol, 184
American Public Media, 177
American Voter, The, 143
"America's Place in the World" surveys, 190
Anderson, Chris, 245*n*
Annenberg Foundation Trust at
    Sunnylands, 129
Annenberg Public Policy Center, 118, 129
Anthrax disease, American understanding of
    dangers of, 185
Antitrust authorities, U.S.
    concentration and/or commercialization
        issues and, 225
    telecommunications industry mergers,
        acquisitions and, 217–218
    voices in policy debates on
        communications and, 226
Antiwar movement, opinion polls and
    understanding participants in, 192
Arbitron, 187*n*
Arbitron ratings, 177
Arcuri, Michael, 156
Asp, Kent, 24
Assignment system, 98, 99–100
Associated Press, 127, 193
AT&T, public opinion polling and, 192
Attack ads. *See also* Political attacks
    by Bush campaign against Kerry in 2004,
        146–147, 150–151
    in congressional elections of 2006, 156
    Lamont's, in 2006 congressional race, 153
    voting behavior in 2000 New Hampshire
        primary and, 143
Attack journalism, 88. *See also* Negativism;
        Political attacks
Audiences. *See* News audiences
Auletta, Ken, 94*n*, 95*n*
Autocratic states, journalism in, 6. *See also*
        Russia; Russian icon-anchors
Autonomy, of journalists, 34–35

Bagdikian, Ben H., 228*n*, 233–234, 245*n*,
    246*n*
Baker, C. Edwin, 189*n*
Baker, Peter, 200–201, 206*n*
Balance, in reporting, 28
Barnhurst, Kevin G., 39*n*

Cairncross, Frances, 246n
"Campaign Ads Are under Fire for Inaccuracy" (Rutenberg), 129
Campaign communication. *See also* Advertising, campaign; Deception in campaigns
  agenda-setting and, 148
  Americanization of, 78–79
  press as custodian of facts in, 120
Campbell, Alastair, 82
Campbell, Colin, 95n
Campbell, Karlyn Kohrs, 229n
Candidates
  campaign ads by, voting behavior and, 143
  development of campaign ads by, 143–144
  as news shapers, 109
  as object of government political message, 74, 74f, 76
Capitalism. *See also* Antitrust authorities, U.S.; Business; Media enterprises
  and globalization of digital communication, 240
  Russian focus groups on, 53, 55–56
Carter, Jimmy, 194
Carvajal, Miguel, 228n
Casey, Bob, Jr., 148
Castells, Manual, 114n
CBS Evening News with Katie Couric, 166
CBS News Internet site, 179
CBS News/*New York Times* surveys
  on influence of television commercials on voters, 142
  launch of, 193
  on national agenda in 2006 congressional elections, 152
  on perceptions of Kerry vs. Bush in 2004 race, 157
  on Persian Gulf Crisis, 197
  on voter impressions of 2004 presidential candidates, 146
Cell phones, story of brain cancers and, 112, 116n
Chaffee, Steven, 38n, 158n
Change to Win Federation, 111
Channel One and Two, Moscow-based networks, 41, 42
Chat groups, Internet, 9–10, 276–277
Chicago Council on Foreign Relations, 239
Cillizza, Chris, 159n
Citizens. *See also* Activists, political
  Internet connections and political knowledge and behavior of, 232–234, 275
  media reform movement by, 261
  need for information in choosing candidates, 118, 185
  need for political information, 269
  news audiences and engagement of, 161–163
  news media guidance for, 272
  photos of breaking events by journalists vs., 251–252, 253, 254
  reliance on the press as custodian of facts, 118–124
  videos by, 4, 234, 257

Civic journalism, 262, 263–265, 272
Civil rights movement, 192, 194
Clinton, Bill
  approval ratings for, 202–203
  Gore's 2000 campaign and, 154
  journalists' access to, 95n
  Lewinsky scandal and approval polls during, 198–200, 201, 204–205
  pseudoevents used by, 80
  strategic communication on health care policy by, 109
  voter impressions of, 145
CNBC, SuperChannel and, 228n
CNN. *See also* Cable television news
  audience demand for, 166, 180
  audience demand for Internet site of, 179
  audience during Persian Gulf crisis of 1990–1991, 163–164
  audience for Hurricane Katrina aftermath on, 173
  audiences for, 1998–2005, 171, 172f
  content analysis of news on, 174
  world penetration of, 239–240
CNN/*USA Today* polls, 197
Coalition Information Center, 95n
Cobb, Roger, 159n
Cohen, Bernard Cecil, 39n
Colbert, Stephen, 249
Cole, Charles, 245n
Combs, James E., 229n
Comedy, late-night, 250
Commercial media systems. *See* Media enterprises
Commercial radio news audiences (U.S.), 175–176, 176f, 177. *See also* Radio
Communication(s). *See also* Agenda-setting; Framing of news; Government news management
  basic model of, 101–102
  policy debates, voices in, 226
  power shift in, 215
  technology changes, deregulation, and opportunities in, 224
Communitarian model of journalism, 272
Commuters, radio news and, 175
Compaine, Benjamin, 243n
Competition among news media
  concentration of media enterprises and, 225
  homogenization of news and, 223–224
  interest groups and, 273
  media abundance and, 213–214
  technological change and, 273
  U.S. government regulation and, 216, 217
Compromise, conflicting interests of news stakeholders and, 9
Congress, U.S.
  elections of 2006 for, 147–148, 152, 153, 156
  FCC's proposed fairness doctrine changes and, 261
  Gingrich and Republicans takeover of, polls on, 202
  polls about, 194
Connecticut, 2006 congressional elections in, 147